BREAD
on the TABLE

BREAD
on the TABLE

Recipes for Making and Enjoying
Europe's Most Beloved Breads

DAVID NORMAN
Owner of Austin's Easy Tiger Bake Shop & Beer Garden

Photographs by Johnny Autry

TEN SPEED PRESS
California | New York

CONTENTS

PREFACE

"It is a mysterious business, this making of bread, and once you are hooked
by the miracle of yeast, you'll be a breadmaker for life."

—JAMES BEARD, *Beard on Bread*

I almost had to make bread. Returning from a year in Europe, where I had grown accustomed to so many types of hearty, substantial bread, my little slice of Gainesville, Florida, offered next to nothing beyond squishy white bread. So when I happened upon a copy of *Beard on Bread*, a compendium on baking by America's most noteworthy food authority, I had to give baking a try. Once I got my hands into the flour, created dough, shaped it, and then saw it come alive and transform into a golden shiny object, I was hooked.

At the time, I was studying literature and dabbling in painting but making bread gave me the same satisfaction that painting did. I was still making something with my hands, with the added bonus of it being quite tasty. Even as I turned my hobby into my first baking job, I still had dreams of becoming an artist, but I felt lucky to be able to head into work and make beautiful things with my hands every day. Knowing that what I made would grace other people's tables, helping them to enjoy a daily meal or celebrate with friends and family, only boosted that good feeling.

With this book, I am hoping to get you similarly hooked on bread baking, if you are not already. Many people, even those who enjoy cooking, find bread baking intimidating. But I believe that with the techniques laid out here you can successfully bake bread from your first loaf, even if you have never spent much time in the kitchen.

Baking bread is not that difficult, but it does take time. During much of that time, the dough is resting and doing its own thing, which means that you can do other things while you are waiting. Nevertheless, you will still need to block out a chunk of time for your bake day.

My method is not a no-knead method, but it is also not the old-fashioned push-and-turn kneading that I learned from the pages of James Beard's book. Rather, it is somewhere in between. Although you can make a really nice loaf of bread using a no-knead recipe, it depends heavily on using a Dutch oven for baking. A Dutch oven helps the bread to hold its shape, and for that reason, the no-knead method is less versatile if you want to make other shapes or types of bread that depend on a more developed dough structure. On the other hand, when I was first using the more labor-intensive Beard method, I often had difficulty figuring out when the dough was developed or how much flour to add. Many times, I realize now, I would not give the dough the chance to relax and absorb the water it needed to develop well. Instead I kept throwing more flour on the table so it would not be sticky!

In this book, we are going to do something in the middle that is just right: We let the magic of the dough do its thing and only intervene from time to time to help it along. Through detailed instructions and plenty of pictures, I will show you how to effectively do both. For novice bakers, you can start with this book's base recipe, a wonderful French country loaf (see page 40), and progress through a variety of breads from several food cultures. Even the serious home bakers among you will find interesting bread varieties and a trick or two that is new to you.

For more advanced bakers, there is a wide variety of more complicated techniques, including scalded flour, sourdough cultures, yeasted starters, grain soakers, and even a bread that involves the first steps of home brewing—done to make the wort that is used as the liquid in the dough. In other words, there is plenty here to keep you interested.

Finally, I hope you will enjoy reading about, making, and eating these breads in context, connected to the traditions and meals whence they come. In no way do I mean the meals and pairings to be prescriptive or to imply that you should not eat the Swedish pâté with a French *pain au levain*. Make your own combinations and start your own traditions. In our family, we like to have what we call a picnic meal

at least once a week. It is our rendition of the way I learned to eat as an exchange student many years ago in Sweden (see page 95). We slice two or three varieties of bread and put them in a basket on the table, and then bring out leftovers from the fridge, some salami and cheese, probably a bowl of olives, and anything else we have on hand.

So I would encourage you, if you are interested in bread baking, to give yourself a "bake day" now and then. Think of other projects you might need to get done around the house, or finish reading that novel in between folding and shaping the dough. If you are planning to make one of the meals from this book to go with the bread you are baking, the prep and cooking can be done while the dough is resting and rising. While I was developing and testing the recipes for this book (and all the recipes, even for the breads that we bake at Easy Tiger, were developed and tested with an ordinary gas oven in my home kitchen), I thoroughly enjoyed being back in touch with the dough in a much more intimate way than a busy bakery allows. Much of what you are about to read has been written in the intervals between working the dough.

INTRODUCTION

"Good bread is the most fundamentally satisfying of all foods; and good bread with fresh butter, the greatest of feasts."

—JAMES BEARD, *Beard on Bread*

Despite these words from Beard, most of the time bread is just part of the feast—eaten alongside, wrapped around, or placed under other food. In these pages, I want to share my years of travel and baking with you through these recipes for a variety of breads and the meals, from a simple sandwich on the street to elaborate dinners, that I have enjoyed with them.

Bread, in its myriad forms, is eaten the world over. I have long been fascinated with how breads have developed alongside different cuisines and how they fit in with their way of eating. Some cultures put bread on the table for every meal, at the ready to sop up any sauce, while elsewhere, the center-piece of a meal is a variety of sliced breads that are served with an assortment of toppings. In France, it is not uncommon to serve extra bread alongside a croque monsieur.

This book is not a comprehensive catalog of world bread and cuisines; it is more personal than that. Instead it is drawn from my own travels and baking experiences over the last thirty-odd years. The book is also informed by what I have learned eating bread in different places, which is that bread traditions developed alongside a complementary culinary tradition. This idea first germinated with me while I was teaching the Art of International Bread Baking, the professional baking program at the French Culinary Institute in New York City. At the time,

each six-week course was divided into two-week sections for French, German, and Italian breads. Academically, I understood that each culture had its own approach to making bread, but my own travels and time spent living abroad informed me even more about how these breads were eaten in different locations. My time spent breaking bread at tables showed me how the food and the bread fit together.

Sometimes there is a particular bread that is eaten with a dish or type of food, like the dark French rye bread, *pain de seigle*, that is served with oysters and other raw seafood. Other breads, like the salt-free bread of Tuscany, can be bewildering until they are eaten with the boldly flavored and often salty local specialties. Sandwiches play their part in all of these cultures, and can range from a simple buttered baguette with thinly shaved ham to a sauce-drenched, five-napkin affair like the *torta ahogada* from Guadalajara.

The breads in this book are presented with a culinary context, from a German *Brotzeit* to a French baker's meal to Tuscan bread with a hunter's stew. Each chapter explores one of the bread-baking traditions that have influenced my career and is followed by a section that puts those breads on the table with recipes for traditional food pairings. I find these pairings transporting, and I hope you will explore them with me.

How I Learned to Eat Bread

In the late summer of 1981, I landed at Kastrup Airport in Copenhagen to begin a year as a high school exchange student. Like countless others before me, I was about to start an adventure that would change and influence my life in ways that were unimaginable at the time. Even so, I never would have predicted that it would be my first step toward becoming a bread baker. In truth, it would be another four years before I kneaded my first dough. But when my host father, Hans-Erik Jonsén, and his son, Michael, brought me back to their home outside of Halmstad, Sweden, I discovered foods and breads I had never tasted before, and other ways of eating that were as foreign as the language.

Both of my parents were from the Midwest. (We moved from northern Minnesota to the Florida Panhandle when I was ten.) They were adventurous cooks; they belonged to a gourmet club, staging elaborate multicourse meals every month or so with several other couples. We always ate well at home. My dad especially liked to try new and different recipes and considered James Beard his culinary hero. Neither of them baked much, though. They made pies, birthday cakes, and cookies with my sister and me, but the only bread I remember was packaged white bread, mostly for sandwiches or toast. I probably had a sandwich or two on rye as my mom's father loved a good Reuben, but the rye available then was barely distinguishable from white bread. So when four or five varieties of bread appeared on the table every morning and evening in Sweden, it was a revelation to me.

In Sweden, two meals each day, breakfast and the evening meal, revolve around bread. Slices from several loaves and some *knäckebröd*, a crispbread, were placed in a basket on the kitchen table, along with a parade of toppings that came out of the refrigerator and cupboard.

In fact, there is a word, *pålägg*, which comes from *på* meaning "on" and *lägga* meaning "to lay." *Pålägg* is everything that you lay on top of *bröd* (bread). Cold cuts (such as ham), summer sausage, salami, cheeses, honey, pâté, pickles, and occasionally some pickled fish and salmon roe in a tube were set out on the table with a tub of butter in the center. Everyone had a small wooden board and a wooden spreader to build their own *smörgås*, or open-faced sandwiches. The Jonsén family always had a pot of tea as well.

Around noon, we would have *middag* (it literally translates to "midday" but means dinner) which is traditionally the one hot meal of the day. Interestingly, bread was not typically served at

middag. More often than not, potatoes were the starch. I loved the sauces and gravies, especially when we went to eat with my host father's parents, as his mother was a great cook. I made sure I soaked up every last bit of sauce or gravy with the potatoes.

Britt, my host mother, was also a great cook. Even better, she was a great baker. Each month she would go to her mother's house for a baking day. Those evenings, she would come home with her share of the spoils and load the cupboard and freezer with a month's supply of cinnamon buns and cookies for *fika*, the all-important Swedish coffee break. My favorite, though, were the loaves of *fullkornsbröd*, dense rye bread studded with cracked rye and rolled in wheat bran. While most of our daily bread came from the grocery store, and it was far better than any bread we could buy at the Piggly Wiggly, these homemade loaves were extra special. Dense and dark, the cracked rye gave the thin slices a pleasant chew. My favorite topping was shavings of farmers' cheese, its dairy twang melding with the earthy, caramelly sweetness of the bread.

Around town, there were PSA billboards encouraging people to eat at least seven slices of bread a day. Based on my experience in the Jonsén family, the encouragement hardly seemed necessary, but I suppose it signaled a change in eating habits that had started even then, as Swedes began eating more fast food and lunches on the go and shifting toward eating *middag* at the end of the day.

Learning Swedish piqued my interest in languages, so I decided to study German at the University of Florida in Gainesville. For my junior year of college, I won a scholarship from the Federation of German-American Clubs to study in Munich. Living in student housing and attending university was quite different from my stay with a family in Sweden, but one thing was familiar—great bread and lots of it. I found so many dark and toothsome varieties of rye breads, some of which reminded me of the Swedish breads I had grown to love and crave, but there were also many new types. I have heard it said that there are more than three hundred different rye breads made throughout Germany.

Living in the student housing, called Studentenstadt, meant that I did not experience the typical rhythm of a family's day and meals. Constrained by my age and budget, many of my meals were eaten in the university canteen or at one of the student-run pubs in the Studentenstadt. Restaurant meals were few and far between. When we did eat out, it was often some cuisine other than German, such as Greek, or when I was especially homesick, Mexican. In the student pubs, we were more likely to have an Asian-influenced one-pot meal, a vegetable curry, or perhaps a Moroccan stew. Though my status as a student partially dictated these choices, there was also a national trend toward Mediterranean and Eastern cuisine during my time in Germany, in part due to a curiosity of the world and relatively inexpensive travel opportunities, but also shaped by a certain amount of reluctance in claiming too much of their Germanness.

One of my favorite rituals and fondest memories is of the brunch that we had nearly every Saturday in the common room on our floor of the Studentenstadt. Unlike my American college dorms, we each had our own room with a private bath and a kitchenette. On Saturday mornings, someone would run to the bakery for fresh rolls, a couple of people would brew coffee, someone else would make a pot of tea, and we would all converge on the common room with whatever we might have in our fridges—cheese, cold cuts, or yogurt—and we would have a meal together. Always fresh from the bakery, among the white rolls known as *semmeln*, were pretzels. My best friend, Martin, taught me the Bavarian way to eat them, with butter.

When I returned to Gainesville and chicken wings, burritos, pizza, and garlic knots, there were two things that I really missed from Germany: great beer and great bread. One day, as I was browsing the bookstore near campus, I came across a copy of *Beard on Bread*. I thought of my father and his dog-eared James Beard cookbooks and decided to give bread baking a try, as this seemed like the only way I would taste great bread without getting on a plane. Starting with the basic white bread recipe, I worked on kneading and proofing and baking simple breads with dynamite flavor.

This was the mid-80's, and while the craft brewing and bread revivals were just getting started on the West Coast, they were a way off from hitting Central Florida. Still, the homebrewing wave had arrived there, and around the same time I started baking bread, I happened upon a display of brewing kits in a shop window. Though the price was high for a student budget, the idea gnawed at me for a few days until I went back and bought the kit, a five-gallon bucket with a spigot and lid with a hole for the air lock, a bottle capper, and a hydrometer, plus my first malt and hops kit. So began my dabbles in fermentation, which thirty years later would lead to heading up the baking program at Easy Tiger Bake Shop and Beer Garden in Austin, where the beer and bread connection seems to have come full circle.

How I Learned to Make Bread

As I finished my studies and started contemplating what was next for me, I was pretty sure that I was not ready to pursue a graduate degree, the logical next step for a literature major. Around that time, I came across a sign for a local cooperative art gallery called the Artitorium. I had been doing some drawing and painting on my own, a creative break from researching and writing that left me with something tangible. The flyer welcomed interested people to join the group for their weekly meeting and potluck dinner. So I went home, pulled down a CorningWare baking dish from my mother, and made the most retro, ironic potluck dish I could think of, a tuna casserole. When I arrived shyly with my hot dish, I found out the potluck part of the get-together had been dropped, but by the end of the meeting, we were all hungry so we heated it up and enjoyed it.

This small group of recent graduates and art students would become my core set of friends, and they were the key reason I stayed in Gainesville for several years after finishing school. But I still needed a job.

I remember applying for a truck driving gig (don't ask) that I was not qualified for and a flower delivery job that I thankfully did not get. Then I read an ad for a position in a small, French-style bakery on the other side of town. Soon I was making tart shells, cookies, quiche, and baguettes and boules at the Uppercrust Bakery. I started in the pastry baker's position, which included filling in for the bread baker on one of his days off. After a few months, I moved up to bread baker, which in the hierarchy of the small shop was the top job. The Uppercrust was a boulangerie, not a patisserie.

At the bakery, we made white and whole wheat country bread and baguettes, all in the prevailing French mode of the time. This meant intensively mixed straight dough (no starters or pre-ferments), shaped directly after mixing and then fermented overnight in a retarder-proofer. We did this in a large walk-in refrigerator that could be set to switch to a warm, moist proofing box to have the loaves risen for baking early in the morning. Although years later I would learn how that way of baking, which had become prevalent in France in the early 1960s, robs the bread of flavor, it was still far superior to any other bread available in Gainesville at the time. In fact, it is probably a good thing that it was on the opposite side of town from my orbit around the university, because if I had discovered it sooner, I may never have picked up that baking book and started making loaves of my own.

I remember talking to Jackie, the owner, about French bread versus the more dense, whole grain breads that I had encountered and loved in Sweden and Germany. Jackie was very much a Francophile, and she associated whole grain breads with health food. For her, it was taste that mattered, and she revered the light, subtle nutty flavors of French bread. Being young, I lacked the confidence to more strongly argue my case, but I also did not fully understand her viewpoint on dense, dark

breads. I am sure it did not help when the only book I could find that had any recipes even close to those breads I was craving was *The Laurel's Kitchen Bread Book*. It must have immediately set off the hippie alarm in her mind. Still, Jackie loved food, and bread was an important and integral part of that for her—never separate.

When I finally left Gainesville (after giving Jackie notice at least three times and then changing my mind), I carried my baking skills with me to Minneapolis. I landed a job in a great neighborhood bakery in Uptown called Gelpe's Old World Bakery. It just happened to be a kosher bakery, so I learned how to make many fine cakes and pastries while following the laws of kashrut, the Jewish dietary rules. Because a basic tenet prohibits observant people from eating meat and dairy products at the same time, the entire shop was divided between the pareve (neutral, with no dairy) side and the dairy side—meat was prohibited from the bakery altogether. Every piece of equipment and tool, from the large mixing bowls and paddles to the scoops and pastry brushes, was in duplicate, clearly marked and kept separate for use with only one set of products. This was all new to me, and I found it fascinating and learned to respect the thoughtfulness that it required of observant people.

After a couple of years and a storm that dumped thirty-some inches of snow on the city on Halloween weekend, I concluded that the years spent below the Mason-Dixon Line had softened this Minnesota native too much. I had also recently had an epiphany. I remember clearly going into the bathroom at Gelpe's and catching a glimpse of myself in the mirror, with a white chef's coat and a funky French military toque that I had picked up at a surplus store, and thinking that I looked like a baker. Pausing, I realized that I really enjoyed what I was doing, that making pastries and breads was fulfilling my creative side, the part that loved to make things. In that moment, I decided that baking was no longer just a job, but would be my career. So after doing some city shopping, I headed west to Seattle and its exciting food scene.

In those last months in Minneapolis, I borrowed a copy of *The Italian Baker* by Carol Field. At Gelpe's, I mostly made pastries, but I was still interested in breads, and here was an approach to bread that was new to me. I made a *biga* (an Italian starter) and tried out some of the book's recipes at home. Here were breads that, although not like the dense whole grain ryes I had in Germany and Sweden, were complex, flavorful, and interesting in texture. I started daydreaming of opening a bakery that would make those kinds of bread.

When I got to Seattle, I was still in pastry mode, thinking that I would land a job in a restaurant or hotel where I could make elaborate desserts and pastry creations. I shopped my résumé around, and in one of the better restaurants, the chef told me about Grand Central Bakery and its head baker, Leslie Mackie. He thought she was looking for bakers. So I called and went for the interview in an industrial area near the port on the south side of the city. The outside of the warehouse that housed the wholesale division was not too promising, but once inside I quickly discovered that here was a bakery doing exactly what I wanted to learn to do.

Leslie hired me as her assistant and I began to feel as if I had come home: bread was, and is, in my soul. For several months, I worked each of the stations, learning to shape, then mix the dough, and finally to bake the breads in the large stone deck oven. At the Uppercrust, we had only a rack oven, and at Gelpe's, I never had occasion to work on the deck oven. Scoring, steaming, and loading dozens of loaves at a time, then pulling them out with the long baker's peel, seemed more like real baking. As Leslie's assistant, I was not just learning the ropes, but helping to keep things running when she was busy elsewhere. Then one day, Leslie and Gwen, the owner of Grand Central Bakery, asked to meet with me. Leslie was leaving to open her own business, which would become the very successful Macrina Bakery, and they wanted me to take over as head baker. Flattered and honored, I knew Leslie's shoes would be hard to fill, but I eagerly accepted the challenge. The steepest learning curve

of my entire life followed, as it was one thing to work each station and another to be in charge of all of it, directing others to produce bread nearly around the clock.

Seattle is a wonderful, beautiful city, with perhaps my ideal climate—yes, even the rain. Perhaps I love it because it happens to be a very good climate for making bread too. One day, though, a salesman from TMB Baking was at the bakery helping to coordinate the installation of a new deck oven and our conversation turned to his other projects. He mentioned something about a new bakery in New York; I asked him if they were looking for a baker. He said he thought something may have happened with their original candidate and offered to put me in touch with them. Soon I was on the phone with François Peltzer, one of the partners, making arrangements to fly to New York for a tryout at TriBakery.

Never before had I needed to try out for a job, which only underscored that this was the big leagues—and indeed it was. As I learned more about TriBakery, the Myriad Restaurant Group, and its impresario, Drew Nieporent, I began to understand better their place in the New York culinary pantheon. Drew's restaurants included the venerable Tribeca Grill, the long-running and well-loved Montrachet, and the ultra-hip Nobu, all within a few blocks of one another in Tribeca. When I was in high school, we took a class trip to New York and saw *Annie* on Broadway; I remember being blown away by the production, which was worlds above any theater experience I had before that. My first meal at Montrachet was just like that, with a level of service that I had not yet experienced, even at some of Seattle's finest restaurants.

Nancy Silverton from La Brea Bakery was the consulting baker on the TriBakery project, so when I was hired, I went to Los Angeles for three weeks to observe La Brea's production. Its production dwarfed Grand Central's, even then, which was well before it had started its parbaked frozen business. One thing that made an impression on me were the giant tubs of olives that a baker had to comb through, double-checking that the mechanical pitters had not missed any. I observed and took detailed notes on all of the breads they produced, their starter-feeding routines, and schedules of fermentation.

Later on during my time in New York, I worked at Bouley Bakery, where most of the bread formulas came from Jacques Mahou in France's Loire Valley. Jacques, a Meilleurs Ouvriers de France, the highest rank a French craftsman can achieve, had two bakeries in Tours and another in a village outside of the city, and David Bouley sent me to visit him there for a week. All three had old-fashioned French-style wood-burning brick ovens in which the fire was built in a box that sits below the baking chamber rather than directly on the oven floor.

My week in the Loire Valley was amazing. At night, I would observe the bakers in one of the two bakeries in Tours. The older bakery was run by a single baker, and the new main bakery had two bakers working overnight. Being able to see and feel the dough and the starters revolutionized my understanding of the baking process, and I was able to make some adjustments when I got back to New York that had a big impact. Because of the difference in the flour and the water absorption, I found that adding about 10 percent more water to the starter gave the starter more life and the breads more lift and bloom. I would have never known what to look for in a starter and dough if I hadn't experienced them in France.

During the day, Jacques and his wife took me sight-seeing all through the Loire Valley. We whizzed down the highway, passing signs that read as if you were walking down the aisle of your favorite wine shop—Vouvray, Sancerre, Chinon. We picnicked in the shadow of the ruins of a cloister. We had dinner at the Michelin-starred Restaurant Charles Barrier and afterward took a tour of the kitchen and bakery. Right there, crammed in a small space behind the kitchen, they had a brick oven with a rotating deck where they made their own breads. Besides being an incredible meal—with *foie gras de*

canard (fattened duck liver), *fricassée de homard* (lobster fricassee), *carré d'agneau rôti* (roasted rack of lamb), and *pigeon de Racan poele* (pan-fried squab)—that bakeshop tucked behind the kitchen was where my soon-to-be dear friend and most influential mentor, Michel Suas, had baked before he left France for the United States.

During what would turn out to be my last year in New York, I spent part of my time in San Francisco, teaching at Michel's baking school, the San Francisco Baking Institute. I was part of the school's team for the United States' largest baking convention, the International Baking Industry Exposition, which is held in Las Vegas every three years. In September of 2001, I woke up in Vegas on a Tuesday morning, got dressed, and headed to the convention hall. As soon as I got into the elevator, people were talking about New York and a plane that had crashed into the World Trade Center. Exiting the elevator, I went straight over to watch the television sets over the bar. As the events unfolded on that morning of terror, the convention was canceled for the day as we tried to absorb what it all meant.

For me, it was surreal to be away from New York that week—and it took several days for a friend and me to rent a car to drive back. Had I been home, I would surely have been at work that morning, only five blocks from the World Trade Center. The bakers on my crew were there that day, all of them Muslim and from Mali and the Ivory Coast, and they were out in the streets helping the people who came flooding uptown. Somehow I had managed to get through to my then girlfriend (and now wife), Paula, to find out that she was okay; she had seen the second tower go down from across the river where she lived in Brooklyn Heights.

Upon my return, everything below Canal Street was closed, including Bouley, but the restaurant and bakery had morphed into the main commissary for feeding the workers at ground zero. At first, many Lower Manhattan restaurants volunteered their resources and food to help out, but as the magnitude of what was required became clear,

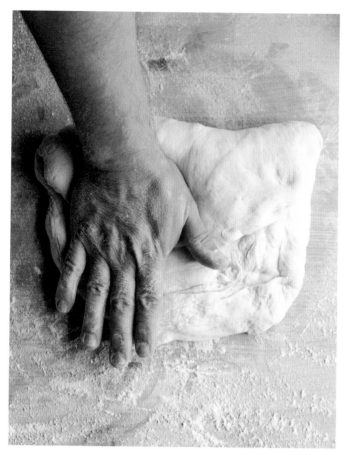

Bouley was awarded the contract to sustain the support role. On the Monday after my return, Paula and I volunteered to help serve the food we were making and were driven on a golf cart to what had been a restaurant right on the edge of the crater that was ground zero. Blue plastic tarps stood in for what had been the façade of the building in which we set up the buffet. The mix of food was broad and somewhat bizarre, as people and companies from all over made donations. At one point, we were serving lobsters given by Bouley's fisherman supplier in Maine alongside stacks of premade Aunt Jemima pancakes. In our rotating rack oven, where usually we baked viennoiserie and pastries, the cooks roasted thirty turkeys at a go.

How I Started Baking Bread in Texas

For her first trip after that, Paula, who is a food and travel writer, flew to Texas to meet Rebecca Rather, the owner of Rather Sweet Bakery in Fredericksburg. She was on assignment for *Food & Wine*, reporting on Rebecca's Christmas tree–trimming party and her signature cookie decorations. Since she was already down there, Rebecca's public relations person also asked if Paula would join a group of journalists who would be staying at a new fitness resort called Hart and Hind, on a ranch deep in the Texas Hill Country. With long hikes up the rugged hills, exercise classes in the fitness room, and a horseback ride led by a character named George, she had a great time. She talked effusively about the beauty of the family ranch where Kit and Carl Detering had set up the resort, but Paula had an exuberance for many of the beautiful places her job took her. When she called from the San Antonio airport and asked me what I thought of the job title ranch manager, I took it with a couple of grains of salt.

We had dinner that night at a little Cuban restaurant in Jersey City after I picked her up in Newark, and as her tale started to unwind, it was clear that this was more than just exuberance, there was a real opportunity. At first it seemed a little crazy, but the more we talked about it over the next couple of weeks, the more intriguing it became. Even before our city had changed so drastically, just a month before, we had been fantasizing about where the next chapter of our lives might play out. Here was an opportunity that would truly only come up once in a lifetime, the chance to see what it was like to live on a ranch in the rural West. While Paula was there on the press junket, the chef had quit, and as Paula and Kit Detering got to sharing stories on their hikes, Kit had asked her, "Why don't you and your boyfriend come down and run the place?" So we booked flights to return in November, for me to see the place and for them to meet me. We were introduced to a group of the Deterings' good friends from the town of Uvalde, thirty miles to the south, and to breakfast tacos and goats splayed open on spits, roasting over an open fire across the Mexican border in Nuevo Laredo. By December, we were packing up a Penske truck with the belongings from our two apartments and headed toward Rio Frio, Texas.

Ostensibly, we were to head up the culinary program for the guests, but with a staff that included just the two of us, a fitness director, and a part-time cleaning person, our job descriptions were broad. On that first trip to Texas, for the interview, I had already gotten Carl interested in building a brick oven, so he ordered a copy of *The Bread Builders*, a book by baker Daniel Wing and well-known brick oven builder Alan Scott, which included complete plans for an oven. Since Carl was in the building-supply business in Houston, he had many of the materials that we needed, except for the fire bricks that would line the oven floor. For those, we hitched the flatbed trailer to the ranch's Chevrolet Suburban and drove to Elgin. I mention that mainly because towing a trailer was the first of many things I would learn to do on the ranch beyond baking and cooking, including operating a backhoe and bulldozer, plowing fields with an old John Deere tractor, and caring for a menagerie of goats, sheep, chickens, and cows.

Baking on the ranch was ideal. On bake days, I would get up early, head to the lodge to put on the coffee, then head out into the woods to gather wood. Commonly called cedar, there was a species of mountain juniper tree that proliferated in the area. In fact, as land was cleared and grazed over the decades, the tree had spread beyond its natural, higher habitat and become a nuisance. One of my bulldozer tasks was to clear parts of the ranch of the overgrowth of cedar. For direct cooking, such as on a grill, the cedar wood was too resinous, but as fuel for the oven, it was perfect. A quick, hot fire was best for our direct-fired oven, where the fire is built right in the baking chamber, and the old, dried cedar branches burned hot and quickly.

Once my fire was going, I would start the dough, mixing it in the old wooden trough I had bought at an antique store, using the techniques you'll learn in this book. The oven could fit ten good-size boules of *pain de campagne* and that was plenty of bread for the week. With no pressure to make bread deliveries or put loaves on the shelf to sell, I could follow the dough's rhythm and pace. There was always plenty of kitchen prep work and other chores to do in between stretching and folding the dough and while the loaves were rising. Timing the fire, the heat of the oven, and the dough so that they would all be ready at the same time was the biggest challenge, but as I baked day in, day out, I learned how to do that too.

I worked hard to take advantage of the tools on hand for optimal results. To create steam in the oven, I placed a long, metal tray designed to feed baby chicks and filled it with bolts; the bolts helped to create a lot of hot surface area that would rapidly heat the water poured in at the beginning of the bake. Because the brick oven was deep and the arched dome higher than the narrow opening, the moisture held well and the loaves sprang to full volume in the steady, intense heat.

While we were running the guest ranch, Paula and I had a very European schedule, with two months off every summer. It was just too hot in July and

August for hiking in the Texas hills and it was one of the perks that made the job so attractive. Our first summer, we took a trip to Tuscany and stayed in the home of our friends Janet and Roberto. Janet was American, but had been living and cooking in Tuscany for a couple of decades. Paula had worked for Janet a few years earlier at a small *agriturismo* that she ran in the Tuscan countryside. Roberto, who was Janet's third Italian husband, had retired from the Italian air force, where he had been a general and involved in the higher levels of NATO; you would never have guessed that by his wild bush of white hair, full Santa Claus beard, and his ever-jovial mood. For three wonderful weeks while they were off sailing the Mediterranean in Roberto's sailboat, Paula and I explored the surrounding towns, such as Siena and Montepulciano, or just lounged at the beach in our base town of Castiglione della Pescaia. We made day trips and had grand lunches, not wanting to navigate the narrow, winding Tuscan roads after dark. We ate porchetta from a trailer by the beach and shopped at the local market, cooking in Janet's well-appointed kitchen in the evenings.

Of course we bought some of the local bread, and it was bland without the salt. It still had more flavor than I had expected, but it wasn't something you would spread with butter and eat by itself for breakfast. Which is the point—saltless Tuscan bread is not served as toast. Instead, it is omnipresent at the table, always alongside the boldly flavored foods of the region, and it is the foil to the salty cured meats. Tuscan prosciutto is saltier than those made in other regions, as is much of the salumi produced there. The bread of Tuscany goes along with the cuisine, fitting in with the food and the way it is eaten there. I was hooked on yet another style of baking.

Going in, we knew that the time at Hart and Hind would be just one chapter in our lives. For four years we enjoyed living in the rocky, prickly, hard-scrabble Texas landscape. We bought horses from a cowboy, George, who had become a great friend. We learned about animal husbandry and cared for

a small herd of registered Red Angus cattle. Carl sent me to Texas A&M University in College Station twice: once to learn about pecans so I could care for the ranch's three orchards and a second time to learn how to artificially inseminate cattle. Yes, I can truthfully claim that I got four heifers pregnant, which added a couple of notches to my belt. Still, as our horse vet, Pete, was quick to remind me, I was not a cowboy. When our friends from Seattle were visiting with their four-year-old son, Calvin, I took him for rides on the horse and tractor and he dubbed me Cowboy Dave. When Pete got wind of that, he made a point of calling me Baker Dave.

Over our four years at Hart and Hind, we helped to grow the business, but in the end, there were still too many weeks without a full house. The Deterings decided to close the guest facilities and return to enjoying the ranch with family and friends—it was time for us to move on. Scouring online, I looked for jobs at Whole Foods Market in Austin. Though I was looking for a baking job, I came across another intriguing position: an auditor for the meat program. The auditor visited the many farms and ranches that raised the animals for the meat they sold, making sure they were being raised in accordance with the standards the grocery chain had established. I took the job, but with the economic slide in 2008, Whole Foods Market was forced to cut personnel, and my position was one of many they trimmed in Austin. At first it was hard being laid off and I struggled to find another place in the meat industry, but it led me back to baking, where I realized I truly belonged. I worked for a time for a local restaurant, Annie's Café, baking overnight in the restaurant kitchen, then met the folks with whom I would partner to open Easy Tiger.

Easy Tiger started when Paula met with a friend of hers, Evelyn Sher, who has a daughter the same age as ours. Evelyn's husband, Bob Gillett, was a partner in a new restaurant group in town, and Evelyn was doing their public relations. They met at 24 Diner, the group's first concept, where chef Andrew Curren was making updated versions of classic diner fare using fresh, high-quality ingredients, much of them from local farms. They talked about some of the group's ideas and plans for the future. At the top of the list that day was the concept of a casual, rustic French place, where bread would be a central part of the menu. Paula told them she happened to know a good baker, so I sent a bag of baguettes and some croissants to the diner. Andrew was so busy that day that he didn't have time to try them, but later that evening he snacked on a croissant. After that, he was on the phone to Bob, making sure that we would get together.

At first, we talked about starting a bakery that would supply their restaurants and perhaps a few wholesale accounts; we considered a retail outlet, but at a site where the rent would be reasonable— not a destination spot. But I knew they had also been interested in a beer garden, and the idea was still in their back pocket when they toured a space on the east end of the Sixth Street entertainment district. Built in the late 1800s, it had housed many different bars over the years. Because it was adjacent to where Waller Creek cuts a deep groove through to the Colorado a few blocks to the south, it was a split-level building, with a lower level containing a large outdoor space in the back.

Immediately, they saw potential for a beer garden in the downstairs bar and outdoor space, so they asked me if I thought we could make a bakery work upstairs. There were some quirky limitations, like an old hardwood floor that was beautiful but not the most practical for installing a 13½-ton deck oven. Still, it seemed like it would work, and the more we thought about the synergies between a beer garden and a bakery, the more it seemed like a natural fit. I would get to bake some pretzels after all—more than I ever could have imagined.

Easy Tiger is decidedly a beer garden, not a biergarten. Though we have some German-influenced food on the menu, such as bratwurst and knackwurst, we also offer other types of sausage, a whole range of overstuffed American sandwiches, and plenty of Texas grilled meats.

Our thirty-odd taps pour predominately American craft beers, in a rotating selection. While we do bake many Bavarian pretzels, the only other bread with ties to Germany is our rye loaf. By the time this book comes out, we will have our second location up and running, and we have invested in some ovens from Germany that work a bit differently from our current deck oven. With these ovens, which can drop temperature more quickly in the middle of the bake, I hope to make more of the heavier, whole grain rye breads that I love so much. Still, the core of Easy Tiger's bread line will remain the French *pain au levain* and other breads from around the world, which I hope to help you bring into your own home with this book.

EQUIPMENT

There is not a lot of specialized equipment necessary for baking bread at home. You just need a few tools to make a better baking environment in your home oven, which has a few handicaps for bread baking. Namely, the difficulty in retaining heat and moisture—the two biggest pitfalls of the home oven. Professional bread ovens are built with a lot of mass to store heat and radiate it back steadily; home ovens are not. The doors for bread ovens are generally small and short in comparison to the size of their baking chamber, and they retain the moisture from steam injected into them and from the loaves themselves during the bake. Home ovens are not designed to do these things, but you can cheat the system (a bit) with the following equipment.

BAKING STONE: To aid in storing and radiating heat, a baking stone or pizza stone is a good investment. I recommend purchasing the largest stone that can fit into your oven to maximize the heated surface area. Rectangular stones are more versatile than round.

BAKING TOWELS: In France, they are known as *couches* (related to the English word *couch*, meaning a resting place) and are made of linen. In Sweden, they are called *bakdukar* and are generally cotton tea towels. While it's easy to buy linen *couches* online, I like to use heavyweight cotton tea towels. I dedicate a few of them to my baking and keep them apart from the rest of my kitchen towels. They are used to proof long loaves of bread in lieu of a basket. To use them, place loaves on the lightly floured towel folded in the middle to keep the loaves from sticking together. Positioning the loaves side by side helps to support them so they can better hold their shape, and laying another towel over the top keeps them from drying out. I also use baking towels to cool rye loaves, because they help keep a more pliable crust.

BANNETONS AND BROTFORMEN BASKETS: Baskets have traditionally been used to support the shape of loaves while they are proofing. French woven wicker banneton, often lined with linen, and German coil Brotformen, available in a variety of shapes, can be purchased online or in some kitchen stores, but they tend to be expensive. Less expensive wicker baskets can also be used. I drape a tea towel in them as a liner; you can even do the same with a mixing bowl.

BOWL SCRAPER AND DOUGH SCRAPER: These are two of the most useful tools for baking. The former is plastic and should be rounded on two corners; the latter, also called a bench scraper or bench knife, is best made of metal and should have a straight edge.

CAST-IRON SKILLET: In our commercial deck oven, steam is generated by a fine mist of water sprayed into a trough that is filled with metal rods that have been heated by the oven. To replicate this steam generator in a home oven, use a cast-iron skillet or metal pan with sides that are low enough to fit in between two oven racks so it can be positioned right below the baking stone.

DIGITAL KITCHEN SCALE: Please, please invest in a digital kitchen scale, preferably one that reads in metric and is accurate to one gram. There is no way to reliably measure dry ingredients without one.

FUNNEL: Buy a metal funnel with a long, flexible nozzle at the auto parts store. The one I use is called a flex-metal filler funnel. This allows you to position the end of the funnel at the top of your improvised steaming pan (or cast-iron skillet or metal pan) and close the oven door most of the way. You then pour water into the funnel, quickly pull out the funnel, and close the door tightly. This partly overcomes the big challenge with home ovens, which is not generating steam but retaining it, though it will never be the same as a steam generator in an enclosed professional bread oven.

INSTANT-READ DIGITAL THERMOMETER: Tracking temperature helps monitor the rate of fermentation, so an instant-read digital thermometer is handy. If your dough is on the cool side, move it to a warm spot in your kitchen, or if it is too warm, refrigerate it for a spell to slow it down.

LOAF PANS: You will need a loaf pan for a couple of the breads in this book. The recipes are based on a heavy-duty 8½ by 4½-inch pan. Other recipes (such as Pain de Mie, page 58) call for a 16 by 4-inch Pullman pan (a loaf pan with a tight-fitting slide-on lid). Or you can split the dough evenly between two standard bread pans and place a large heavy baking sheet with a weight on top to act as the lid.

PEEL: A baking peel is nice to have for sliding your loaves onto the baking stone, though you can also do this with a thin cookie sheet. If you buy a peel, get one that is at least 14 inches wide.

SCORING BLADE: Sharp blades are necessary to score loaves neatly without tearing the surface of the dough. In a commercial bakery, we use double-edged razor blades attached to a narrow metal stick. You can find blades attached to a plastic handle that, as long as you keep them clean and dry after using, should hold up for several bakes. A single-edged razor blade or a utility knife also works, or even a sharp serrated knife, though it is hard to get most knives as sharp as a razor blade.

STAINLESS-STEEL BOLTS: Large stainless-steel bolts or a heavy-gauge stainless-steel chain offer a lot of surface area for the water to come into contact with when you are using your home steam generator in a cast-iron skillet (see page 14) or metal pan.

INGREDIENTS

Bread is made from just a handful of simple ingredients: flour, water, salt, and yeast. Because of this, you should be mindful about selecting good-quality ingredients. One exciting development on the grain and flour front is the new local mills springing up. Just outside of Austin, we are lucky to have Barton Springs Mill, where we can get stone-ground wheat, rye, corn, and other grains.

Though I emphasize that the flavors of bread develop through fermentation, starting with flour that has good flavor also makes quite a difference in the flavor of the finished loaf. Try different brands of flour in your favorite recipe to see which you prefer.

Flour

UNBLEACHED ALL-PURPOSE FLOUR

For my basic flour, I prefer to use certain brands of all-purpose flour rather than bread flour, because in most instances I prefer its lower amount of gluten-forming protein. While bread flour is made of high-protein hard spring wheat, all-purpose flour is often a blend of lower-protein soft wheat and hard red winter wheat. Not all all-purpose flours are equal, however; a few are made from hard red winter wheat exclusively and these perform best for my recipes. I use flour from Central Milling, which you can get online or at Costco. Central Milling also produces the Whole Foods Market 365 Organic All-Purpose Flour, an excellent baking flour. King Arthur's Unbleached All-Purpose Flour is also made from hard red winter wheat and works well in these bread recipes.

Regardless of which brand you choose, please use unbleached flour. Flour naturally turns white as it ages, and its baking properties become more consistent over time. In bleached flour, bleaching agents are used to artificially age the flour. Besides not being necessary, bleaching robs the flour of flavor.

RYE FLOUR

Medium rye flour, which has some of the bran sifted out, used to be a staple at the grocery store but is much harder to find these days. Luckily, it can be ordered online. Most of the rye flour you see in stores now is the whole grain variety, sometimes called dark rye. It can be used in any of the rye bread recipes in this book, even where medium rye would be more traditional.

DUSTING FLOUR

You will see that I am quite adamant that you resist the urge to add flour to the work surface when you are first mixing and kneading the dough. However, once the dough has developed its structure through kneading and resting, you will want a light dusting of flour on the counter so that the dough does not stick while you are handling it for folding and shaping. For this dusting, I always use all-purpose flour no matter what the mix of flours is in the dough. With a handful cupped in my up-turned palm, fingers spread slightly, I cast a thin coat onto the table with a flick of my wrist. If during the shaping the dough still sticks to the surface, you can add a little more, but if the dough just slides without gripping at all, you will want to brush some away.

When you have a fully risen loaf, scored and ready to slide off your baking peel onto the hot baking stone in your oven, it is critical that it not stick at all. All-purpose flour does absorb water and can become sticky in contact with wet dough, so I like to use rice flour for dusting the peel. Because it is only starch, it will not absorb water at room temperature and a light dusting will protect the loaf from sticking to the wooden peel. Semolina and cornmeal, which are more granular and take longer to absorb water, also work well for dusting the peel, but they are more noticeable on the bottom of the baked loaf. In France, bakers who work with

FLOUR AND MILLING

Flour is made from grains, which are essentially the seeds of plants in the grass family. Grains have three basic components: the germ that sprouts into the baby plant; the endosperm, a store of carbohydrates and proteins that provide nutrients for the sprout as it develops roots and leaves; and a protective outer layer called bran.

Modern mills grind the grains into flour in progressive steps, called breaks, between sets of rollers that turn in opposite directions. The rollers can be grooved or smooth and are set progressively closer together at each break, grinding the particles more and more finely. Between each break, the crushed grain is sent through a giant sifter with screens that have progressively smaller mesh. This separates the particles into several streams. The bran and germ are removed from the endosperm, which continues through the subsequent breaks to be ground into white flour. Whole wheat flour from a roller mill is achieved by recombining all of the streams at the end of the process.

Stone mills grind the flour between two stone disks, one of which remains stationary, while the other rotates. The spacing between the stones determines how fine the flour becomes. Some of the bran can be sifted out to achieve a lighter flour, though highly refined white flour is difficult to achieve with a stone mill. Stone mills, however, can produce whole grain flour with exceptional aroma and flavor, especially when used fresh from the mill.

In high-extraction flour, a special kind used for the Miche (page 76), a higher percentage of the whole kernel is used than in refined white flour. The best version of this flour comes from a stone mill, where it has been sifted to remove some of the coarser bran but still has the germ and much of the outer layers of the endosperm. These layers contain more minerals and other components that carry more flavor than the very center of the kernel.

wood-fired ovens often dust their peels with finely ground olive pits.

Rice flour can also help prevent breads from sticking that are set to proof for long periods, especially under refrigeration, such as Easy Tiger Pretzels (page 164). If you want to proof your loaves slowly overnight in the refrigerator, a blend of half rice flour and half all-purpose flour can be used to dust the proofing basket or the *couche* and help the bread to release easier the next day.

Salt

Sea salt, either fine or coarse, is excellent for use in bread baking. Some French bakeries use coarse, moist *sel gris*, or gray sea salt, in their dough. However, the recipes in this book were developed and tested using kosher salt, which I often default to because it is readily available and has a clean, pure salt flavor. Avoid using normal table salt, as it can have an off-flavor from the additives and iodine.

When weighing your ingredients—you are weighing, right?—salts are interchangeable. You may want to adjust slightly when measuring by volume, using a little less than level spoonfuls for very fine salt, or mounding slightly for very coarse salt.

Water

Tap water is usually fine for bread making, unless your water has an off-flavor (sometimes Austin water tastes grassy) or is very soft. Purified water, either through a home filter system or bottled, is great if you prefer not to use tap water. Do not use distilled water or water that has been softened, as it has been stripped of minerals that are good for dough structure and fermentation.

Yeast

I prefer to use instant yeast. It is dried using a more modern, lower-heat process than active dry yeast, so more of the yeast cells are still active. I find that active dry yeast can impart an undesirable, residual yeasty flavor in the final bread. Instant yeast has a long shelf life and ferments reliably and

efficiently. It is convenient because most of the time it can be added directly into the flour and does not need to be hydrated or proofed in water before-hand. Exceptions come when there is less water and time for the yeast to hydrate well, like in the sponge for the Vörtbröd (Swedish "Wort" Bread; see page 116), when it is helpful to make a slurry and hydrate the yeast before incorporating it into the dough.

There is some confusion in the terminology used for different brands of yeast, but leading brands of "rapid-rise" or "fast-acting" yeast are really the same as instant yeast. If you are unable to find instant yeast, I recommend substituting rapid-rise or fast-acting yeast; just be sure to measure for the weight that is called for in the recipe.

Fresh yeast, also called compressed yeast, can be used, but it is much harder to find and does not keep well. If you do use fresh yeast, triple the amount by weight of the instant yeast called for in these recipes. Make sure that the yeast truly is fresh. It should break and crumble cleanly and not be soft or mushy at all. Some people feel that fresh yeast is necessary when making traditional or family recipes where they, or perhaps a relative, have always used it, but the appropriate amount of instant yeast will produce the same results.

If you make a lot of sweet yeasted doughs, such as the Vörtbröd (page 116), consider buying an osmotolerant yeast, often referred to as "Gold Label," because that is how the leading brand, Saf-Instant, distinguishes it from its Red Label instant yeast made for lean dough. A high amount of sugar (where the sugar is 10 percent the weight of the flour or higher) creates an environment where it is harder for yeast to exchange nutrients and gas through its cell walls. Traditionally, that has required an increase in the amount of yeast added to sweet dough to make up for the inefficacy. The selected strains of yeast in Saf-Instant Gold yeast are able to work effectively in the high sugar environment so that additional yeast is not necessary for good fermentation.

TIPS FOR SUCCESSFUL BREAD MAKING

Here are some guidelines for better, more consistent baking. More detailed techniques and instructions follow, but these are important fundamentals to think about for all the breads you make.

Organize Before You Start

As with any cooking or baking, it is a good idea to gather your *mise en place.* Your ingredients and tools should all be collected before you begin. Read through the recipe and make sure you have what you need for each stage. Even after many years of baking, I notoriously get dough on the cabinet door because I always forget to get out a bowl scraper before my hands are covered in sticky dough.

Invest in a Digital Scale

Weighing all the ingredients makes bread making much easier. You will have better success right from the beginning if you use a digital scale, and they can be had for around $25. I know I mentioned this in the Equipment section as well, but it is that important.

Adjust the Water, Not the Flour

Flour absorbs different amounts of water, depending on many factors, and you always want the flour, salt, yeast, and any other ingredients to remain in the same proportion to each other. That means adjusting the amount of water if the dough is not the right consistency, not the flour. It takes a little practice, but I give you clues in each recipe of what to look and feel for. In the beginning of a recipe, I instruct you to hold back a small amount of the water, about 5 percent, which is about a tablespoon for every 300 grams (1¼ cups) of water in the recipe. As everything comes together, you can add it to the dough if needed. In fact, sometimes you may need to add additional water beyond what is called for in

the recipe. During kneading, do not flour the work surface or add flour to the dough. It will be sticky at first, but as it develops it will become less sticky.

Let the Dough Develop Partially on its Own

Kneading takes effort and time, but resting the dough at 15-minute intervals does a lot of the work for you. After combining the ingredients and working the water into the flour, stretch the dough and fold it over itself and then let it rest. This stretching and folding develops the dough more effectively and is easier than more traditional kneading (pushing on the dough with the heel of your hand), which can also tear the dough.

After partially developing the dough with this initial stretching, folding, and resting, I then give it four more folds, at 15-minute intervals, over the course of an hour. Each fold only takes a moment, and there is always something to do in the kitchen or around the house in between.

I have found that not only is this less work than traditional kneading, it develops the dough better and more reliably.

Temperature is Important

Dough temperature is hard to control at home. Even if you hit the target temperature after kneading, a small batch of dough can change temperature during fermentation. You may have to move the dough around to different spots in your kitchen.

Ideally, I like most wheat-based dough to be in the range of 72°F to 76°F and rye dough to be a bit warmer, between 78°F and 82°F. You can easily measure the temperature of the dough with an instant-read thermometer.

If your kitchen and flour are cold, use warmer water. Conversely, when they are warm, use colder water. In the heat of Texas summer, our tap water can be warm enough to bathe in, so I add a couple of ice cubes to cool it down.

Temperature influences the rate at which the yeast ferments the dough. If your dough is warmer, the fermentation time will be quicker; if your dough is colder, it will take more time.

Preheat the Oven

Plan ahead and make sure that you heat the oven, baking stone, and the steaming pan thoroughly. I like to give it at least an hour, which sounds like overkill, but trust me, it is not. Your oven thermostat will read the air temperature and say that it has come up to temperature in as little as 10 minutes, but the walls of the oven, the baking stone, and the steaming pan do not truly heat up in such a short time. Those are the places that can store enough heat to help give the loaf the burst of energy it needs to "bloom" or spring in the oven and to develop a nice crust. When scored properly and with good heat, the loaf "blooms" outward, not just rising but opening up like a flower.

Do Not Peek During Baking

It is especially important to keep the oven closed during the beginning of the bake so the heat and steam stay inside. When putting the bread in the oven, open and close the door as quickly as you can and keep it closed for at least 10 to 20 minutes, depending on the size of the loaf and the total bake time. An exception can be made for bread with a hearty portion of rye flour, like the Rugbrød (Danish rye; page 108) or the Bauernbrot (German farmer's bread; page 148). You want to let some of the moisture out and help reduce the temperature after about 5 minutes of baking by cracking open the door briefly.

Listen to the Bread

Color can tell you when a loaf is done, but you can also turn it over and rap on the bottom to check for doneness. It should sound hollow. If you hear a heavy thump when you rap on the loaf, return it to the oven for 5 minutes, then check again.

ADJUST THE WATER, NOT THE FLOUR

One of the important things I learned as a professional baker is how flour can absorb different amounts of water, depending on many factors, such as the variety of the wheat, its growing conditions, the way it is milled, its age, and even how it has been stored. In contrast to most home baking recipes—which tell you to add more flour to a dough to achieve the desired consistency—in a professional kitchen, I learned to vary the water. For a consistent product, we want to make sure that the flour, salt, yeast, and any other ingredients stay in the same proportion to each other, then adjust the water as needed. That is why I encourage you to avoid adding flour to the work surface or the dough when stretching and folding. It can seem sticky and messy for a while, but if you stay with it, using your scraper and letting your dough develop, you will have a better and moister loaf.

DOUGH FEEL

While the gluten is absorbing the water, the dough will remain sticky and feel "wet" to the touch, even in dough with a relatively low hydration (percentage of water). It is more useful to develop a feel for how stiff or soft the dough is by judging the resistance it has when you squeeze it. To feel if a dough is the right consistency, pinch it between your thumb and two or three fingers in several places and gauge how soft or stiff the dough feels. Refer to the following chart.

DOUGH FEEL	CONSISTENCY	EXAMPLE
Stiff	Solid with very little give	Biga (page 183)
Medium-stiff	Some give, like a rubber bouncy ball	Semolina
Medium-soft	More give but with some resistance; you should feel a core	Pain de Campagne (page 40)
Soft	Fingers almost touch	Ciabatta (page 188)

STEPS TO MAKING GREAT BREAD

Now we will dive a little deeper into the general techniques for making bread at home. While each recipe has its own instructions, read through this section to get an overview on my bread-making process. There is also more detailed instruction here about adjusting the water for different types of flour, as well as how to improve fermentation with starters and alternative methods of mixing.

Mixing and Kneading

To make a bread dough, there are two steps: mixing to combine all the ingredients and kneading to start to develop the gluten. I prefer to both mix and knead with my hands, so I can feel how the dough is coming together, which allows me to make adjustments. You could use a wooden spoon for the mixing, but your hands are going to get sticky during the kneading anyway (and then you will just have a dirty spoon to clean).

Start with a bowl large enough to allow the dough to at least double in volume. Weigh each of your dry ingredients (flours, salt, and yeast) and put them in the bowl. Blend these dry ingredients together with your fingers to evenly distribute them. If there is a starter in the recipe, divide it into pieces and scatter them on top of the flour. Make a well in the center of the flour. Pour the water into the well, holding back a small amount, about 5 percent or a tablespoon for every 300 grams (1¼ cups) in the recipe for later, until you know if the flour will need it all. Keep in mind, even the same brand of flour can vary from batch to batch (see page 23).

Make sure you have a plastic bowl scraper at hand, then start to blend the water into the flour with your fingers. As the flour begins to absorb the water and the mixture starts to thicken, plunge both hands in and squeeze the dough. Concentrate on getting the water worked into the flour first, as the starter is already hydrated, and then start to work in the starter as you squeeze. Work from the side of the bowl closest to you across to the other side, squeezing with both hands. Rotate the bowl a quarter turn and squeeze your way through the dough again. You will feel the dough starting to become a more cohesive mass, and the water and starter will become more fully incorporated. Use your bowl scraper from time to time to scrape the sticky dough from the sides of the bowl into the center. Keep rotating the bowl and squeezing the dough until everything is fully incorporated, 1 to 2 minutes. The dough will be a shaggy and sticky mass.

Now is the best time to check the feel of the dough and adjust the water to achieve the right consistency. Each recipe will let you know the proper consistency for that bread, but for general guidance, see "Dough Feel" on page 23. Remember, it is better to have a dough that is a little wet than one that is too dry.

Turn out the dough onto an unfloured work surface, using the bowl scraper to get as much as you can out of the bowl and off your hands, and incorporate any small pieces into the dough. Resist the urge to add flour to the work surface or the dough at this stage. Kneading and resting the dough will develop the gluten and make it less sticky. Adding flour before you give the dough a chance to develop will only make for a dry loaf.

Starting with the edge closest to you, grab the dough with both hands, palms down, and pull it gently toward you. Stretch it up and flip it over the top of the dough mass by 2 or 3 inches and press it into the surface. Scrape up the dough with a dough scraper, rotate it a quarter turn, and repeat the same movement as before. Keep rotating, stretching, and folding the dough, working your way to the far

PRE-FERMENTS: USING STARTERS TO ADD FLAVOR

Pre-ferments, also commonly known as starters, provide an effective way to build complex flavors and more interesting textures in your bread. Basically, you are taking a portion of the total flour in the dough and some of the water and fermenting it ahead of time. For many breads in this book, we will make a simple, yeast-based pre-ferment, which is actually a very basic dough in itself. In France, they call this *pâte fermentée*, and it is the same as baguette dough. We use this technique at Easy Tiger for our baguettes as well as some other yeasted doughs. Instead of mixing a separate batch of *pâte fermentée*, we make extra baguette dough to use as the starter on the next shift. This makes for a very effective and production-friendly starter.

Other starters in this book include a *poolish* and *biga*, both made from flour, water, and yeast, without the addition of salt. *Poolish* is made with equal parts flour and water (by weight) and has a batter-like consistency, whereas *biga*, the Italian term for a starter, is a very stiff dough, with only half as much water as flour. Both have a very small amount of yeast, which ferments the flour slowly, building flavor for the final dough.

Sourdough breads use a special kind of starter that is made by capturing and cultivating wild yeast and benevolent bacteria in a sourdough culture. Included in this book are instructions for starting and using a traditional French-style *levain* and a rye sourdough starter that is used for many of the Scandinavian and German breads.

side of the mass, a total of 4 or 5 times, which will take 3 to 5 minutes. With each stretch and fold of the dough, you will feel it developing, becoming more cohesive, less sticky, and easier to stretch. The stretches should be gentle enough not to tear the dough.

When most of the dough holds together and easily pulls off the work surface as you stretch it, slide the dough scraper under it and gather it into a ball. The dough will not be fully developed yet and will still be a little sticky.

Smooth the surface of the dough by cupping your hands on the bottom of the far side of the ball and pulling it gently toward you, allowing the dough to grip the work surface, then move your hands to the left, rotating the dough. Return your hands to the far side of the ball and pull and rotate it again one or two times more. This will stretch and tighten the surface and help shape the dough into a smooth ball. Put the ball back into the bowl with the smooth surface facing up and allow it to rest for 15 minutes.

Turn out the dough on a lightly floured work surface, with the smooth side down. Gently press out the dough to flatten it into a round about 2 inches thick. Take the edge closest to you and stretch it up and over the top of the dough, about two-thirds of the way to the opposite side, and press into the surface. Grab the edge opposite you and stretch and fold it toward you over the first fold, about two-thirds of the way to the closest edge, and press into the surface. Rotate the dough a quarter turn and repeat with two more folds, first away from you and then toward you.

Turn the dough over so the seams are underneath and pull into a ball by cupping your hands on the far side, pulling toward you, and rotating counterclockwise, stretching the surface tight. Repeat one or two times to form a ball. You will notice that the dough is more developed and will stretch tighter than before. Be careful not to stretch too tight; if the surface starts to tear, stop tightening. Return the ball to the bowl, smooth surface facing up, and let rest for 15 minutes.

Repeat this stretching and folding three times at 15-minute intervals for a total of four folds over an hour. The smooth, elastic dough will develop a good gluten network. After the final fold, cover the bowl with a tea towel or plastic wrap and let sit in a warm, draft-free place to ferment.

Fermentation

Let the dough rest and ferment according to the recipe. During this phase, the yeast (either instant yeast or the wild yeasts of a sourdough starter) is converting the dough's sugars into carbon dioxide and alcohol, building flavor and further developing the dough. The carbon dioxide is captured by the gluten network, leavening and lightening the dough. Most wheat-based doughs should double in volume and feel airy when gently touched. Dough with a large percentage of rye flour will still grow and become airy, but will not increase in volume as much as a wheat-based dough.

Many recipes in this book call for folding the dough again during the fermentation process, a step that is also known as punching down the dough. This can help further strengthen the dough and also redistributes the yeast, reinvigorating the fermentation and helping to even out the dough's temperature. To do this, turn out the dough on a lightly floured surface, smooth side down. Press it gently to flatten a bit. It is okay to press out some of the gases, but do it gently and not too thoroughly. Grabbing the edge opposite you, stretch the dough up and over the top of the dough mass, about two

thirds toward the center. Gently press the dough down, then stretch the edge closest to you and fold it over the top of the first fold. Press it in gently. Rotate the dough a quarter turn and repeat two more folds over the top, one away from you, one toward you. Turn the dough over, cup your hands behind it, and gently pull toward you to stretch the surface. At the same time, move your hands to the left, rotating the dough counterclockwise about a quarter turn, rounding it. Repeat one or two times to form a ball. Return the dough to the bowl, covering it again for the remaining fermentation time.

Shaping

There are two basic shapes for most of the breads in this book: round and oblong. For each of them, the goal is the same: to give good structure to the loaf so that the final rising, aka proofing, can leaven the bread well.

Dust the work surface lightly with all-purpose flour and turn out the dough so that the smooth side is down. Divide the dough according to the recipe. For most wheat-based breads, we do an initial shaping that starts to stretch the gluten; regardless of the final shape, we make a round at this stage. Then we give the dough a rest and do a final shaping to tighten the structure. This final shape builds on that initial stretch, pulling the surface tauter and giving the dough a nice, tight structure. Just be careful not to stretch to the point where the dough starts to tear. If it does, stop stretching and let the dough rest according to the instructions in the recipe.

Proofing

After the dough is shaped, it is set to proof, what a baker calls the final rise. Proofing is the final stage of leavening the dough, which builds the fermentation gases in the loaf to make it lighter and help it achieve the desired interior texture of the bread, what is known as crumb structure. This process also helps hold and direct the shape of the proofing bread and makes it easier to transfer it to the oven when ready.

AUTOLYSE

Professor Raymond Calvel (see page 37) developed this method of resting dough to allow the flour to fully hydrate and the gluten to start to form in order to reduce mixing times. This was in reaction to the long, high-speed mixing that had become popular in France in the late 1950's and 1960's and that was responsible for loss of flavor and texture in traditional French breads of the time. Indeed, it is not hard to find plenty of bland, tasteless bread in France today, though there are many excellent artisan bakers working there— you just need to seek them out.

For the *autolyse*, flour and water are mixed together until just combined and then allowed to rest for about 20 minutes. During the rest period, the gluten-forming proteins absorb the water and start to link. When mixing is resumed, the structure becomes more organized and the gluten is strengthened in a shorter period of time, which reduces the oxidation of the dough. It is this "bleaching" of the dough during oxidation that robs flavor.

Salt is omitted during the *autolyse*, as salt attracts water more readily than the gluten. Yeast is also typically left out, as we do not want fermentation to begin yet, but since we use instant yeast in this book, it is best to blend the yeast into the flour before adding the water for the *autolyse*. If you do not, the instant yeast does not dissolve properly during the short mixing time left after the *autolyse*. Dough-type starters, like the *pâte fermentée* or our *levain*, are also left out of the *autolyse* stage.

Others have experimented with using longer *autolyse* times, often 24 hours and sometimes even more. This is done for a different reason and must be done with care. It allows the enzymes (see page 121) to break down more of the starch into sugars. In particular, a Parisian baker named Phillipe Gosselin uses a long, cold overnight *autolyse*, then mixes in the yeast and salt the next day and slowly allows the dough to warm up and the fermentation to begin. Peter Reinhart picked up this technique and developed it further for home bakers in his book *The Bread Baker's Apprentice*. He particularly likes the residual sugars that are released by the enzymes but not fully fermented, leaving the bread with a sweetness and contributing to a darker caramelization.

Some people advocate using the *autolyse* technique even when hand mixing their dough. I have tried this a few times, comparing it with the method presented here, and I can find no discernible advantages. Even though I put the salt and the yeast (and pre-ferment) into the mix in the beginning, the rest periods during the first hour of folding the dough accomplish the thorough hydration of the dough and the formation of the gluten network. I do think it helps to make a better dough when using a mixer and would highly recommend it when mixing by machine.

Free-form hearth loaves, those that will be baked directly on the baking stone in your oven, are often proofed in baskets (see Equipment, page 14) or between folds of cloth, called *couche* in French, which help hold an oblong shape and keep adjacent loaves from sticking to one another. Breads that are baked in loaf pans or on sheet pans are generally proofed in or on the baking pan. During proofing, breads should be covered so they do not dry out and form a skin. Use a tea towel at this point, as plastic wrap can stick to the surface of the bread and cause it to rip or deflate when pulled off. Proof bread in a warm (but not too hot), draft-free place, ideally somewhere between 75°F and 80°F.

I find proofing to be the hardest part of the bread-making process. It takes some practice. Each recipe gives a suggested proofing time, but many factors—including the temperature of the dough and room, humidity, how the dough was fermented before it was shaped, and how it was handled during shaping—can affect the outcome. Start looking at and gently touching the loaves 10 to 15 minutes before the time given. One method of testing if a dough is proofed is to gently push it with your fingertips; if it springs back slowly, it is ready to be baked. If it springs back quickly, it needs more time. If it does not spring back at all, it is overproofed. However, factors such as the wetness of the dough and the tightness of the shaping can affect the springback, so it is not always the most reliable test. Use this method as a starting point, and with experience, you will be able to feel how much air is in the dough and know when it is proofed simply by touch.

A dough is overproofed when the surface is no longer smooth and taut. If you overproof a loaf, there is a risk that it will deflate and collapse either while scoring or in the oven. But if you catch it early on, before the dough completely collapses, it is possible to reshape the loaf and let it proof again. The results will not be as good as if it were correctly proofed the first time around, but you can usually still get a decent loaf. Just watch it more carefully the next time, and make sure you set a timer.

Baking

Next comes the trickiest part of baking at home: trying to duplicate the intense and steady heat of a bread oven and create enough moisture so that the loaf can achieve its full bloom (see page 22). When a loaf of bread is first introduced to the heat of the oven, all the fermentation gases and moisture trapped inside expand and allow the loaf to fill out to its full volume. High, steady heat and some moisture in the baking chamber promote this oven spring, as it is called, while scoring helps direct and control how it happens.

It is important to thoroughly preheat the oven, baking stone, and steaming pan (see page 22). Place the steaming pan on a rack on the lowest rung and the stone on a rack one rung above the steaming pan. You should turn on your oven at least 1 hour before baking your bread. I usually do this at the beginning of the final proof, or sooner for breads that have a shorter proofing time.

You will need a baking peel or an inverted baking sheet to transfer the loaf onto the baking stone. Dust the peel with rice flour (see page 19). Turn the proofed loaf out of the basket or baking towel onto the peel with the seam side down (except in the case of the Bauernbrot; see page 148).

Next you need to score the loaf. Scoring the surface of the bread not only makes for a prettier loaf, but also helps direct how the loaf will expand when it first hits the heat of the oven. A razor blade is the best tool for this job, though a small, sharp serrated knife will also work. Quickly draw the blade across the loaf, making cuts about ⅛ inch deep. For many scores, the blade is nearly flat against the surface of the loaf, while others are perpendicular; specific scoring instructions are included with each recipe.

Besides proper scoring, a moist oven is necessary for good oven spring and for good crust formation. Using a metal funnel with a long, flexible nozzle (see page 14), place the end of the nozzle at the edge of the steaming pan and close the door as much as you can. Pour about 60 grams (¼ cup) water through the funnel. As soon as the water hits the steaming pan, pull out the nozzle and shut the door tight. Let the steam settle for 30 seconds or so (you can pre-steam right before you score the loaf).

Now give the peel or baking sheet a little shake to make sure the loaf moves freely. Open the oven, place the peel in the center of the baking stone, and quickly pull it out from under the loaf. (If the recipe makes two loaves and your stone can fit them both at once while still leaving them room to expand without touching, load the first loaf accordingly, then quickly score and load the second loaf.) Close the oven door immediately.

Crack the door open just enough to stick the funnel nozzle into the edge of the steaming pan and add another 117 to 235 grams (½ to 1 cup) water. Remove the funnel as soon as all the water hits the steaming pan and close the door tightly.

Resist the temptation to open the oven door to peek at your loaf too soon. You want the oven to stay moist while the loaf is expanding and you want the heat to stay as steady as possible. After about two-thirds of the recommended bake time, you can take a peek. You want the crust to be a deep brown color. Slip the loaf out, turn it over, and rap the bottom—if it is done baking, it should sound hollow. If it still gives a heavy thud, return the loaf to the oven for 5 to 10 minutes.

Cool the bread on a wire cooling rack until completely cool.

USING A STAND MIXER

Although I really enjoy mixing bread dough by hand, there are times when I do find it convenient to mix by machine. All of the breads in this book can be made in a stand mixer. Here is the basic technique for doing so. These instructions will not be repeated for every recipe, so refer back to this section when you wish to use your mixer. Any time there is a significant deviation from these basic instructions, it will be noted in the individual recipe.

For the starter, combine all the ingredients in the bowl of your stand mixer. Using the dough hook, mix on low speed until the ingredients come together and start to pull off the sides of the bowl. You may have to stop the mixer and use a scraper on the sides and bottom a couple of times to help it along. You can also go up one or two notches in speed depending on your mixer and the amount of dough in the bowl; this will help pick everything up. You do not need to fully develop the starter as the long fermentation will further develop the gluten structure, so stop when everything is fully incorporated and the dough has just started to pull away from the sides of the bowl.

If you want to mix your final dough in a stand mixer, it is useful to do what is called an *autolyse*. Instructions on how to do this follow; read the sidebar on page 28 if you want to learn more about the method.

Put the flour and instant yeast, if using, into the bowl of the mixer fitted with the dough hook. Blend the yeast into the flour with your fingers. Add most of the water, holding back about 5 percent, which is about a tablespoon for every 300 grams (1¼ cups) of water in the recipe. Leaving some of the water out in the beginning will allow you to make adjustments to the dough consistency if you need to.

Mix the flour and water on low speed until the dough comes together, all the water is incorporated, and there are no lumps of flour. If it seems too dry and some of the flour is not being picked up, you can add the rest of the water. Shut the mixer off and with your thumb and a couple of fingers, grab the dough and pull upward. A piece should break off fairly easily. Push that piece back into the top of the dough and allow the dough to rest for 20 minutes in the bowl.

After the rest, grab the dough between your thumb and a couple of fingers and gently pull on the dough a bit as before. Notice how the dough now stretches without breaking immediately; the gluten web has already started to form. This will make the rest of the mixing take less time and give a better development to the final dough.

Now is the best time to check the dough feel as well. Feel the whole mass of dough in the bowl by squeezing it with your fingers. Refer to the recipe and the chart on page 23 to determine if the dough is the correct consistency. If it feels too stiff, turn the mixer on and add the water you held back.

Add the salt and mix on low speed. Once you cannot see any salt on the surface, after 1 to 1½ minutes, stop the mixer and add the starter, divided into three or four pieces. Resume mixing on low speed for 2 or 3 minutes, until all the starter is incorporated, then bump the speed up one or two notches.

Watch the dough carefully; it should pull off the sides of the bowl and start to look smooth, but not get too shiny or start to go slack. It is better to undermix than overmix, as the dough will build more strength during fermentation.

Stop the mixer and pinch off a small piece of dough. Gently stretch it with your hands, rotating and pulling it out to see if you can form a "window," or a thin film of dough, before it breaks. A thin, clear window indicates that the dough is fully developed, but for our purposes, you want to stop mixing before that point, so you should still have a "cloudy" window as it starts to tear.

Cover the bowl with a damp tea towel or plastic wrap and allow the dough to ferment according to the recipe, including giving it any folds included in the fermentation section (but not the four folds that are a part of the hand-kneading technique).

French Bread

Learning from the Masters

FRENCH BREAD is arguably the world's most iconic bread. From the ubiquitous baguette to a rustic country loaf, French bread inspires bakers around the globe. French baking has been central to my career, grounding my technique no matter what type of bread I am baking.

Much like formal French cuisine, the techniques for making French breads have been codified over the ages. Although the formula may not vary much from baker to baker, the skill of the baker brings out flavors and nuances that create a signature style. In the annual Parisian competition for the best baguette in the city, which besides a cash prize carries the honor of supplying the French president baguettes for a year, the winning recipe could start off with the same list of ingredients as a pale, cottony selection from the *supermarché* (supermarket). Yet the flour type, use of a starter, mixing time, mixing speed, dough temperature, fermentation time, shaping technique, proofing conditions, scoring, oven type, baking temperature, and length of the bake all impact the final loaf.

Early in my career, I had an opportunity to attend one of the first seminars put on by the fledgling Bread Bakers Guild of America. It was taught by the renowned baking expert Professor Raymond Calvel. Professor Calvel taught generations of bakers and millers in France and traveled the world teaching the craft of French bread baking. For me and a handful of American bakers who assembled in Berkeley, California, it was our first chance to see the techniques and methods of a skilled, educated baker up close. This was shortly after I had taken over as head baker at Seattle's Grand Central Bakery. It helped push me through the first great learning curve of my baking career, as I was tackling the responsibility of all bread production for a bakery's wholesale division.

French bread went through a period of decline starting in the late 1950s with the advent of high-speed mixers. Bakers used them to knead their dough intensely, forcing more air into it, then shortened the fermentation time. This made it possible for them to shorten their hours and increase their production, often a necessity as the French government regulated the price of many bread varieties, most notably the baguette. However, it also led to an inferior flavor and texture, which precipitated a decline in bread consumption in France. Professor Calvel worked tirelessly to fight against this trend and developed techniques to help shorten the production cycle while still building great flavor. The technique he is most known for, the autolyse (see page 28), involves a resting period that allows the gluten structure to start to form so that a much shorter kneading time is necessary to develop the dough, preventing the bleaching out of the color and flavor from the dough.

What I learned from Calvel fundamentally influenced my understanding of the techniques of making bread. To this day, I make baguettes the way I learned at that seminar and use the mixing, fermenting, and shaping methods I first encountered there for numerous other breads. Even so, I still had much to learn several years later when I took over as the instructor for the professional bread baking program at the French Culinary Institute in New York City. Teaching others meant not only knowing how to make good bread, but understanding the reasons and science behind the methods to be able to pass that information along to others. From the esteemed deans of the school, André Soltner, Alain Sailhac, Jacques Torres, and Jacques Pépin, I gained an even deeper appreciation for the importance of skilled technique in cooking and baking. In an article for the *New York Times*, Pépin explained the proper way to *slice* a baguette. I often give this article to my bakers to show them that even cutting a baguette has a proper technique.

Later, when I was the head baker at Bouley Bakery, also in New York City, I had the opportunity to visit Tours, France, and learn more from Jacques Mahou, a master baker and owner of three bakeries, all with traditional wood-fired ovens. As a consultant, Mahou had provided most of the original recipes for David Bouley's bread program and Bouley sent me over to spend a week with Mahou in France. Most of Mahou's breads were based on a *levain*, the French sourdough starter, and he taught me some of the older ways of building and using a *levain*. While in most modern bread formulas the ratios of all the ingredients are relative to the weight of the flour, Mahou's technique adjusted the proportion of salt and starter as the amount of water changed. He also adjusted the amount of *levain* in the final dough depending upon the season, adding more if the weather was cold and less during warmer months.

Perhaps the most important part of that whole trip was getting to see and touch his starter—to feel its consistency, watch it develop between feedings, and learn to observe which characteristics meant it was ready to add to the final dough. Because North American flour typically absorbs more water than its French counterpart, my starter in New York was drier and stiffer than his and less lively as a result. When I returned to Bouley Bakery, I increased the amount of water in our starter by 10 percent so that it would feel like the one in France. I saw an immediate improvement in the starter and all the breads we made with it. They were more alive and vigorous in their fermentation and rose to greater volume in the oven and came out with a better crust. Inside, the crumb structure was improved, and naturally, the bread was moister and tasted better. I got

all that just from what I learned by seeing and touching Mahou's dough.

To introduce and understand the basic techniques of bread making, we will start with *pain de campagne*, a classic French country bread. Made with a yeasted starter, this robust loaf is not only a great master recipe for learning the fundamentals of bread making, but will also be a welcome addition to your table.

While I am not a huge fan of adding a whole lot of extra ingredients into bread dough, there are some classic fruit and nut additions that harmonize well. In the variations on the *campagne* recipe, we take a look at some of these, learning when and how to incorporate them.

For sourdough fans, there are instructions on how to build and maintain a *levain* and a couple of variations of *pain au levain* leavened with that starter.

PAIN DE CAMPAGNE

French Country Bread

**MAKES 2 ROUND
LOAVES**

STARTER 13 to 37 hours

MIXING & KNEADING 1 hour 20 minutes

FERMENTATION 1½ to 2 hours

SHAPING 30 minutes

PROOFING 1 to 2 hours

BAKING 40 to 50 minutes

A classic bread for anyone's repertoire, here *pain de campagne* serves as a master recipe that will introduce you to my bread-making techniques. With a lengthy fermentation time, a touch of rye flour, and a yeasted starter, this is a full-flavored, versatile bread that showcases the fundamentals of good bread making.

Referred to as *pâte fermentée* in French and often translated as "pre-fermented dough," or simply "pre-ferment," the starter is a basic bread dough itself. In the bakeshop, we use our baguette dough as *pâte fermentée*, which makes for an effective, production-friendly method, as we simply make extra dough with each batch of baguettes to set aside as the starter for the next day. There are several breads in this book that use this same starter.

STARTER

ALL-PURPOSE FLOUR	480 grams	3¾ cups
SALT	10 grams	2 teaspoons
INSTANT YEAST	2 grams	½ teaspoon
WATER	310 grams	1⅓ cups

Put the flour, salt, and yeast in a large bowl and blend together with your fingers to evenly distribute them. Make a well in the center of the flour and add the water.

Using your hand, draw the flour into the water, stirring and blending with your fingers. As it begins to come together, squeeze the dough with your hands to better incorporate the water into the flour. Starting at the near side of the bowl, grasp the dough with both hands and squeeze it between your thumbs and fingers. Rotate the bowl and continue to squeeze the dough, working in the water and working out any clumps of flour. Use a plastic bowl scraper to scrape down the sides and bottom of the bowl, folding the dough over on top of itself.

The dough should be medium-stiff, having some give but also a pretty solid core, like a rubber bouncy ball.

Because this dough will ferment a long time, you do not need to develop the gluten much; just squeeze and work the dough until it is fully combined with no lumps. Form the dough into a rough ball in the bowl and cover it with plastic wrap, or place in a container with a lid.

Let the dough sit at room temperature for 1 hour, then refrigerate for at least 12 hours or up to 36 hours.

DOUGH

ALL-PURPOSE FLOUR	600 grams	5 cups
WHOLE RYE FLOUR	120 grams	1 cup plus 1½ tablespoons
SALT	16 grams	1 tablespoon
INSTANT YEAST	3 grams	¾ teaspoon
STARTER	All from above	
WATER	470 grams	2 cups
RICE FLOUR	For dusting	

Mixing and Kneading

Put the all-purpose flour, rye flour, salt, and yeast in a large bowl and blend together with your fingers to evenly distribute them. Divide the starter into six pieces and scatter them on top of the flour. Make a well in the center of the flour and add the water, holding back a small amount (25 grams, or 1 tablespoon plus 2 teaspoons) until you see if the flour needs it all.

Make sure you have a plastic bowl scraper at hand, then start to blend the water into the flour with your fingers. As the flour begins to absorb the water and

CONTINUED

the mixture starts to thicken, plunge both hands in and squeeze the dough between your thumbs and fingers. Concentrate on getting the water worked into the flour first, as the starter is already hydrated, and then start to work in the starter as you squeeze. Work from the side of the bowl closest to you across to the other side, squeezing with both hands. Rotate the bowl a quarter turn and squeeze your way through the dough again. You will feel the dough starting to come together as a more cohesive mass, and the water and starter will become more fully incorporated. Use your bowl scraper from time to time to scrape the sticky dough from the sides of the bowl into the center. Keep rotating the bowl and squeezing the dough until everything is fully incorporated, a total of 1 to 2 minutes. It will remain a shaggy and sticky mass.

The dough should be medium-soft, having definite give but also some resistance; you should be able to feel a core when you squeeze it. Add the reserved water if the dough is not soft enough. Add the water a little at a time, squeezing it into the dough as you have been. You may even have to add more water to get the right consistency if it still feels too stiff. It is better to have a dough that is a little wet than one that is too dry.

Turn out the dough onto an unfloured work surface, using the bowl scraper to get as much as you can out of the bowl and off your hands, and incorporate any small pieces into the dough. Resist the urge to add flour to the work surface or the dough at this stage. Kneading and resting the dough will develop the gluten and make it less sticky. Adding flour before you give the dough a chance to develop will only make for a dry loaf.

Starting with the edge closest to you, grab the dough with both hands, palms down, and pull it gently toward you. Stretch it up and flip it over the top of the dough mass by 2 or 3 inches and press it into the surface. Use your dough scraper to gather the mass together and scrape it all off the work

surface, rotate it a quarter turn, and repeat the same movement as before. Keep rotating, stretching, and folding the dough, working your way to the far side of the mass, a total of 4 or 5 times, which will take 3 to 5 minutes. With each stretch and fold of the dough, you will feel it developing, becoming more cohesive, less sticky, and easier to stretch. The stretches should be gentle enough not to tear the dough.

When most of the dough holds together and easily pulls off the work surface as you stretch it, slide the dough scraper under it and gather it into a ball. The dough will not be fully developed yet and will still be a little sticky.

Smooth the surface of the dough by cupping your hands on the bottom of the far side of the ball and pulling it gently toward you, allowing the dough to grip the work surface, then move your hands to the left, rotating the dough. Return your hands to the far side of the ball and pull and rotate it one or two more times. This will stretch and tighten the surface and help shape the dough into a smooth ball. Put the ball back into the bowl with the smooth bottom surface up and allow it to rest for 15 minutes.

Turn out the dough on a lightly floured work surface, with the smooth side down. Gently press out the dough to flatten it into a round about 2 inches thick. Take the edge closest to you and stretch it up and over the top of the dough, about two-thirds of the way to the opposite side, and press into the surface. Grab the edge opposite you and stretch and fold it toward you over the first fold, about two-thirds of the way to the closest edge, and press into the surface. Rotate the dough a quarter turn and repeat with two more folds, first away from you and then toward you.

Turn the dough over so the seams are underneath and pull into a ball by cupping your hands on the far side, pulling toward you, and rotating counter-clockwise, stretching the surface tight. Repeat one or two times to form a ball. You will notice that the dough is more developed and will stretch tighter than before. Be careful not to stretch too tight; if the surface starts to tear, stop tightening. Return the ball to the bowl, smooth surface facing up, and let rest for 15 minutes.

Repeat this stretching and folding three times at 15-minute intervals for a total of four folds over an hour. The smooth, elastic dough will develop a good gluten network.

Fermentation

After the final fold, return the ball to the bowl, smooth side up, cover with a tea towel or plastic wrap, and let sit in a warm, draft-free place until the dough has doubled in volume and feels airy when gently touched, about 1 hour. Turn out the dough onto a lightly floured surface, smooth side down. Press it gently to flatten a bit until it is about 2 inches thick. It is okay to press out some of the gases, but do it gently and not too thoroughly. Grabbing the edge opposite you, stretch the dough up and fold it over the top, about halfway toward you. Gently press the dough down, then stretch the edge closest to you and fold it over the first fold. Press it in gently. Rotate the dough a quarter turn and repeat two more folds, one away from you and one toward you.

Turn the dough over so the seam side is down. Cup your hands behind the dough and gently pull it toward you to stretch the surface. At the same time, move your hands to the left, rotating the dough counterclockwise about a quarter turn, rounding it. Repeat one or two times to form a ball. Return the ball to the bowl with the smooth side up and cover until it doubles in volume again, 30 minutes to 1 hour.

Shaping

Dust the work surface lightly with all-purpose flour and turn out the dough so that the smooth side is down. Divide the dough into two equal pieces with a bench knife or bowl scraper.

Gently press one piece of the dough to flatten it into a rough circle about 1 inch thick. Grab the edge opposite you and stretch it up and over the top of the dough, about two-thirds of the way toward you. Gently press into the surface with the heel of your hand. Rotate the dough a quarter turn and grab the edge opposite you, stretching and folding it over the first fold, about two-thirds of the way toward you, pressing it gently. Repeat two or three more times until you have a loose ball shape, then turn the ball over so the seam side is down.

Cup your hands behind the ball with your pinkie fingers and the sides of your hands on the table, then gently pull your hands toward you. At the same time as you are gently pulling, move your hands to the left, causing the ball to rotate counterclockwise about a quarter turn. The dough should grip the table and the surface will tighten. Move your hands behind the ball again, pulling gently and rotating the ball. Set aside and cover with a tea towel, repeating with the second piece of dough. Let the dough rest for 15 to 20 minutes so the gluten relaxes a bit.

Turn the first ball over so the smooth side is down and gently press the ball to flatten it into a round about 2 inches thick. Stretch and fold the opposite edge about two-thirds of the way toward you and gently press into the dough with the heel of your hand. Rotate the dough a quarter turn and stretch and fold another flap about two-thirds of the way toward you over the first flap and press it in. Repeat three more times, then turn the ball over so the seam side is down.

CONTINUED

Cup your hands behind the ball so that your pinkie fingers and the sides of your hands are touching the table and pull the dough ball toward you. At the same time, move your hands to the left so that the ball rotates counterclockwise about a quarter turn. Move your hands back behind the ball and repeat pulling and rotating the ball, stretching and tightening the surface of the dough. Keep rounding until you have a smooth, tight surface and a nice round shape, taking care not to pull so hard that the surface starts to tear.

Let the first ball rest with the seam side down and repeat with the second ball. Let that one rest for a couple of minutes while you prepare the baskets for proofing. Evenly flour two baskets or bowls with a light coat of all-purpose flour. Invert the balls into the baskets so that the seam side is up.

Proofing

Preheat the oven to 500°F with the baking stone and steaming pan in place (see page 22).

Cover the loaves with a tea towel and let rise for 1 to 2 hours, depending on the room temperature (see page 21). Check the loaves after 45 minutes to 1 hour, and again every 15 to 20 minutes if they are not ready. They should feel lighter and full of air.

If your baking stone is large enough to bake both loaves at once, allowing them to expand and not touch, you can proof both loaves together. If not, have a space cleared in your fridge so that you can hold the second loaf while the first bakes.

Baking

Dust the peel with rice flour (see page 17) and turn out one of the loaves onto the peel with the seam side down close to the front edge of the peel.

Using a funnel (see page 14), steam the oven with about 60 grams (¼ cup) water. Let the steam settle for 30 seconds or so while you score the loaf.

To score the loaf in a box cut pattern, hold the blade perpendicular to the surface of the loaf about 2 inches from the edge and quickly draw the blade along one side in a rounded line that follows the curve of the round edge. Make a second cut along the opposite edge, a third cut along the top edge, and a fourth cut along the bottom edge, following the curve of the edge of the loaf each time. The cuts should cross each other slightly at the ends, be evenly centered and about ⅛ inch deep.

Open the oven and place the tip of the peel on the baking stone where you want the loaf to end up. Leave room for the second loaf if the stone is large enough; center the loaf if it is not. Quickly pull the peel out from under the loaf, letting it gently drop onto the baking stone Close the oven door immediately. If your stone can fit two loaves at once, quickly score the second loaf and place it onto the baking stone.

Crack the door enough to stick the funnel nozzle into the edge of the steaming pan and add an additional 117 to 235 grams (½ to 1 cup) water. Remove the funnel as soon as the water hits the steaming pan and close the door tightly. Lower the oven to 450°F. Place the second loaf in the refrigerator if it does not fit.

After about 40 minutes, check your loaf. You want the crust to be a deep brown color and the loaf to sound hollow when it is tapped on the bottom. If it still gives a heavy thud, return it to the oven for 5 to 10 minutes more.

Cool the bread on a wire cooling rack until completely cool.

PAIN AUX PRUNEAUX ET NOISETTES

Bread with Prunes and Hazelnuts

MAKES 2 TRIANGLE-SHAPED LOAVES

STARTER 13 to 37 hours

MIXING & KNEADING 1 hour 20 minutes

FERMENTATION 1½ to 2 hours

SHAPING 40 minutes to 1 hour

PROOFING 45 minutes to 2 hours

BAKING 40 to 50 minutes

Dried fruits make great additions either on their own or together with nuts, as they are here. Hazelnuts have always been a favorite of mine, and with the prunes, they make an elegant bread. The unique triangle shape adds to the elegance.

STARTER

ALL-PURPOSE FLOUR	180 grams	1¼ cups plus 2½ tablespoons
SALT	4 grams	1 teaspoon
INSTANT YEAST	1 gram	¼ teaspoon
WATER	117 grams	½ cup

Put the flour, salt, and yeast in a large bowl and blend together with your fingers to evenly distribute them. Make a well in the center of the flour and add the water.

Using your hand, draw the flour into the water, stirring and blending with your fingers. As it begins to come together, squeeze the dough with your hands to better incorporate the water into the flour. Starting at the near side of the bowl, grasp the dough with both hands and squeeze it between your thumbs and fingers. Rotate the bowl and continue to squeeze the dough, working in the water and working out any clumps of flour. Use a plastic bowl scraper to scrape down the sides and bottom of the bowl, folding the dough over on top of itself.

This dough should be medium-stiff, having some give but also a pretty solid core, like a rubber bouncy ball.

Because this dough will ferment a long time, you do not need to develop the gluten much; just squeeze and work the dough until it is fully combined with no lumps. Form the dough into a rough ball in the bowl and cover it with plastic wrap, or place in a container with a lid.

Let the dough sit out at room temperature for an hour, then refrigerate for at least 12 hours or up to 36 hours.

DOUGH

ALL-PURPOSE FLOUR	160 grams	1¼ cups
WHOLE WHEAT FLOUR	110 grams	1 cup
SALT	6 grams	1 teaspoon
INSTANT YEAST	1 gram	¼ teaspoon
STARTER	All from above	
WATER	190 grams	¾ cup plus 1 tablespoon
HAZELNUTS	40 grams	⅓ cup
PRUNES	40 grams	⅓ cup
RICE FLOUR	For dusting	

Mixing and Kneading

Put the all-purpose flour, whole wheat flour, salt, and yeast in a large bowl and blend together with your fingers to evenly distribute them. Divide the starter into six pieces and scatter them on top of the flour. Make a well in the center of the flour and add the water, holding back a small amount (10 grams, or about 2 teaspoons) until you see if the flour needs it all.

Make sure you have a plastic bowl scraper at hand, then start to blend the water into the flour with your fingers. As the flour begins to absorb the water and the mixture starts to thicken, plunge both hands in and squeeze the dough. Concentrate on getting the water worked into the flour first, as the starter is already hydrated, and then start to work in the starter as you squeeze. Work from the side of the bowl closest to you across to the

CONTINUED

other side, squeezing with both hands. Rotate the bowl a quarter turn and squeeze your way through the dough again. You will feel the dough starting to come together as a more cohesive mass, and the water and starter will become more fully incorporated. Use your bowl scraper from time to time to scrape the sticky dough from the sides of the bowl into the center. Keep rotating the bowl and squeezing the dough until everything is fully incorporated, 1 to 2 minutes. It will remain a shaggy and sticky mass.

The dough should be medium-soft, having definite give but also some resistance; you should be able to feel a core when you squeeze it. Add the reserved water if the dough is not soft enough. Add the water a little at a time, squeezing it into the dough as you have been. You may even have to add more water to get the right consistency if it still feels too stiff. It is better to have a dough that is a little wet than one that is too dry. Turn out the dough onto an unfloured work surface, using the bowl scraper to get it all out of the bowl and scraping as much off your hands as you can. Resist the urge to add flour to the work surface or the dough at this stage.

Starting with the edge closest to you, grab the dough with both hands, palms down, and pull it gently toward you. Stretch it up and flip it over the top of the dough mass by 2 or 3 inches and press it into the surface. Grab the new edge closest to you and stretch it gently up and flip it over the top. Repeat this stretching and flipping of the dough four or five times, working your way to the far side of the mass. The stretches should be gentle enough not to tear the dough apart. As you continue this process, the dough will hold together better and be easier to stretch.

Scrape up the dough with a dough scraper, rotate it a quarter turn, and repeat the stretching and flipping through the dough mass four or five times, 3 to 5 minutes. With each stretch and flip of the dough, you will feel it developing, becoming more

cohesive and less sticky. When most of the dough holds together and pulls off the work surface as you stretch it, slide the dough scraper under it and gather it into a ball. The dough will not be fully developed yet and will still be a little sticky.

Cup your hands around the bottom of the far side of the ball and pull it gently toward you, allowing the dough to grip the work surface, then move your hands to the left, rotating the dough counterclockwise. Return your hands behind the dough and pull and rotate again one or two times. This will tighten the surface and help shape the dough into a smooth ball. Return the ball to the bowl with the smooth side up and let it rest for 15 minutes.

Dust the work surface lightly with all-purpose flour and turn out the dough so that the smooth side is down. Gently press the dough to flatten it into a round about 2 inches thick. Grab the edge closest to you and stretch it up and over the top of the dough, about two-thirds of the way to the opposite side, and press into the surface. Grab the edge opposite you and stretch and fold it toward you over the first fold, about two-thirds of the way to the closest edge, and press into the surface. Rotate the dough a quarter turn and repeat two more folds, one away from you and one toward you.

Turn the dough over so the seam side is down. Form a ball by cupping your hands around the bottom of the far side of the dough and pulling it toward you, rotating the dough counterclockwise. Repeat one or two times to form a ball. You will notice that the dough is more developed and will stretch tighter than before. Be careful not to stretch it too tight; if the surface starts to tear, stop tightening. Return the ball to the bowl, smooth side up, and let rest for 15 minutes.

Repeat this stretching and folding one more time and let rest for 15 minutes.

Just before the third fold, add the hazelnuts and prunes to the dough and work them in by gently squeezing the dough from one end to the other, as you did with the water. Work your way through the dough three or four times until the nuts and fruit are fully incorporated, then stretch and fold the dough a third time. Gather into a ball and return it to the bowl, seam side down, and let rest for 15 minutes.

Repeat this stretching and folding a fourth (and final) time.

Fermentation

After the final fold, return the ball to the bowl, smooth side up, cover with a tea towel or plastic wrap, and let sit in a warm, draft-free place, until the dough has doubled in volume and feels airy when gently touched, about 1 hour. Turn out the dough onto a lightly floured surface, smooth side down. Press it gently to flatten a bit until it is about 2 inches thick. It is okay to press out some of the gases, but do it gently and not too thoroughly. Grabbing the edge opposite you, stretch the dough up and fold it over the top, about halfway toward you. Gently press the dough down and then stretch the edge closest to you and fold it over the first fold. Press it in gently. Rotate the dough a quarter turn and repeat two more folds, one away from you and one toward you.

Turn the dough over so the seam side is down. Cup your hands behind the dough and gently pull it toward you to stretch the surface. At the same time, move your hands to the left, rotating the dough counterclockwise about a quarter turn, rounding it. Repeat one or two times to form a ball. Return the ball to the bowl with the smooth side up and cover until it doubles in volume again, 30 minutes to 1 hour.

CONTINUED

Shaping

Dust the work surface lightly with all-purpose flour and turn out the dough so that the smooth side is down. Divide the dough into two equal pieces with a bench knife or bowl scraper.

Gently press one piece of the dough to flatten it into a rough circle about 1 inch thick. Grab the edge opposite you and stretch it up and over the top of the dough, about two-thirds of the way toward you. Gently press into the surface with the heel of your hand. Rotate the dough a quarter turn and grab the edge opposite you, stretching and folding it over the first fold, about two-thirds of the way toward you, pressing it gently. Repeat two or three times until you have a loose ball shape, then turn the ball over so the seam side is down.

Cup your hands behind the ball with your pinkie fingers and the sides of your hands on the table, then gently pull your hands toward you. At the same time as you are gently pulling, move your hands to the left, causing the ball to rotate counterclockwise about a quarter turn. The dough should grip the table and the surface will tighten. Move your hands behind the ball again, pulling gently and rotating the ball. Set aside and cover with a tea towel, repeating with the second piece of dough. Let the dough rest for 15 to 20 minutes so the gluten relaxes a bit.

Turn the first ball over so the smooth side is down and gently press to flatten it into a round about 2 inches thick. Stretch and fold the opposite edge about two-thirds of the way toward you and gently press into the dough with the heel of your hand. Rotate the dough a quarter turn and stretch and fold another flap about two-thirds of the way toward you over the first flap and press it in. Repeat three more times, then turn the ball over so the seam side is down.

Cup your hands behind the ball so that your pinkie fingers and the sides of your hands are touching the table and pull the dough ball toward you. At the same time, move your hands to the left so that the ball rotates counterclockwise about a quarter turn. Move your hands back behind the ball and repeat pulling and rotating the ball, stretching and tightening the surface of the dough. Keep rounding until you have a smooth, tight surface and a nice round shape, taking care not to pull so hard that the surface starts to tear.

Set aside and cover with a tea towel, repeating with the second piece of dough. Let the dough rest for 15 to 20 minutes so the gluten relaxes a bit.

Pat out the first ball gently into a circle. Stretch and fold the opposite edge about halfway toward the center and press into the dough with the heel of your hand. Rotate and fold flaps twice more onto the dough to form a triangle shape. Pinch the seam closed with your fingertips. Place on a lightly floured towel on a board or baking sheet, seam side up, and cover with another tea towel while you repeat with the second piece of dough. Fold a bit of the towel up between the loaves so they do not stick together.

Proofing

Preheat the oven to 500°F with the baking stone and steaming pan in place (see page 22). Cover the loaves with a tea towel and let rise for 45 minutes to 2 hours, depending on the room temperature. They will proof a little faster than the boules, as you push out less of the gas making this shape. They should feel lighter and full of air.

Baking

Dust the peel with rice flour (see page 17) and turn out the loaves onto the peel with the seam side down, with some space between them.

FRUITS AND NUTS

Many kinds of dried fruits and nuts can be added to a country dough separately or in combination. Fruit and nut breads go especially well with rich, creamy cheeses.

Try these suggestions:

- Pecans and raisins
- Walnuts and dried cranberries
- Golden raisins (perhaps with anise or fennel seeds)

- Dried figs
- Prunes
- Dried apricots

Add between 150 and 200 grams (5 and 7 ounces) of fruits, nuts, or a combination of the two per kilogram (2.2 pounds) of dough.

Using a funnel (see page 14), steam the oven with about 60 grams (¼ cup) water. Let the steam settle for 30 seconds or so while you score the loaf.

Place a strip of parchment or even plain paper about 1 inch wide down the middle of one triangle. Use a fine-mesh sieve to lightly dust all-purpose flour over the loaf. Do not flour too heavily or it will not form a good crust. Carefully remove the strip of paper, leaving an unfloured stripe. To score the loaf, make five shallow, angled cuts down the unfloured part. Repeat with the second loaf.

Open the oven and slide the peel out from under the loaves, dropping them onto the baking stone. Close the oven door immediately.

Crack the door enough to stick the funnel nozzle into the edge of the steaming pan and add an additional 180 grams (¾ cup) water. Remove the funnel as soon as the water hits the steaming pan and close the door tightly. Lower the oven to 450°F.

After about 40 minutes, check your loaf. You want the crust to be a deep brown color and the loaf to sound hollow when it is tapped on the bottom. If it still gives a heavy thud, return the loaves to the oven for 5 to 10 minutes.

Cool the bread on a wire cooling rack until completely cool.

PAIN DE SEIGLE

French Dark Rye Bread

MAKES 2 OBLONG LOAVES

STARTER 13 to 37 hours

MIXING & KNEADING 1 hour 20 minutes

FERMENTATION 20 to 30 minutes

PROOFING 30 to 45 minutes

BAKING 35 to 45 minutes

When I first got to New York City, as the head baker for the opening of Drew Nieporent's TriBakery, I made a version of this French rye bread. When Drew and some of the other New Yorkers tried it, they seemed to like it but said it did not taste like rye. The majority of the flour for the bread was a whole grain, dark rye flour, so this perplexed me. To me, this bread expresses perhaps the purest rye flavor. Then I realized what they were missing was not the flavor of rye, but of caraway, the ubiquitous spice in a New York deli–style rye bread. Even the "unseeded" versions of the bread these fellows grew up on are seasoned with caraway powder, and that is flavor they associate with rye. This traditional French rye bread is about the pure, earthy flavor of the grain.

This is also one of the easiest rye breads to make and it will seem familiar if you have made the *pain de campagne*. We start with the same starter, or *pâte fermentée*. To this, we add whole rye flour, salt, and yeast—a pretty basic French bread, really, just using mostly rye flour. The dough will be stickier than wheat-based dough and won't develop as fully, but the starter does a good job of giving the bread some strength and structure.

distribute them. Make a well in the center of the flour and add the water.

Using your hand, draw the flour into the water, stirring and blending with your fingers. As it begins to come together, squeeze the dough with your hands to better incorporate the water into the flour. Starting at the near side of the bowl, grasp the dough with both hands and squeeze it between your thumbs and fingers. Rotate the bowl and continue to squeeze the dough, working in the water and working out any clumps of flour. Use a plastic bowl scraper to scrape down the sides and bottom of the bowl, folding the dough over on top of itself.

This dough should be medium-stiff, having some give but also a pretty solid core, like a rubber bouncy ball.

Because this dough will ferment a long time, you do not need to develop the gluten much; just squeeze and work the dough until it is fully combined and with no lumps. Form the dough into a rough ball in the bowl and cover it with plastic wrap, or place in a container with a lid.

Let the dough sit out at room temperature for an hour, then refrigerate for at least 12 hours or up to 36 hours.

STARTER

ALL-PURPOSE FLOUR	190 grams	1½ cups
SALT	4 grams	1 teaspoon
INSTANT YEAST	1 gram	¼ teaspoon
WATER	125 grams	½ cup

Put the flour, salt, and yeast in a large bowl and blend together with your fingers to evenly

DOUGH

WHOLE RYE FLOUR	400 grams	3½ cups
SALT	10 grams	2 teaspoons
INSTANT YEAST	4 grams	1 teaspoon
STARTER	All from above	
WATER	280 grams	1 cup plus 3 tablespoons
RICE FLOUR	For dusting	

CONTINUED

Mixing and Kneading

Put the rye flour, salt, and yeast in a large bowl and blend together with your fingers to evenly distribute them. Divide the starter into four pieces and scatter them on top of the flour. Make a well in the center of the flour and add the water, holding back a small amount (14 grams or about 1 tablespoon) until you see if the flour needs it all.

Make sure you have a plastic bowl scraper at hand, then start to blend the water into the flour with your fingers. As the flour begins to absorb the water and the mixture starts to thicken, plunge both hands in and squeeze the dough between your thumbs and fingers. Concentrate on getting the water worked into the flour first, as the starter is already hydrated, then start to work in the starter as you squeeze. Work from the side of the bowl closest to you across to the other side, squeezing with both hands. Rotate the bowl a quarter turn and squeeze your way through the dough again. You will feel the dough starting to come together as a more cohesive mass, and the water and starter will become more fully incorporated. Use your bowl scraper from time to time to scrape the sticky dough from the sides of the bowl into the center. Keep rotating the bowl and squeezing the dough until everything is fully incorporated, a total of 1 to 2 minutes. It will remain a shaggy and sticky mass.

The dough should be medium-soft, having definite give but also some resistance; you should be able to feel a core when you squeeze it. Add the reserved water if the dough is not soft enough. Add the water a little at a time, squeezing it into the dough as you have been. You may even have to add more water to get the right consistency if it still feels too stiff. It is better to have a dough that is a little wet than one that is too dry.

Turn out the dough onto an unfloured work surface, using the bowl scraper to get it all out of the bowl and scraping as much off your hands as you can. Resist the urge to add flour to the work surface or the dough at this stage.

Starting with the edge closest to you, grab the dough with both hands, palms down, and pull it gently toward you. Stretch it up and flip it over the top of the dough mass by 2 or 3 inches and press it into the surface. Grab the new edge closest to you and stretch it gently up and flip it over the top. Repeat this stretching and flipping of the dough four or five times, working your way to the far side of the mass. The stretches should be gentle enough not to tear the dough apart. As you continue this process, the dough will hold together better and be easier to stretch.

Scrape up the dough with a dough scraper, rotate it a quarter turn, and repeat the stretching and flipping through the dough mass four or five times, 3 to 5 minutes. With each stretch and flip of the dough, you will feel it developing, becoming more cohesive and less sticky. When most of the dough holds together and pulls off the work surface as you stretch it, slide the dough scraper under it and gather it into a ball. The dough will not be fully developed yet and will still be a little sticky.

Dust the work surface lightly with all-purpose flour and turn out the dough so that the smooth side is down. Fold the edges into the center.

Turn the dough over so that the seam side is down. Form a ball by cupping your hands around the bottom of the far side of the dough and pulling it gently toward you, allowing the dough to grip the work surface, then move your hands to the left, rotating the dough counterclockwise. Repeat one or two times to form a ball. Because of the rye flour, you won't be able to pull the surface tight, but you will be able to make it smooth. Return the ball to the bowl with the smooth side up, cover with a tea towel, and let rest for 30 minutes.

CONTINUED

Dust the work surface lightly with all-purpose flour and turn out the dough so that the smooth side is down. Gently press the dough to flatten it into a round about 2 inches thick. Grab the edge closest to you and stretch it up and over the top of the dough, about two-thirds of the way to the opposite side, and press into the surface. Grab the edge opposite you and stretch and fold it toward you over the first fold, about two-thirds of the way to the closest edge, and press into the surface. Rotate the dough a quarter turn and repeat two more folds, one away from you and one toward you.

Turn the dough over so the seam side is down. Form a ball by cupping your hands around the bottom of the far side of the dough and pulling it toward you, rotating the dough counterclockwise. Repeat one or two times to form a ball.

Fermentation

After the final fold, return the ball to the bowl, smooth side up, cover with a tea towel or plastic wrap, and let sit in a warm, draft-free place, until the dough has expanded and feels airy when gently touched, 20 to 30 minutes. It will not have increased in volume significantly.

Shaping

Preheat the oven to 475°F with the baking stone and steaming pan in place (see page 22).

Dust the work surface lightly with all-purpose flour and turn out the dough so that the smooth side is down. Divide the dough into two equal pieces with a bench knife or bowl scraper and round each piece into a ball. Place the balls of dough, seam side down, on the work surface, cover with a tea towel, and let rest for 5 to 10 minutes.

For this type of rye bread, you should press out the gases evenly and thoroughly to achieve an even crumb structure, without any large holes. Gently press one piece of the dough, keeping the dough

ball round; it helps with the tapered shape of an oblong loaf.

Grab the closest edge with both hands and stretch and fold it about two-thirds of the way to the opposite edge and gently press into the surface with the heel of one hand. Grab the opposite edge and stretch it over the first fold, about two-thirds of the way toward you, pressing it into the surface. Return to the opposite edge, grip it at the right end with your right hand. With the palm of your left hand down, stretch out your left thumb and place it lengthwise on the surface of the dough just to the left of your right hand so that you can stretch the dough over your thumb. Use your right hand to pull the opposite edge over your thumb all the way down to meet the closest edge and press them together with the heel of your right hand to form a seam. Move your thumb to the left a bit and stretch the opposite edge down to the closest edge in 1-inch increments, rotating the dough slightly with each stretch and sealing the edges together with the heel of your hand as you go. The round shape will help to form a taper at each end.

With the seam side down, cup both hands over the center of the loaf and roll the loaf back and forth on the work surface to make a cylinder shape. If it sticks, add a tiny dusting of flour. If it slides instead of rolls, there is too much flour so you need to brush some away. Angle your hands downward slightly to help shape the tapered ends of the loaf. Roll a few more times until you have a smooth, even loaf with a well-sealed seam. For this bread, you want a mostly even, straight cylinder with a slight taper, not a football shape with pointy ends. Set aside and cover with a tea towel, repeating with the second piece of dough.

Proofing

Lay a towel on top of a cutting board or baking sheet and dust lightly with all-purpose flour. Place a loaf, seam side up, on the towel. With a fold of the towel in between, place the second loaf, seam side up, on the towel next to the first. Fold the ends of the towel over the tops of the loaves (you can add a second towel over the tops of the loaves if the ends do not cover the tops and prevent the loaves from forming a dry skin). Let rest for 30 to 45 minutes.

Baking

Dust the peel with rice flour (see page 17) and turn out one of the loaves onto the peel with the seam side down close to the front edge of the peel.

Using a funnel (see page 14), steam the oven with about 60 grams (¼ cup) water. Let the steam settle for 30 seconds or so while you score the loaf.

Score each loaf across the width, perpendicular to the long edges with a razor blade or sharp serrated knife. Make seven or eight cuts evenly spaced down the length of the loaf.

Open the oven and slide the peel out from under the loaves, dropping them onto the baking stone. Close the oven door immediately.

Using the funnel, add 235 grams (1 cup) more water to the steaming pan (rye breads like a lot of steam). Close the oven door tightly as soon as all the water hits the steaming pan.

After 5 minutes, lower the oven to 425°F and open the door a crack to allow some of the steam to escape for 30 seconds or so. Close the door and let bake until the crust is evenly browned and the loaf is slightly hollow sounding when rapped on the bottom, 30 to 40 minutes.

Cool the bread on a wire cooling rack until completely cool.

PAIN DE MIE

Pullman Bread

**MAKES 1 PULLMAN LOAF
OR 2 STANDARD LOAVES**

MIXING & KNEADING 2 hours 25 minutes

FERMENTATION 30 to 40 minutes

PROOFING 1 hour 20 minutes

BAKING 30 to 50 minutes

Traditionally baked in a straight-sided long Pullman loaf pan with a lid on top, *pain de mie* can be cut into perfectly square slices that are ideal for sandwiches. *Mie* is the French term for the crumb, or interior of the loaf, as opposed to the *croute*, or crust, of which this bread has virtually none.

This dough is enriched with the addition of milk, sugar, and butter. There are some special techniques involved in achieving a well-developed dough with fat and sugar. *Pain de mie* is one bread along a spectrum of enriched breads in the French baking tradition, and is at the lower end of the scale in the proportion of added enrichments, but these techniques are helpful in making any bread of this type up to the highly enriched brioche doughs.

One challenge in making an enriched dough is that fat can surround the gluten-forming proteins in flour and prevent them from forming a good network. This is desirable in pastries, cakes, and cookies, where you want to "shorten" the gluten and prevent it from making a tough, chewy product; but in bread making, the gluten network gives the loaf structure because it helps to trap the fermentation gases, leavening the dough. Therefore, whenever possible, it is best to hold significant amounts of fat out of the dough while the gluten is forming and add them into the well-developed gluten network later.

I also advise that you hold the sugar and salt from the dough until the gluten has had the chance to absorb the amount of liquid it needs. Both sugar and salt readily attract water, and the gluten proteins need to absorb enough moisture early in the mixing process so they can make the proper bonds. This can be especially true in an enriched bread, where the hydration is relatively low at the beginning.

This is one of the few breads where we do not use a starter, as we get a lot of flavor from the butter, milk, and sugar, but you certainly could use *pâte fermentée* in this dough if you wanted. If you do, add about 220 grams (around 8 ounces) of starter to this recipe.

Besides the Croque Monsieur (page 89) in this chapter, *pain de mie* makes excellent tea sandwiches and toast as well. For a traditional Pullman loaf, use a 16 by 4-inch Pullman loaf pan; you can also use two standard 8½ by 4½-inch loaf pans with a baking sheet for a lid.

DOUGH

ALL-PURPOSE FLOUR	650 grams	5 cups plus 1 tablespoon
INSTANT YEAST	4 grams	1 teaspoon
MILK	400 grams	1¾ cups
SUGAR	26 grams	2 tablespoons
SALT	13 grams	1 tablespoon
BUTTER, COLD	65 grams	4 tablespoons plus 2 teaspoons

Mixing and Kneading

Put the flour and yeast in a large bowl and blend together with your fingers to evenly distribute them. Make a well in the center of the flour and add the milk.

Make sure you have a plastic bowl scraper at hand, then start to blend the milk into the flour with your fingers. As the flour begins to absorb the milk and the mixture starts to thicken, plunge both hands in and squeeze the dough between your thumbs and fingers. Work from the side of the bowl closest to you across to the other side, squeezing with both hands. Rotate the bowl a quarter turn and squeeze

CONTINUED

your way through the dough again. You will feel the dough starting to come together as a more cohesive mass, and the milk and starter will become more fully incorporated. Use your bowl scraper from time to time to scrape the sticky dough from the sides of the bowl into the center. Keep rotating the bowl and squeezing the dough until everything is fully incorporated, a total of 1 to 2 minutes.

The dough should be medium-stiff, having definite give but also a pretty solid core, like a rubber bouncy ball.

Add the sugar and the salt on top of the mixture and keep squeezing to work the ingredients into the dough until everything is fully incorporated, 1 to 2 minutes more. It will remain a shaggy and sticky mass.

Turn out the dough onto an unfloured work surface, using the bowl scraper to get it all out of the bowl and scraping as much off your hands as you can. Resist the urge to add flour to the work surface or the dough at this stage.

Starting with the edge closest to you, grab the dough with both hands, palms down, and pull it gently toward you. Stretch it up and flip it over the top of the dough mass by 2 or 3 inches and press it into the surface. Grab the new edge closest to you and stretch it gently up and flip it over the top. Repeat this stretching and flipping of the dough four or five times, working your way to the far side of the mass. The stretches should be gentle enough not to tear the dough apart. As you continue this process, the dough will hold together better and be easier to stretch.

Scrape up the dough with a dough scraper, rotate it a quarter turn, and repeat the stretching and flipping through the dough mass again four or five times, 3 to 5 minutes. With each stretch and flip of the dough, you will feel it developing, becoming more cohesive and less sticky. When most of the dough holds together and pulls off the work surface

as you stretch it, slide the dough scraper under it and gather it into a ball. The dough will not be fully developed yet and will still be a little sticky.

Cup your hands around the bottom of the far side of the ball and pull it gently toward you, allowing the dough to grip the work surface, then move your hands to the left, rotating the dough counterclockwise. Return your hands behind the dough and pull and rotate again one or two times. This will tighten the surface and help shape the dough into a smooth ball. Return the ball to the bowl with the smooth side up and let it rest for 15 minutes.

Dust the work surface lightly with all-purpose flour and turn out the dough so that the smooth side is down. Gently press the dough to flatten it into a round about 2 inches thick. Grab the edge closest to you and stretch it up and over the top of the dough, about two-thirds of the way to the opposite side, and press into the surface. Grab the edge opposite you and stretch and fold it toward you over the first fold, about two-thirds of the way to the closest edge, and press into the surface. Rotate the dough a quarter turn and repeat two more folds, one away from you and one toward you.

Turn the dough over so the seam side is down. Form a ball by cupping your hands around the bottom of the far side of the dough and pulling it toward you, rotating the dough counterclockwise. Repeat one or two times to form a ball. You will notice that the dough is more developed and will stretch tighter than before. Be careful not to stretch it too tight; if the surface starts to tear, stop tightening. Return the ball to the bowl, smooth side up, and let rest for 15 minutes.

Repeat this stretching and folding two more times at 15-minute intervals.

After the third stretch and fold, when the dough has rested for about 10 minutes, take your cold butter out of the refrigerator and pound it with a rolling pin until it is softened and pliable. Butter softened in this way will incorporate into the dough more easily than butter that has softened by warming up to room temperature.

On a lightly floured surface, turn out the dough with the smooth side down and press it with your hands to flatten it until it's about ½ inch thick. Evenly distribute the softened butter in small pieces, about 1 teaspoon each, over the surface of the dough. Work the butter into the dough by stretching and flipping the dough from one side to the other as you did initially. Grab the edge closest to you, stretch it a bit toward you, then fold it and let rest for 15 minutes. Repeat this stretching and folding three times at 15-minute intervals for a total of four folds over an hour. This will develop into a smooth, elastic dough with a good gluten network.

Fermentation

After the final fold, return the dough to the bowl, smooth side up, cover with a tea towel or plastic wrap, and let sit in a warm, draft-free place for 30 to 40 minutes.

Shaping

Spray the Pullman pan or two 8½ by 4½-inch pans generously with baking spray, including the lids.

Dust the work surface lightly with all-purpose flour and turn out the dough so that the smooth side is down.

If using a Pullman pan, press the dough into a 14 by 8-inch rectangle. If using two 8½ by 4½-inch loaf pans, divide the dough into two equal pieces with a bench knife or bowl scraper and pat out each piece into an 8 by 6-inch rectangle.

For this bread, you should press out the gases evenly and thoroughly to achieve a more even crumb structure, without any large holes. For each rectangle, grab the long edge closest to you with both hands, fold about two-thirds of the way to the

opposite side, and press into the dough with the heels of your hands. Grab the opposite edge and fold it toward you over the first fold, about two-thirds of the way to the closest edge, and again seal it with the heels of your hands.

Return to the opposite edge, grip it at the right end with your right hand. With the palm of your left hand down, stretch out your left thumb and place it lengthwise on the surface of the dough just to the left of your right hand so that you can stretch the dough over your thumb. Pull the top edge all the way down to meet the bottom edge and press them together with the heel of your right hand to form a seam. Move your thumb to the left a bit and stretch the top edge down to the bottom edge in 1-inch increments, sealing the edges together with the heel of your hand as you go.

Roll the dough back and forth to make an even, straight cylinder the length of your pan. Carefully put the cylinder into the pan with the seam side down. It should touch the ends but not the sides of the pan. Repeat with the second piece of dough if needed.

Proofing

Preheat the oven to 450ºF with the steaming pan in place (see page 22). You do not need a baking stone.

Cover the pan(s) with a tea towel and let rise until the center of the loaf is just even with the top of the pan(s), about 1 hour.

If using a Pullman pan, slide on the lid. If using standard loaf pans, place both pans on a baking sheet and lightly spray the bottom of a second baking sheet with baking spray. Place the second baking sheet on top of the loaf pans as a cover and place a skillet or something else heavy and ovenproof on top of the second baking sheet. Let rise for 10 minutes more.

CONTINUED

Baking

Using a funnel (see page 14), steam the oven with about 60 grams (¼ cup) water. Let the steam settle for 30 seconds or so. Even though the pans are covered, a moist baking chamber helps distribute the heat more evenly.

Open the oven and slide the covered pan or pans onto the center oven rack. Close the oven door. Lower the oven to 375°F.

After 30 to 40 minutes, carefully remove the lid and check your loaves. If they are still very pale on top, return the pan to the oven for 10 minutes; if they are evenly browned on top, remove from the pans and give the bottoms a light thump. If they do not yet sound hollow or if the sides seem very soft, return the loaves to the oven without the pan for 5 to 10 minutes.

Cool the bread on a wire cooling rack until completely cool.

LEVAIN NATUREL

Building a Sourdough Starter

INITIAL ACTIVITY 24 to 72 hours

ESTABLISHMENT FEEDINGS Every 8 hours for 7 days

MAINTENANCE Use for baking or feed once a week; maintain in the refrigerator

USE Pull from refrigerator 11 to 13 hours before using in a recipe

Sourdough baking can seem intimidating, but once you cultivate a good, healthy starter, you should be able to make sourdough breads with ease. There is a bit of a commitment involved in getting the starter going, as it needs to be fed every 8 hours for about a week. Once it is established, however, then you only need to feed it once a week, keeping it in the refrigerator in between bakes. You will have to plan ahead before baking, though, as you will need to "wake up" the starter a day before you want to make your dough. That is really no more trouble than making a yeasted starter (such as a *pâte fermentée*) ahead of time, though.

When I moved to Texas, I met people who had sourdough starters that they had maintained for years. Some of them had even been passed down for a generation or two. While I am not sure how many of these cultures were used regularly for bread baking—often they were used in biscuits or pancakes and usually for flavor, not as the main leavening—the tradition these folks were following delighted me.

Still, the health of a starter is far more important than its age. While some bakeries may get marketing mileage out of saying their starter is decades old, many bakers routinely start a new culture to ensure that they have a good, healthy, active starter. At Easy Tiger, I have started the *levain* from scratch three times so far in the six years we have been open.

Professional bakers have a distinct advantage when it comes to sourdough baking in that we use our starter every single day. This means our starter gets regular and consistent feedings. With the maintenance instructions that follow, you can keep a healthy starter active so that you can use it whenever you want.

Sourdough cultures are complex communities of different strains of yeast and lactobacilli. There are myriad ways to make and maintain them and variations in hydration, temperature, and feeding schedule that all influence the baking characteristics of the dough and the flavor and texture of the bread. I am going to show you how to build a traditional *levain naturel* with a doughlike consistency, what American bakers often refer to as a stiff *levain*, as opposed to a liquid *levain*, which has a more batter-like consistency. This *levain* will be the base sourdough starter for several recipes, such as the Pain au Levain (page 70) and Miche (page 75). We will also make a rye sourdough starter to use in the sourdough rye breads in the following chapter.

This is the one section of the book where I want you to put aside the experiential, bake-by-feel side of things and put on your scientist's cap. While the process is not difficult, you are more likely to succeed if you follow the proportions, temperatures, and especially the timing schedule closely until you have an active, mature starter. Once the culture is established, there is less that can go wrong; a strong, healthy starter has defenses against contamination by undesirable microbes.

Because we are looking to ferment grains and not fruits, I prefer to use only flour to initiate a starter rather than adding fruit, which some bakers use because the wild yeast it contains can speed up starter activity initially. I have almost always been able to get a starter going this way without a problem. I tried an experiment once where I started two cultures at the same time, one using grapes and one using only flour; the starter made with the grapes was more sluggish and a lot less active during the first week than the starter made

CONTINUED

without grapes. Then they evened out and became identical as they were fed together on exactly the same schedule. I could not discern any difference in the breads made from the two starters once they were mature. I have repeated this trial with the same results, though I would not say I am ready for peer review just yet.

Start with a good-quality unbleached all-purpose flour and a whole rye flour. Using organic flours is a plus, but is not necessary. Filtered water (not distilled water) is also a good idea. Use a clean bowl to mix the flours and water. Storing it in a transparent cylindrical container that is at least three times taller than its diameter helps to gauge the activity of your starter. I love to use a quart-size glass canning jar and a permanent marker to mark the starting and ending levels right on the side of the jar. It is a good idea to sanitize the jar in the dishwasher or put it in some boiling water for a few minutes before you use it for the first time. Again, once you get your starter established, contamination is unlikely, but in this initial phase, it does not hurt to take some precautions and give the desirable microbes every advantage.

INITIAL STARTER

ALL-PURPOSE FLOUR	75 grams	⅔ cup
WHOLE RYE FLOUR	25 grams	¼ cup
FILTERED WATER AT 75°F TO 80°F OR SLIGHTLY WARMER THAN ROOM TEMPERATURE	60 grams	¼ cup

In a very clean small bowl, blend the all-purpose and rye flours with your fingers then add the water and knead until completely incorporated. Continue kneading in the bowl for a few minutes to

form a cohesive ball. Place the ball in a 1-quart jar and push down, flattening the top. (I use a skinny silicone spatula or the handle end of a long wooden spoon.) Try to press the dough into the bottom of the jar all the way around, eliminating air pockets around the edges as much as possible. This will help you to more accurately gauge the level of the rise, so that you can monitor the progress and maturity of the starter. Mark the level of the top of the dough mass on the side of the jar with a permanent marker. You can put a lid loosely on top of the jar or cover it with a tea towel. Let sit in a warm, draft-free place until the next day.

Begin checking the starter after 24 hours to see if there is any activity. You may not see much rise in the level of the starter at the beginning, but you should see distinctive bubbles in the dough itself. If there are no bubbles or only a few bubbles, leave the starter out for up to 72 hours, checking every 12 hours or so. If you do not see any obvious activity after 72 hours, or if the starter turns gray and has an unpleasant off-smell, discard it and start again.

Feeding Day 1 | *First Three Feedings*

Once you see activity, it is time to start feeding your starter. It is important to be diligent about the feedings, keeping to a schedule of a feeding every 8 hours—establishing a time that fits in your daily schedule for a week is key. For example, if you feed the starter at 6 a.m., you will need to feed it again at 2 p.m. and 10 p.m. If you are not an early riser, you could feed at 8 a.m., 4 p.m., and midnight. The midday feeding is probably the most challenging for folks who work during the day and cannot sneak away. Be sure to record the time of your first feed so that you will be able to feed it every 8 hours. I like to do the first feed just before bedtime, then I feed again when I wake up.

SOURDOUGH TERMINOLOGY

Levain naturel is the French term for a sourdough starter, which is often referred to as a natural starter in English. I use the terms *sourdough* and *levain* interchangeably.

As a baker in New York City, I used the word *levain* to describe our breads as naturally leavened, as there was often a strong negative reaction to the term *sourdough* from customers who immediately thought of the very tangy West Coast style. Even then, my breads tended to have a milder, though still complex, sour flavor.

These days, I trend back toward using the term *sourdough*, because in English at least, the term *natural* sets up a dichotomy that implies that breads leavened with baker's yeast are somehow unnatural, which is not true at all.

INITIAL STARTER	100 grams	3½ ounces
FILTERED WATER AT 75°F TO 80°F OR SLIGHTLY WARMER THAN ROOM TEMPERATURE	60 grams	¼ cup
ALL-PURPOSE FLOUR	75 grams	⅔ cup
WHOLE RYE FLOUR	25 grams	¼ cup

Measure 100 grams (3½ ounces) of the starter and put in a clean bowl. Add the water and break up the starter a little with your hand. It does not have to be completely dissolved. Add the all-purpose and rye flours and knead until completely incorporated. Continue kneading in the bowl for a few minutes to form a cohesive ball. Discard the rest of the starter, which you will no longer need. Clean the jar well in hot water (if you use soap, rinse well to remove any traces of it). Push the fed starter down into the bottom of the jar as before, flattening the top and marking the level on the side.

Repeat this feeding two more times, every 8 hours, and discard the leftover starter each time.

Feeding Days 2 Through 7

After the first three feedings, you should only feed all-purpose flour and water to the starter, eliminating the rye flour.

STARTER	100 grams	3½ ounces
FILTERED WATER AT 75°F TO 80°F OR SLIGHTLY WARMER THAN ROOM TEMPERATURE	60 grams	¼ cup
ALL-PURPOSE FLOUR	100 grams	1 cup plus 1½ teaspoons

Measure 100 grams (3½ ounces) of the starter and put in a clean bowl. Add the water and all-purpose flour, as you did for the first three feedings, and then knead into a ball once again. Discard the rest of the starter and clean the jar and push the ball into the jar as before, flattening the top and marking the level on the side.

CONTINUED

Before each feeding, note the level of the starter; it will gradually increase before it starts to collapse in on itself at the top. The eventual goal is for the starter to triple its height in 8 hours, which indicates good yeast activity and means the starter will leaven your dough well. Even if the starter triples its height early in the process, it is best to keep up the 8-hour feedings for 7 full days in order to achieve the right acidity in the starter. You may want to shorten the feeding interval if the rise peaks in less than 8 hours and you notice a decrease in the height of the rise (less than the three times the original height). But if the 8-hour feeding interval is easier to maintain, keep that up; you will still have a healthy starter after 7 days.

Maintaining Your Starter

Now that you have established your starter, you can keep it in the refrigerator and only need to feed it once a week. This can happen when you use your starter to make a dough. All you need to do is feed a portion of the reserved starter, let it begin to ferment at room temperature for about an hour, and then slow that fermentation to a crawl by putting it back in the refrigerator. For maintenance feedings, the proportion of flour to starter is higher. Always use this same recipe and discard the extra starter.

STARTER	50 grams	1¾ ounces
FILTERED WATER AT 75°F TO 80°F OR SLIGHTLY WARMER THAN ROOM TEMPERATURE	90 grams	¼ cup plus 2 tablespoons
ALL-PURPOSE FLOUR	150 grams	1 cup plus 3 tablespoons

Measure 50 grams of the starter and put in a clean bowl. Discard the excess starter and clean out your storage jar. Add the water and all-purpose flour, as you did for the first three feedings, and then knead with your hands until well incorporated. Return to your clear storage container. Let the starter sit out at room temperature for an hour or so, so that the fermentation gets started (you will not see much change in that time, but the fermentation is getting going). Return to the refrigerator.

Preparing the Starter for Baking

Take the *levain* out of the refrigerator 11 to 13 hours before making a dough and feed it according to the individual bread recipe.

PAIN AU LEVAIN

French-Style Sourdough

**MAKES 2
ROUND LOAVES**

STARTER 3 hours (11 to 13 hours, if starter needs a wake-up feed)

MIXING & KNEADING 1 hour 20 minutes

FERMENTATION 1½ to 2 hours

PROOFING 45 minutes to 1 hour

BAKING 35 to 45 minutes

This is one of my favorite breads to make and to eat, a French sourdough that is the ancestor of *pain de campagne*. It is at the core of the Easy Tiger bread line and one of our best-selling breads. We shape it into a boule, like the ones here, a bâtard, and a larger country loaf called a *miche*. Our Easy Tiger recipe was developed based on the method I learned from Jacques Mahou, a baker in Tours, France, while I worked at Bouley Bakery. Over the years, I have made many versions of this bread, always with the goal of creating a complex, full flavor with mild acidity, which is in contrast to the sharp West Coast–style sourdoughs.

Like the *pain de campagne*, this dough has some rye flour in it, giving it that country bread touch, but I also like to add whole spelt flour. Spelt is an older relative of wheat and is an increasingly popular ancient grain. I love its flavor and it rounds out this bread in a beautiful way. You can substitute whole wheat flour or even all-purpose for the spelt flour if you prefer.

To get the flavor profile we want, with depth and complexity but without sharp acid notes, you need to build the dough on the *levain* relatively soon after it has been fed, about three hours after the final feeding. This also assures that the *levain* has really strong leavening power. For any of you who think of sourdough baking as being sluggish or unreliable, I think you will be surprised at how well this starter ferments the dough.

This recipe requires a mature sourdough starter, which must be made at least 1 week in advance.

Sourdough Starter | *Levain*

If you are making this bread from the Levain Naturel (page 64) that you have been maintaining and storing in your refrigerator, take the *levain* out and feed it as follows, 11 to 13 hours before you want to make your bread dough. After this step, you will need to feed it again and let it ferment another 3 hours before making the dough. If your starter is already active—either because you just brought a new starter to maturity or you just used it for baking another bread and have been actively feeding it—skip to the final feed step.

WAKE-UP FEED

LEVAIN (PAGE 64)	200 grams	7 ounces
ALL-PURPOSE FLOUR	200 grams	1½ cups
WATER AT 90°F	120 grams	½ cup

Place the starter in a clean bowl and mix in the flour and water by hand, stirring and blending with your fingers, until well incorporated. Cover with a tea towel and let ferment at room temperature for 8 to 10 hours, depending on your schedule.

FINAL FEED

LEVAIN	165 grams	5.8 ounces
ALL-PURPOSE FLOUR	165 grams	¾ cup
WATER	100 grams	⅓ cup plus 2 tablespoons

About 3 hours before you want to make your bread dough, place the starter in a clean bowl and mix in the flour and water by hand, stirring and blending with your fingers, until well incorporated. Cover with a tea towel and let ferment at room temperature for 3 hours. You will use all of the *levain* from this feed in the dough.

CONTINUED

DOUGH

ALL-PURPOSE FLOUR	660 grams, plus more for dusting	5 cups plus 2½ tablespoons
WHOLE SPELT FLOUR	170 grams	1½ cups
WHOLE RYE FLOUR	34 grams	5 tablespoons
SALT	28 grams	1 tablespoon plus 2 teaspoons
LEVAIN FROM FINAL FEED	All from page 71	
WATER	690 grams	3 cups
RICE FLOUR	For dusting	

Mixing and Kneading

Put the all-purpose, spelt, and rye flours and the salt in a large bowl and blend together with your fingers to evenly distribute them. Divide the *levain* into six pieces and scatter them on top of the flour. Make a well in the center of the flour and add the water, holding back a small amount (35 grams, or 2 tablespoons plus 1 teaspoon) until you see if the flour needs it all.

Make sure you have a plastic bowl scraper at hand, then start to blend the water and *levain* into the flour with your fingers. As the flour begins to absorb the water and the mixture starts to thicken, plunge both hands in and squeeze the dough. Concentrate on getting the water worked into the flour first, as the *levain* is already hydrated, then start to work in the starter as you squeeze. Work from the side of the bowl closest to you across to the other side, squeezing with both hands. Rotate the bowl a quarter turn and squeeze your way through the dough again. You will feel the dough starting to come together as a more cohesive mass, and the water and starter will become more fully incorporated. Use your bowl scraper from time to time to scrape the sticky dough from the sides of

the bowl into the center. Keep rotating the bowl and squeezing the dough until everything is fully incorporated, 1 to 2 minutes. It will remain a shaggy and sticky mass.

The dough should be medium-soft, having definite give but also some resistance; you should be able to feel a core when you squeeze it. Add the reserved water if the dough is not soft enough. Add the water a little at a time, squeezing it into the dough as you have been. You may even have to add more water to get the right consistency if it still feels too stiff. It is better to have a dough that is a little wet than one that is too dry.

Turn out the dough onto an unfloured work surface, using the bowl scraper to get it all out of the bowl and scraping as much off your hands as you can. Resist the urge to add flour to the work surface or the dough at this stage.

Starting with the edge closest to you, grab the dough with both hands, palms down, and pull it gently toward you. Stretch it up and flip it over the top of the dough mass by 2 or 3 inches and press it into the surface. Grab the new edge closest to you and stretch it gently up and flip it over the top. Repeat this stretching and flipping of the dough four or five times, working your way to the far side of the mass. The stretches should be gentle enough not to tear the dough apart. As you continue this process, the dough will hold together better and be easier to stretch.

Scrape up the dough with a dough scraper, rotate it a quarter turn, and repeat the stretching and flipping through the dough mass four or five times, 3 to 5 minutes. With each stretch and flip of the dough, you will feel it developing, becoming more cohesive and less sticky. When most of the dough holds together and pulls off the work surface as you stretch it, slide the dough scraper under it and gather it into a ball. The dough will not be fully developed yet and will still be a little sticky.

Cup your hands around the bottom of the far side of the ball and pull it gently toward you, allowing the dough to grip the work surface, then move your hands to the left rotating the dough counterclockwise. Return your hands behind the dough and pull and rotate again one or two times. This will tighten the surface and help shape the dough into a smooth ball. Return the ball to the bowl with the smooth side up and let it rest for 15 minutes.

Dust the work surface lightly with all-purpose flour and turn out the dough so that the smooth side is down. Gently press out the dough to flatten it into a round about 2 inches thick. Grab the edge closest to you and stretch it up and over the top of the dough, about two-thirds of the way to the opposite side, and press into the surface. Grab the edge opposite you and stretch and fold it toward you over the first fold, about two-thirds of the way to the closest edge, and press into the surface. Rotate the dough a quarter turn and repeat two more folds, one away from you and one toward you.

Turn the dough over so the seam side is down. Form a ball by cupping your hands around the bottom of the far side of the dough and pulling it toward you, rotating the dough counterclockwise. Repeat one or two times to form a ball. You will notice that the dough is more developed and will stretch tighter than before. Be careful not to stretch it too tight; if the surface starts to tear, stop tightening. Return the ball to the bowl, smooth side up, and let rest for 15 minutes.

Repeat this stretching and folding three times at 15-minute intervals for a total of four folds over an hour. This will develop into a smooth, elastic dough with a good gluten network.

Fermentation

After the final fold, return the ball to the bowl smooth side up, cover with a tea towel or plastic wrap, and let sit in a warm, draft-free place until the dough has doubled in volume and feels airy when gently touched, about 1 hour. Turn out the dough on a lightly floured surface, smooth side down. Press it gently to flatten a bit until it is about 2 inches thick. It is okay to press out some of the gases, but do it gently and not too thoroughly. Grabbing the edge opposite you, stretch the dough and fold it over the top, about halfway toward you. Gently press the dough down, then stretch the edge closest to you and fold it over the first fold. Press it in gently. Rotate the dough a quarter turn and repeat two more folds, one away from you and one toward you.

Turn the dough over so the seam side is down. Cup your hands behind the dough and gently pull it toward you to stretch the surface. At the same time, move your hands to the left, rotating the dough counterclockwise about a quarter turn, rounding it. Repeat one or two times to form a ball. Return the ball to the bowl with the smooth side up and cover again with a tea towel or plastic wrap until it doubles in volume again, 30 minutes to 1 hour.

Shaping

Dust the work surface lightly with all-purpose flour and turn out the dough so that the smooth side is down. Divide the dough into two equal pieces with a bench knife or bowl scraper.

Gently press one piece of the dough to flatten it into a rough circle about 1 inch thick. Grab the edge opposite you and stretch it up and over the top of the dough, about two-thirds of the way toward you. Gently press into the surface with the heel of your hand. Rotate the dough a quarter turn and grab the edge opposite you again, stretching and folding it over the first fold, about two-thirds of the way toward you, pressing it gently. Repeat two or three times until you have a loose ball shape, then turn the ball over so the seam side is down.

CONTINUED

Cup your hands behind the ball with your pinkie fingers and the sides of your hands on the table, then gently pull your hands toward you. At the same time as you are gently pulling, move your hands to the left, causing the ball to rotate counterclockwise about a quarter turn. The dough should grip the table and the surface will tighten. Move your hands behind the ball again, pulling gently and rotating the ball. Set aside and cover with a tea towel, repeating with the second piece of dough. Let the dough rest for 15 to 20 minutes so the gluten relaxes a bit.

Turn the first ball over so the smooth side is down and gently press the ball a bit. Stretch and fold the opposite edge about two-thirds of the way toward you and press into the dough with the heel of your hand. Rotate the dough a quarter turn and stretch and fold another flap about two-thirds of the way toward you over the first flap and press it in. Repeat three times, then turn the ball over so the seam side is down. Cup both hands behind the ball so that your pinkie fingers and the sides of your hands are touching the table and pull the dough ball toward you. At the same time, move your hands to the left so that the ball rotates counterclockwise about a quarter turn. Move your hands back behind the ball and repeat pulling and rotating the ball, stretching and tightening the surface of the dough. Keep rounding until you have a smooth, tight surface and a nice round shape, taking care not to pull so hard that the surface tears.

Let the first ball rest with the seam side down and repeat with the second ball. Let that one rest for a couple of minutes while you prepare the baskets for proofing. Evenly flour your baskets or bowls with a light coat of flour. Invert the balls into the baskets so that the seam side is up.

Proofing

Preheat the oven to 500°F with the baking stone and steaming pan in place (see page 22).

Cover the loaves with a tea towel and let rise for 1 to 2 hours. Check the loaves after 45 minutes to 1 hour, and again every 15 to 20 minutes if they are not ready. They should feel lighter and full of air.

Baking

Dust the peel with rice flour (see page 17) and turn out one of the proofed loaves onto the peel with the seam down close to the front edge of the peel.

Using a funnel (see page 14), steam the oven with about 60 grams (¼ cup) water. Let the steam settle for 30 seconds or so while you score the loaf.

Score the loaf with a razor blade. There are many different ways to score a boule—a box cut like the Pain de Campagne (see page 40) or a diamond pattern across the top are two common scores. Experiment or just score evenly across the loaf with cuts about ⅛ inch deep so the loaf will rise evenly.

Open the oven and place the tip of the peel on the baking stone where you want the loaf to end up. Leave room for the second loaf if the stone is large enough; center the loaf if it is not. Quickly pull the peel out from under the loaf, letting it drop onto the baking stone. Close the oven door immediately. If your stone can fit two loaves, quickly score the second loaf and place it onto the baking stone.

Crack the door enough to stick the funnel nozzle into the steaming pan and add an additional 235 grams (1 cup water) or so. Remove the funnel as soon as the water hits the steaming pan and close the door tightly. Lower the oven to 450°F. Place the second loaf in the refrigerator if it does not fit. After about 35 minutes, check your loaf. You want the crust to be a deep brown color and the loaf to sound hollow when it is tapped on the bottom. If it still gives a heavy thud, return it to the oven for 5 to 10 minutes.

Cool the bread on a wire rack.

MICHE

Large Country Loaf with Stone-Ground Flour

MAKES 1 LARGE ROUND LOAF	STARTER 11 to 13 hours	PROOFING 1 to 2 hours
	MIXING & KNEADING 1 hour 20 minutes	BAKING 50 minutes to 1 hour
	FERMENTATION 1½ to 2 hours	

Besides the baguette, the extra-large round loaves at Poilâne are perhaps the most famous of French breads. These loaves are called *miches*, a word that can also be slang for breasts or buttocks. I used to think the name for the bread came from the slang, imagining lonely, slightly naughty-minded bakers in the middle of the night likening their pillows of soft dough to more fleshly pleasures. When I dug a little deeper into the etymology, I found out that it is the opposite: The slang was inspired by the shape of the bread. Just another reminder of the central importance of bread to French culture.

Though *miche* refers to a large round loaf and not a particular type of dough, most of us think of a country bread made with darker, stone-ground flours and a sourdough *levain*. For this version, we will use wheat flour that is somewhere between white flour and whole wheat, often called high-extraction flour (see page 18).

This recipe requires a mature sourdough starter, which must be made at least 1 week in advance.

Sourdough Starter | *Levain*

If you are making this bread from the Levain Naturel that you have been maintaining and storing in your refrigerator, take the *levain* out and feed it as follows, 11 to 13 hours before you want to make your bread dough. After this step, you will need to feed it again and let it ferment another 3 hours before making the dough. If your starter is already active—either because you just brought a new starter to maturity or you just used it for baking another bread and have been actively feeding it—skip to the final feed step.

WAKE-UP FEED

LEVAIN (PAGE 64)	200 grams	7 ounces
ALL-PURPOSE FLOUR	200 grams	1½ cups
WATER AT 90°F	120 grams	½ cup

Place the starter in a clean bowl and mix in the flour and water by hand, stirring and blending with your fingers, until well incorporated. Cover with a tea towel and let ferment at room temperature for 8 to 10 hours, depending on your schedule.

FINAL FEED

LEVAIN	165 grams	5.8 ounces
ALL-PURPOSE FLOUR	165 grams	¾ cup
WATER	100 grams	⅓ cup plus 2 tablespoons

About 3 hours before you want to make your bread dough, place the starter in a clean bowl and mix in the flour and water by hand, stirring and blending with your fingers, until well incorporated. Cover with a tea towel and let ferment at room temperature for 3 hours. You will use all of the *levain* from this feed in the dough.

CONTINUED

DOUGH

HIGH-EXTRACTION FLOUR (SEE PAGE 18)	830 grams	7½ cups
WHOLE RYE FLOUR	34 grams	5 tablespoons
SALT	28 grams	1 tablespoon plus 2 teaspoons
LEVAIN FROM FINAL FEED	All from page 77	
WATER	690 grams	3 cups
RICE FLOUR	For dusting	

Mixing and Kneading

Put the high-extraction and rye flours and the salt in a large bowl and blend together with your fingers to evenly distribute them. Divide the *levain* into four pieces and scatter them on top of the flour. Make a well in the center of the flour and add the water, holding back a small amount (35 grams, or 2 tablespoons plus 1 teaspoon) until you see if the flour needs it all.

Make sure you have a plastic bowl scraper at hand, then start to blend the water and *levain* into the flour with your fingers. As the flour begins to absorb the water and the mixture starts to thicken, plunge both hands in and squeeze the dough. Concentrate on getting the water worked into the flour first, as the *levain* is already hydrated, then start to work in the starter as you squeeze. Work from the side of the bowl closest to you across to the other side, squeezing with both hands. Rotate the bowl a quarter turn and squeeze your way through the dough again. You will feel the dough starting to come together as a more cohesive mass, and the water and starter will become more fully incorporated. Use your bowl scraper from time to time to scrape the sticky dough from the sides of the bowl into the center. Keep rotating the bowl and squeezing the dough until everything is fully incorporated, 1 to 2 minutes. It will remain a shaggy and sticky mass.

The dough should be medium-soft, having definite give and also some resistance; you should be able to feel a core when you squeeze it. Add the reserved water if the dough is not soft enough. Add the water a little at a time, squeezing it into the dough as you have been. You may even have to add more water to get the right consistency if it still feels too stiff. It is better to have a dough that is a little wet than one that is too dry.

Turn out the dough onto an unfloured work surface, using the bowl scraper to get it all out of the bowl and scraping as much off your hands as you can. Resist the urge to add flour to the work surface or the dough at this stage.

Starting with the edge closest to you, grab the dough with both hands, palms down, and pull it gently toward you. Stretch it up and flip it over the top of the dough mass by 2 or 3 inches and press it into the surface. Grab the new edge closest to you and stretch it gently up and flip it on top. Repeat this stretching and flipping of the dough four or five times, working your way to the far side of the mass. The stretches should be gentle enough not to tear the dough apart. As you continue this process, the dough will hold together better and be easier to stretch.

Scrape up the dough with a dough scraper, rotate it a quarter turn, and repeat the stretching and flipping through the dough mass four or five times, 3 to 5 minutes. With each stretch and flip of the dough, you will feel it developing, becoming more cohesive and less sticky. When most of the dough holds together and pulls off the work surface as you stretch it, slide the dough scraper under it and gather it into a ball. The dough will not be fully developed yet and will still be a little sticky.

Cup your hands around the bottom of the far side of the ball and pull it gently toward you, allowing the dough to grip the work surface, then move your hands to the left, rotating the dough counterclockwise. Return your hands behind the dough and pull and rotate again one or two times. This will tighten the surface and help shape the dough into a smooth ball. Return the ball to the bowl with the smooth side up and let it rest for 15 minutes.

Dust the work surface lightly with all-purpose flour and turn out the dough so that the smooth side is down. Gently press out the dough to flatten it into a round about 2 inches thick. Grab the edge closest to you and stretch it up and over the top of the dough, about two-thirds of the way to the opposite side, and press into the surface. Grab the edge opposite you and stretch and fold it toward you over the first fold, about two-thirds of the way to the closest edge, and press into the surface. Rotate the dough a quarter turn and repeat two more folds, one away from you and one toward you.

Turn the dough over so the seam side is down. Form a ball by cupping your hands around the bottom of the far side of the dough and pulling it toward you, rotating the dough counterclockwise. Repeat one or two times to form a ball. You will notice that the dough is more developed and will stretch tighter than before. Be careful not to stretch it too tight; if the surface starts to tear, stop tightening. Return the ball to the bowl, smooth side up, and let rest for 15 minutes.

Repeat this stretching and folding three times at 15-minute intervals for a total of four folds over an hour. This will develop into a smooth, elastic dough with a good gluten network.

Fermentation

After the final fold, return the ball to the bowl, smooth side up, cover with a tea towel or plastic wrap, and let sit in a warm, draft-free place until the dough has doubled in volume and feels airy when gently touched, about 1 hour. Turn out the dough on a lightly floured surface, smooth side down. Press it gently to flatten until it is about 2 inches thick. It is okay to press out some of the gases, but do it gently and not too thoroughly. Grabbing the edge opposite you, stretch the dough and fold it over the top about halfway toward you. Gently press the dough down, then stretch the edge closest to you and fold it over the top of the first fold. Press it in gently. Rotate the dough a quarter turn and repeat two more folds, one away from you and one toward you.

Turn the dough over so the seam side is down. Cup your hands behind the dough and gently pull it toward you to stretch the surface. At the same time, move your hands to the left, rotating the dough counterclockwise about a quarter turn, rounding it. Repeat one or two times to form a ball. Return the ball to the bowl with the smooth side up and cover with a tea towel or plastic wrap until it doubles in volume again, 30 minutes to 1 hour.

Shaping

Dust the work surface lightly with all-purpose flour and turn out the dough, smooth side down.

Gently press the dough to flatten it into a rough circle about 1 inch thick. Grab the edge opposite you and stretch it up and over the top of the dough, about two-thirds of the way toward you. Gently press into the surface with the heel of your hand. Rotate the dough a quarter turn and grab the edge opposite you again, stretching and folding it over the first fold, about two-thirds of the way toward you, pressing it gently. Repeat two or three times until you have a loose ball shape, then turn the ball over so the seam side is down.

Cup your hands behind the ball with your pinkie fingers and the sides of your hands on the table, then gently pull your hands toward you. At the same time as you are gently pulling, move your hands to the left, causing the ball to rotate counterclockwise about a quarter turn. The dough should grip the table and the surface will tighten. Move your hands behind the ball again, pulling

CONTINUED

gently and rotating the ball. Set aside and cover with a tea towel for 15 to 20 minutes so the gluten relaxes a bit.

Turn the ball over so the smooth side is down and gently press the ball a bit. Stretch and fold the opposite edge about two-thirds of the way toward you and press into the dough with the heel of your hand. Rotate the dough a quarter turn and stretch and fold another flap about two-thirds of the way toward you over the first flap and press it in. Repeat three times, then turn the ball over so the seam side is down. Cup both hands behind the ball so that your pinkie fingers and the sides of your hands are touching the table and pull the dough ball toward you. At the same time, move your hands to the left so that the ball rotates counterclockwise about a quarter turn. Move your hands back behind the ball and repeat pulling and rotating the ball, stretching and tightening the surface of the dough. Keep rounding until you have a smooth, tight surface and a nice round shape, taking care not to pull so hard that the surface starts to tear.

Let the ball rest with the seam side down for 5 minutes while you prepare the basket for proofing. Evenly flour your basket or bowl with a light coat of flour. Invert the ball into the basket so that the seam side is up.

Proofing

Preheat the oven to 500°F with the baking stone and steaming pan in place (see page 22).

Cover the loaf with a tea towel and let rise for 1 to 2 hours. Check the loaf after 45 minutes to 1 hour, and again every 15 to 20 minutes if not ready. It should feel lighter and full of air.

Baking

Dust the peel with rice flour (see page 17) and turn out the proofed loaf onto the peel with the seam down close to the front edge of the peel.

Using a funnel (see page 14), steam the oven with about 60 grams (¼ cup) water. Let the steam settle for 30 seconds or so while you score the loaf.

Score the loaf with a razor blade. I like to make four cuts on the top, each about 4 inches long, in a square around the loaf, but not connecting with one another; all the cuts should be about ⅛ inch deep. Start on the left side a couple of inches in from the edge and about one-third of the way down from the top. Quickly slash straight down, stopping 1 inch from the bottom edge. Next, place the blade 1 inch to the right of the bottom end of the first cut and slash quickly to the right to about 1 inch from the right edge. Place the blade about 1 inch above the end of that second cut and slash quickly up the left side to about 1 inch from the top edge. Finally, place the blade about 1 inch from the end of the third cut and slash quickly across the top to about 1 inch from the left edge. This last cut should end up above the start of the first cut.

Open the oven and place the tip of the peel on the baking stone. Quickly pull the peel out from under the loaf, letting it gently drop onto the baking stone. Close the oven door immediately.

Crack the door enough to stick the funnel nozzle into the edge of the steaming pan and add an additional 235 grams (1 cup) water or so. Remove the funnel as soon as the water hits the steaming pan and close the door tightly. After about 10 minutes, lower the oven to 400°F.

After about 40 minutes, check your loaf. You want the crust to be a deep brown color and the loaf to sound hollow when it is tapped on the bottom. If it still gives a heavy thud, return it to the oven for 5 to 10 minutes.

Cool the bread on a wire cooling rack.

FRENCH BREAD ON THE TABLE

BREAD IS CENTRAL to French culture and an essential part of daily eating. If you are not eating a fresh croissant for breakfast, you are probably taking yesterday's bread and toasting it for a *tartine beurre*, spread with jam or perhaps Nutella. In France, when you sit down to a meal—at home or a restaurant—a basket of bread will be on the table. Unless you are in the fanciest of restaurants, you will not have a separate bread plate; the French simply place bread on the tablecloth next to their main plate. Finishing your plate by mopping up all the sauce with bread is not only accepted but expected, so much so that there is a French verb meaning just that; *saucer*, as they say.

I once made bread for a dinner honoring Jacques Pépin, whom I knew from my days teaching at the French Culinary Institute. It took the master chef a moment to remember me, but when I explained our connection, he was happy to know that the meal would include good bread. The event was at my friend's Austin restaurant, Launderette, and we had planned to serve the bread with the fourth course of chicken with truffles, foie gras, and sauce *aligot*. As soon as the first course started, though, we got a request from Pépin's table for a basket of bread. It was a good thing I had brought plenty, because from that moment on we had to send the bread out to all the tables that followed his lead.

Over the years, I have traveled in France and eaten some amazing meals, everywhere from neighborhood bistros to Michelin-starred restaurants. But it was the lunch baker Jacques Mahou and his wife served me in their home in Tours that influenced me more. In all three of Jacques's bakeries, the breads were baked in wood-burning brick ovens. Per tradition, as the heat slowly diminishes after the overnight bake

has finished, a casserole is prepared in a sturdy cast-iron pot and set in the oven to cook. One day during my visit, Jacques roused me from bed (as I had spent the night with his bakers in the *petrin* below the shop) and the steaming pot was set in the middle of the table. I cannot remember exactly what was in that pot, but I remember feeling connected to centuries of tradition, sharing a meal and bread with this respected baker's family.

I've had a similar experience on my many visits to the home of my most important mentor, Michel Suas, even after he left France. Suas had made pastries and baked bread at Restaurant Charles Barrier, also in Tours, before moving to the San Francisco Bay Area. I have had the privilege of sharing many beautiful meals with Michel and his wonderful wife, Evelyn, in their house high atop the hill overlooking the Pacific Ocean. Without fuss or formality, those meals inevitably follow a very French progression from a light appetizer to a main dish to a salad with a perfect vinaigrette and finish with a well-selected cheese. Bread from the San Francisco Baking Institute or Thorough Bread and Pastry, both of which the couple own, is always on the table.

Of course, cheese is also paramount to French cuisine, and fine cheese demands fine bread to accompany it. As with wine, different cheeses pair well with different types of bread. While there are certainly no hard-and-fast rules, in general, younger, lighter cheeses benefit from the subtle nuttiness of a well-crafted baguette, while a robust *pain au levain* stands up to more pungent, mature cheeses. Very ripe cheese and blue cheese generally harmonize well with nut and fruit breads like Bread with Prunes and Hazelnuts (page 46). My Northern European experience often leads me toward a rye bread, especially with a firmer Alpine-style cheese—not a common cheese pairing in France. It is fun to include a variety of breads with a selection of cheese, so you can taste how they play off each other, bringing out nuances in both the breads and cheeses with different combinations.

In general, the French do not slather butter on their table bread when it accompanies the meal. When the cheese comes out, however, that's when the *beurre* also appears. I heartily agree with this, as I find the butter marries the flavors and textures of bread and cheese together perfectly. Make sure to let the butter come to room temperature along with the cheese by bringing everything out of the fridge well before serving.

LA CHARBONÉE DE BOULANGER

SERVES 4 TO 6

As one of the dishes that could be cooked in the dying heat of the baker's oven, this stew was mentioned in Raymond Calvel's seminal book, *The Taste of Bread*. It piqued my interest and I did some research into it, but even my French friends had never heard of it. Finally, I tracked down James MacGuire, who was on the team that translated Calvel's book into English. He told me that Calvel explained the dish as cubes of pork shoulder braised in the manner of boeuf bourguignon. This version is entirely my own interpretation of the dish.

About 2 pounds pork shoulder roast, cut into 2-inch cubes

Salt and pepper

½ large yellow onion, sliced

2 carrots, sliced

4 sprigs thyme

2 sprigs savory

3 bay leaves

1 bottle red wine, preferably a Chinon or other Loire Valley red

3 tablespoons vegetable oil with a high smoke point, such as grapeseed oil

3 tablespoons all-purpose flour

15 pearl onions, peeled and left whole

15 small button mushrooms

1 to 2 cups chicken stock

5 cloves garlic, skin-on, lightly smashed

Small potatoes, peeled and boiled if desired for serving, or serve with Pain de Campagne (page 40) or Pain au Levain (page 70).

Season the pork generously with salt and pepper. Place half of the yellow onion and half the carrots, 1 sprig thyme, 1 sprig savory, and 2 bay leaves in a baking dish or bowl, cover with the pork cubes, and add just enough wine to cover the meat, pouring it over the top and reserving at least ½ cup. Cover and refrigerate overnight.

Strain the solids from the marinade, reserving all the liquid. Reserve the pork and discard the vegetables and herbs. Dry the pork thoroughly with paper towels.

Preheat the oven to 450°F, or if you have been baking bread, leave the baking stone in and lower the oven to 200°F once the bread is out.

In a Dutch oven or other heavy, ovenproof pan with a lid, heat the oil over high heat, then brown the pork in batches so as not to overcrowd the pan. Brown the pork well on all sides, then remove and reserve; brown the rest of the meat. Turn the heat to medium and brown the remaining yellow onion, remaining carrots, flour, pearl onions, and mushrooms. Return the meat to the pan and deglaze with the reserved marinade and the reserved ½ cup of the wine. Add enough chicken stock so that the liquid almost covers the meat. Add the garlic and remaining thyme, savory, and bay leaf. Cover the pot and bake for 1 hour. Turn the oven to 250°F and bake for 1 more hour. Serve with the potatoes or bread, if desired.

VINAIGRETTE

MAKES ENOUGH FOR 1 HEAD ROMAINE OR LEAF LETTUCE

After the main course, it is refreshing to have a green salad. Our friend Evelyn always mixed her vinaigrette right in the bottom of the wooden salad bowl, then put the lettuce on top and tossed. With a vinaigrette, the key is balance, getting the acid just right so that it is not overbearing but is bright enough to make a refreshing middle course. Classic vinaigrette is three to four parts oil to one part vinegar.

1 tablespoon red wine vinegar

½ teaspoon Dijon mustard

Salt and pepper

¼ cup olive oil

In a large bowl, whisk together the vinegar and mustard, season with salt and pepper, then slowly drizzle in the oil while whisking briskly. Taste and adjust seasonings. If it is too acidic, add more oil, or add a few drops more vinegar if it needs more bite.

CROQUE MONSIEUR

MAKES 2 SANDWICHES

A croque monsieur may seem like a simple grilled ham and cheese sandwich, but basting it with béchamel takes it to another level. This is a bar snack, which in France probably means a wine bar, and it pairs nicely with a Beaujolais Village or a Sauvignon Blanc, wines with a crisp acidity to balance the cheese. I also enjoy a croque monsieur with a crisp pilsner. Add a fried egg to make the sandwich a croque madame. And don't forget to serve this with a side of bread to sop up any cheese and sauce that ooze out.

Bread that is a day or two old works best for this—the slices can even sit out overnight so they dry out just a bit. If you're short on time, you can dry the bread slices in a low oven (200°F) for a few minutes.

BÉCHAMEL

1 tablespoon unsalted butter

1 tablespoon plus 1 teaspoon all-purpose flour

¾ cup whole milk

Pinch of freshly grated nutmeg

Salt and ground white pepper

SANDWICHES

4 slices Pain de Mie (page 58)

2 slices boiled ham

2 slices Emmenthaler cheese, plus ¾ cup grated

4 tablespoons unsalted butter, melted

To make the béchamel, melt the butter in a heavy saucepan over medium heat. Add the flour, stirring constantly with a wooden spoon, and cook for a minute or two. Whisk in ¼ cup of the milk until smooth with no lumps, then whisk in the remaining ½ cup milk. Continue to cook, whisking constantly, until thick enough to coat a spoon, 2 to 3 minutes. Add the nutmeg and season to taste with salt and pepper. Keep warm.

Adjust the oven rack 4 inches from the broiler and heat the broiler.

To make the sandwiches, spread one side of each bread slice generously with the béchamel. Top 2 of the bread slices with a piece of ham, followed by a piece of cheese. Place a second slice of bread on top of the cheese, sauce side down. Brush both sides of the sandwich with melted butter and cook in a cast-iron skillet over medium heat until browned and crispy on one side, 4 to 5 minutes. You can also weight down the sandwich with a second pan on top. Flip the sandwiches and cook the other side until browned and crispy, another 4 to 5 minutes. Remove from the heat.

Leaving the sandwiches in the pan, sprinkle the grated cheese on top. Broil the sandwiches until the cheese is melted and browned on top, 3 to 5 minutes. Serve at once.

OYSTERS WITH MIGNONETTE

MAKES SEVERAL DOZEN OYSTERS OR A FULL TOWER OF FRUITS DES MER

I grew up on Florida's Gulf Coast, the Redneck Riviera, where raw oysters meant cocktail sauce and saltine crackers. In fact, I remember well my first raw oyster. We were having a garden party at the beach condo we were renting when we first moved to Northwest Florida, and among the guests was a family we knew through my aunt. I had a big crush on the daughter, who was a year older than me. When she slurped down an oyster, I knew I had to follow suit. I nudged a mollusk onto a saltine and smothered it with cocktail sauce, and after only a slight hesitation, popped it into my mouth. Charlotte failed to recognize the significance of the Midwestern transplant performing the ritual that was her Gulf Coast birthright, and remained unimpressed, but I began a lifelong love affair with the slippery, sweet, and salty bivalve.

For the brinier oysters from the colder waters of the Atlantic, serve this classic French mignonette sauce, along with Pain de Seigle (page 52), a good salted butter, and a crisp, white wine with good minerality, such as a Muscadet or a Sancerre. It is best to make the mignonette a day ahead, so the flavors have plenty of time to marry.

1 teaspoon peppercorns

Pinch of coarse sea salt

¾ cup good-quality red wine vinegar

1 shallot, diced (about 2 tablespoons)

2 to 3 dozen fresh oysters

Crushed ice or rock salt for serving

Using a mortar and pestle, coarsely crush the peppercorns with the salt; don't overdo it, or the pepper will disappear into the vinegar.

Transfer to a bowl and add the vinegar and shallot and stir to combine. Refrigerate for at least 1 day. The mignonette keeps for up to 1 month in the refrigerator and continues to be more refined over several days, so make it in advance if you can.

Shuck the oysters and serve them on a platter embedded in crushed ice or rock salt, along with the mignonette sauce.

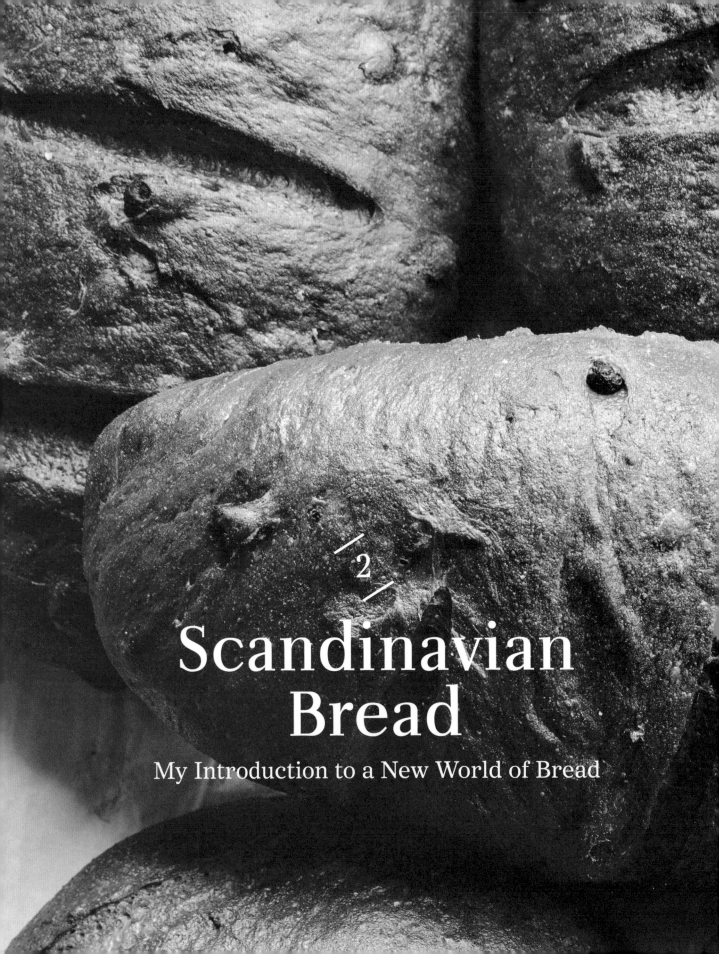

Scandinavian Bread

My Introduction to a New World of Bread

IN SWEDEN, where I was a high school exchange student, there are two categories of bread. *Matbröd*, meaning literally "food bread," is eaten with savory meals, most often sliced thinly and topped with other ingredients to make open-faced sandwiches. *Kaffebröd* is sweet bread served for *fika*, the ubiquitous Swedish coffee break.

Most *matbröd* is made with a blend of rye flour and wheat flour in varying proportions and can range from dense, hearty whole grain loaves to lofty, light loaves. Often they are fairly sweet. During the First World War, authorities pushed bakers to include more sugar beets, which were abundant, to stretch the flour, which was more scarce, and Swedes developed a taste for sweeter breads during that time. From my bedroom window, I could watch the sugar beet harvest in the fields bordering the village.

Spices also flavor many Scandinavian rye breads. *Brödkrydor*, or bread spice, is a blend of anise and fennel that you can purchase at the grocery store. The peel from Seville oranges, called *pomerans* in Swedish, is used as a spice and coriander is also common. Caraway is used in some breads as well.

For me, the flavor of rye is earthy, reminiscent of the forest. Indeed, distinguished food science author Harold McGee writes that rye has "mushroom, potato and green notes" in his book *On Food and Cooking*. These flavors build a great background for the smoked and cured meats and creamy cheeses of the northern lands, but rye also has a strong affinity for the flavors of the sea. Perhaps it is the contrast of land and sea flavors that makes them work well together.

Keep in mind that rye differs from wheat in ways that influence the handling and performance of bread dough. Wheat flour has a magical combination of proteins that link up to form gluten, providing beautiful, airy, and light loaves. Rye, too, has similar proteins, but not in the right proportions to form the same gluten network as wheat. You can mix and mix rye dough but you will never achieve the elastic dough that wheat flour produces. However, there are other elements in rye flour that form enough structure to capture fermentation gases and produce a fine and evenly crumbed loaf of bread. They require less mixing and more gentle handling.

In several of these bread recipes, a portion of the rye flour is scalded by mixing with boiling water prior to incorporating it into the final dough. This gels the starch in the flour into a thick paste, helping give the dough better structure and enhancing the flavor. It also makes it easier to slice the baked bread thinly.

Sourdough is important in making rye bread, not only for its traditional leavening and flavor, but also to help control excessive enzymatic activity to which rye is prone. Although a wheat-based *levain* can be used to make sourdough rye bread, the more traditional flavor comes from a rye sourdough starter, cultured and fed with rye flour exclusively. See how to start and maintain a rye sourdough starter on page 100.

Flatbreads are also a large part of the Scandinavian bread culture. Crisp *knäckebröd*, sometimes called hardtack in the Upper Midwest, is always on the breakfast table alongside the soft loaf breads. In Norway, a whole family of flatbreads is cooked on a griddle instead of in an oven. In the past, both *knäcke* and Norwegian lefse were made in large quantities on a single bake day, then dried and stored to eat through the long northern winter.

FULLKORNSBRÖD

Whole Grain Rye Bread

**MAKES 2 OBLONG
LOAVES**

SCALD 1 to 24 hours

MIXING & KNEADING 45 minutes

FERMENTATION 1 hour

PROOFING 1 hour

BAKING 1 hour to 70 minutes

This hearty, compact rye bread is studded with rye chops, also called cracked rye, which are whole rye grains cut into large pieces like steel-cut oats. The two loaves are gently rolled in wheat bran before proofing. This recipe was adapted slightly from Britt Jonsén, my Swedish host mother. She would bake this *fullkornsbröd* with her mother on their monthly baking days, and it was a favorite of mine. Ideally, start this bread two days in advance: one day to make the scald and one day to bake and rest the bread.

Scald

Although you can make this the same day, it is best to let it sit overnight.

WHOLE RYE FLOUR	480 grams	4¼ cups
RYE CHOPS (CRACKED RYE)	140 grams	¾ cup plus 1½ tablespoons
SALT	15 grams	1 tablespoon
WATER	1 kilogram	4¼ cups

Put the flour, rye chops, and salt in a large heatproof bowl and blend together with your fingers to evenly distribute them. Bring the water to a rolling boil in a saucepan and carefully pour over the flour mix, immediately stirring with a wooden spoon. Stir until there are no lumps; the mixture will be quite thick.

Cover with a tea towel and leave in the bowl at room temperature overnight (up to 24 hours) for the best results.

If making the dough straightaway, let the scalded flour rest for 20 minutes in the bowl, then turn out onto a rimmed baking sheet, spreading it out to let it cool to room temperature before proceeding. Return the scalded flour to a large clean bowl just before mixing and kneading.

DOUGH

WATER AT 90°F	60 grams	¼ cup
INSTANT YEAST	18 grams	1½ tablespoons
SCALDED FLOUR	All from above	
ALL-PURPOSE FLOUR	700 grams	5½ cups
WHEAT BRAN	20 grams, plus more for topping the loaves	¼ cup plus 3 tablespoons
RICE FLOUR	For dusting	

Mixing and Kneading

Put the warm water into a small heatproof bowl. Add the yeast and whisk briefly to moisten. Let sit for 5 to 10 minutes, then whisk again to form a thick slurry. Normally, instant yeast can be blended into the flour without being rehydrated, but because most of the liquid for this dough is already in the scald, the yeast would not fully dissolve during the hand mixing, so it is better to make this slurry.

Make sure you have a plastic bowl scraper at hand. Add the yeast slurry to the bowl of the scalded flour. Plunge both hands in and start squeezing the yeast slurry into the scald, working from the side of the bowl closest to you across to the other side, until well incorporated. Add the all-purpose flour and wheat bran and start squeezing them into the scald. Work from the side of the bowl closest to you across to the other side, squeezing with both hands. Rotate the bowl a quarter turn and squeeze your way through the dough again. You will feel the dough starting to come together as a more cohesive mass, and the water and scald will become more fully incorporated. Use your bowl scraper from time to time to scrape the sticky dough from the sides of the bowl into the center. Keep rotating the bowl and squeezing the dough until everything is fully incorporated, 1 to 2 minutes.

CONTINUED

The dough should be medium stiff, having some give, like a rubber band. Add the reserved water if the dough is not soft enough. You may have to add more water to get the right consistency if it feels too stiff. It is better to have a dough that is a little wet than one that is too dry.

Turn out the dough onto an unfloured work surface, using the bowl scraper to get it all out of the bowl and scraping as much off your hands as you can. Resist the urge to add flour to the work surface or the dough at this stage.

Starting with the edge closest to you, grab the dough with both hands, palms down, and pull it gently toward you. Stretch it up and flip it over the top of the dough mass by 2 or 3 inches and press it into the surface. Grab the new edge closest to you and stretch it gently up and flip it over the top. Repeat this stretching and flipping of the dough four or five times, working your way to the far side of the mass. The stretches should be gentle enough not to tear the dough apart. As you continue this process, the dough will hold together better and be easier to stretch.

Scrape up the dough with a dough scraper, rotate it a quarter turn, and repeat the stretching and flipping through the mass four or five times for a total of 3 to 4 minutes. Use a plastic dough scraper to help scrape up the dough that sticks to the counter. With each stretch and flip of the dough, you will feel it developing, becoming more cohesive and less sticky. However, because of the rye flour, it will not become as elastic and stretchy as dough made mostly with wheat.

Dust the work surface and your hands lightly with all-purpose flour.

Work the dough into a ball by folding the edges into the center and return it to the bowl with the seam underneath. Cover with a damp tea towel.

Fermentation

Let the dough sit in a warm, draft-free place until it feels airy when touched but is not quite doubled in volume, about 1 hour. After fermentation, you will not fold this dough.

Shaping

Dust the work surface lightly with all-purpose flour and turn out the dough so that the smooth side is down. Moisten a tea towel and pour some wheat bran onto a rimmed baking sheet or plate.

Divide the dough into two equal pieces with a bench knife or bowl scraper. Gently press one piece of the dough with the heels of both hands into a rough rectangle. Grab the long edge closest to you and stretch, fold it about two-thirds of the way to the opposite side, and gently press into the dough with the heels of your hands. Grab the edge opposite you and stretch it over the first fold, about two-thirds of the way toward you, pressing it into the dough with the heels of your hands. Again, grab the opposite edge and fold toward you, this time all the way to meet the closest edge and seal the seam where the two edges meet with the heel of your hand from one end to the other. Gently roll the loaf back and forth to make a cylinder and further seal the seam. Keep the cylinder as even and straight as you can, not tapering the ends.

Gently roll one of the finished loaves on the moistened tea towel, then in the wheat bran to coat the surface. Place the loaf with the seam side up on a tea towel. Repeat the shaping of the second loaf and coating it with bran.

With a fold of the towel pulled up to separate the two loaves, place the second loaf, seam side up, on the towel next to the first. Cover the loaves with a second towel if the first does not cover them.

Proofing

Preheat the oven to 450°F with the baking stone and steaming pan in place (see page 22).

Let the loaves rise until close to double in size, about 1 hour.

Baking

Dust the peel with rice flour (see page 17) and turn out one of the loaves onto the peel with the seam side down.

Using your funnel (see page 14), steam the oven with 60 grams (¼ cup) water. This bread is not scored.

Open the oven and place the tip of the peel on the baking stone where you want the loaf to end up. Leave room for the second loaf if the stone is large enough; center the loaf if it is not. Quickly pull the peel out from under the loaf, letting it gently drop onto the baking stone. Close the oven door immediately. If your stone can fit two loaves at once, quickly place the second loaf onto the baking stone; place it in the refrigerator if it does not fit.

Using the funnel, add 235 grams (1 cup) more water to the steaming pan. Close the oven door tightly as soon all the water hits the steaming pan. Rye breads like a lot of steam.

After 5 minutes, lower the oven to 350°F and open the door a crack to allow some of the steam to escape for about 30 seconds. Close the door and bake until the crust is an even, light brown color and the loaf is slightly hollow sounding when rapped on the bottom, 55 minutes. If it still gives a heavy thud, return it to the oven for 5 to 10 minutes.

Wrap the loaves in tea towels and completely cool on a wire cooling rack, preferably for 24 hours, before slicing.

RYE SOURDOUGH STARTER

INITIAL ACTIVITY 24 to 48 hours

ESTABLISHMENT FEEDINGS Every 8 hours for 4 or 5 days

MAINTENANCE Use for baking or feed once a week; maintain in the refrigerator

USE Pull from refrigerator 24 to 48 hours before using in a recipe

Rye bread benefits from a sourdough starter not only for traditional leavening and better flavor, but also to help control the excessive enzymatic activity to which it is prone. From the outset, rye has more of the enzymes that convert starch into simpler sugars than wheat, and this can be exacerbated by wet conditions during growing and harvesting if the grains start to sprout. This conversion to sugar is important for fermentation, but if too much of the starch turns to sugar, the structure of the loaf during baking is compromised, resulting in a sticky, gummy crumb. Acid from a sourdough starter is one of the most effective ways to keep the enzymes in check.

Although there are many ways to make and maintain a rye sourdough starter, I like this method because unlike the Levain Naturel (page 64), you only need to feed it once before using it in a recipe. It gives good flavor and acid balance, and if well maintained, it also has good leavening power. The secret is the small amount of starter in proportion to the flour and water in the feedings, giving the microbes plenty of fuel for an extended fermentation.

When you are making this starter, be sure to use very clean bowls and utensils. You might even consider sterilizing the jar that holds the starter with boiling water to be safe.

Rye ferments readily, so this starter should get going quickly and develop into maturity in 4 to 5 days. Be prepared to feed the starter every 8 hours during that initial time. Once it reaches maturity, it is easy to maintain by either using it to bake or doing a maintenance feeding once a week.

INITIAL STARTER

WHOLE RYE FLOUR	100 grams	¾ cup plus 2½ tablespoons
WATER AT 75°F TO 80°F OR SLIGHTLY WARMER THAN ROOM TEMPERATURE	100 grams	¼ cup plus 3 tablespoons

In a very clean medium bowl, blend the flour and water with your fingers into a thick paste. (Unlike the Levain Naturel (page 67), this starter is more liquid than solid.) Place in a 1-quart jar or other see-through, cylindrical container. Mark the level of the top of the starter on the side of the jar with a permanent marker. You can put a lid loosely on top of the jar or cover it with a tea towel. Let sit in a warm, draft-free place for 24 to 48 hours.

Start checking the starter after 24 hours to see if there is any activity. Once you notice some bubbling activity within the paste, start feeding it on an 8-hour schedule. If you do not see any obvious activity after 48 hours, or if the starter turns gray or has an unpleasant off-smell, discard it and start again.

Feeding Days 1 Through 4 or 5

Once you see activity, it is time to start feeding your starter. It is important to be diligent about the feedings, keeping to a schedule of a feeding every 8 hours—establishing a time that fits in your daily schedule for up to 4 days is key. For example, if you feed the starter at 6 a.m., you will need to feed it again at 2 p.m. and 10 p.m. If you are not an early riser, you could feed at 8 a.m., 4 p.m., and midnight. The midday feeding is probably the most challenging for folks who work during the day and cannot sneak away. Be sure to record the time of your first feed so that you will be able to feed it every 8 hours. I like to do the first feed just before bedtime, then I feed again when I wake up.

CONTINUED

INITIAL STARTER	100 grams	¼ cup plus 3 tablespoons
WATER AT 75°F TO 80°F OR SLIGHTLY WARMER THAN ROOM TEMPERATURE	100 grams	¼ cup plus 3 tablespoons
WHOLE RYE FLOUR	100 grams	¾ cup plus 2½ tablespoons

Measure 100 grams (¼ cup pus 3 tablespoons) of the starter and put in a clean bowl. Add the water and break up the starter a little with your hands. It does not have to be completely dissolved. Add the rye flour and knead until completely incorporated. Discard the rest of the starter. Clean the jar in hot water (if you use soap, rinse well to remove any traces of it). Put the fed starter into the jar and mark the level with a marker on the side of the jar.

Repeat this feeding every 8 hours for 4 to 5 days and discard the leftover starter each time. Before each feeding, note the level of the starter; it will gradually increase before it starts to collapse in on itself at the top. The goal is for the starter to double its height within 8 hours before it starts collapsing in on itself. A mature starter should have a pleasant acidic smell.

Once the starter is mature, you can use it right away in a bread recipe or keep it in the refrigerator and feed it once a week.

Maintaining Your Starter

If you do not use your starter for baking for a week or more, take it out of the refrigerator and feed it once a week. Always use this same recipe and discard the extra starter.

RYE SOURDOUGH STARTER	10 grams	2 teaspoons
WHOLE RYE FLOUR	100 grams	¾ cup plus 2½ tablespoons
WATER AT 80°F TO 90°F	100 grams	¼ cup plus 3 tablespoons

Measure 10 grams (2 teaspoons) of the starter and put in a clean, medium bowl. Discard the excess starter and clean out your storage jar. Mix the flour and water into the starter and knead with your hands until you have a smooth paste. Return the mixture to the storage jar. Let the starter sit out at room temperature for 3 hours, so that the fermentation gets started (you will not see much change in that time, but the fermentation is getting going). Return to the refrigerator.

Wake-Up Feed

Twenty-four to 48 hours before you wish to bake bread, pull the starter from the refrigerator and immediately feed it the following:

RYE SOURDOUGH STARTER	20 grams	4 teaspoons
WHOLE RYE FLOUR	100 grams	¾ cup plus 2½ tablespoons
WATER AT 80°F TO 90°F	100 grams	¼ cup plus 3 tablespoons

Measure out 20 grams (4 teaspoons) of the starter. Discard the excess starter (you'll have extra to set aside later for future bakes), clean out your storage jar, and set it aside. Place the starter in a clean medium bowl and mix in the flour and water by hand, stirring and blending until you have a smooth paste. Cover the bowl with a tea towel and place in a warm, draft-free place for 12 hours.

Measure out the amount of starter you need for your bread recipe into a separate bowl, and return the rest of the fed starter back to the jar and refrigerate it.

GOTLANDSBRÖD

Gotland's Bread

MAKES 2 ROUND LOAVES

STARTER 12 to 14 hours (24 to 26 hours if starter needs a wake-up feed)

SCALD 1 to 24 hours

SPONGE 2 hours

MIXING & KNEADING 15 minutes

FERMENTATION 60 to 70 minutes

PROOFING 20 to 30 minutes

BAKING 55 to 65 minutes

Gotland is an island in the Baltic Sea off the eastern coast of Sweden. Though I have never been to Gotland, when I was working at Bouley Bakery in New York, I had a visit from a Swedish baker named Erik Olofson. The Stockholm bakery where Erik worked was part of Rosendals Trädgård, a market garden, orchard, café, and bakery. In the bakery, there is a wood-fired stone oven designed by the Finnish architect Heikki Hyytiäinen. The oven includes two baking chambers, one above the other, with access from two sides. One side opens to the outdoors, for loading the wood and sweeping the ash, and the other side opens indoors, for loading and unloading the bread.

This is my adaptation of Erik's recipe for *Gotlandsbröd*. He had spent a summer on Gotland "with its innumerable bakeries and stone ovens," as he describes it in his book *Bröd & Marmelad*. In the book, he tells of learning the recipe from a woman who was the third generation in her family to make and sell it in markets all around the island.

You will need dried bitter orange peel, which is available online from home brewing companies.

This recipe requires a mature rye sourdough starter, which must be made 4 to 5 days in advance (see page 100), and making a scald, which is best done a day in advance. In addition, it's best to rest the loaves overnight before slicing.

STARTER

RYE SOURDOUGH STARTER (PAGE 100)	18 grams	1 tablespoon plus 1 teaspoon
WHOLE RYE FLOUR	180 grams	1⅔ cups
WATER AT 80°F OR SLIGHTLY WARMER THAN ROOM TEMPERATURE	180 grams	¾ cup

If your rye sourdough starter is refrigerated, feed it the wake-up feed (page 102).

After the 12-hour wake-up feed or if you are using an unrefrigerated mature starter, measure 18 grams (1 tablespoon plus 1 teaspoon) of the starter into a small bowl; put the rest in the storage jar and return to the refrigerator.

Add the flour and warm water to the starter in the bowl and mix by hand until you have a smooth paste. Cover with a tea towel and let ferment in a warm, draft-free place for 12 to 14 hours.

Scald

Although you can make this the same day, it is best to let it sit overnight.

WHOLE RYE FLOUR	280 grams	2½ cups
WATER	560 grams	2⅓ cups

Put the flour in a large heatproof bowl. Bring the water to a rolling boil in a kettle or small saucepan, then carefully pour over the flour, immediately stirring with a wooden spoon. Stir until there are no lumps; the mixture will be quite thick.

Cover with a tea towel and let rest overnight as your sourdough starter is fermenting.

BITTER ORANGE PEEL

DRIED BITTER ORANGE PEEL	15 grams

Put the orange peel in a small saucepan and add enough water to cover. Bring to a boil, then simmer until softened, 20 to 30 minutes. Drain and let cool. Put in a covered container or bowl covered with plastic wrap and store at room temperature overnight.

CONTINUED

SPONGE

ANISE SEEDS	4 grams	1 teaspoon
FENNEL SEEDS	4 grams	1 teaspoon
ALL-PURPOSE FLOUR	90 grams	¾ cup
STARTER	All from page 105	
BITTER ORANGE PEEL	All from page 105, drained and chopped	
WATER	50 grams	3 tablespoons plus 1 teaspoon
SCALDED FLOUR	All from page 105	

Grind the anise and fennel seeds in a mortar and pestle or a spice grinder. Adding a couple pinches of salt from the 20 grams in the dough below can help grind them finer. Put the ground spices and flour in a large bowl and blend together with your fingers to evenly distribute them.

Add the starter, flour and spice blend, the chopped orange peel, and water to the bowl of scalded flour. Mix and squeeze with your hands until there are no lumps. You should have a smooth sponge. Cover with a tea towel or plastic wrap and let stand in a warm place until doubled in volume, about 2 hours.

DOUGH

ALL-PURPOSE FLOUR	300 grams	2⅓ cups
SALT	20 grams	1 tablespoon plus 1 teaspoon
DARK BEET-SUGAR SYRUP OR CANE SYRUP	150 grams	¼ cup plus 3 tablespoons
SPONGE	All from above	
RICE FLOUR	For dusting	

Mixing and Kneading

Put the flour and salt in a small bowl and blend together with your fingers to evenly distribute them. Add this flour mixture and the syrup to the bowl with the sponge.

Make sure you have a plastic bowl scraper at hand. Plunge both hands in and start squeezing the flour and syrup into the sponge. Work from the side of the bowl closest to you across to the other side, squeezing with both hands. Rotate the bowl a quarter turn and squeeze your way through the dough again. You will feel the dough starting to come together as a more cohesive mass, and the flour, syrup and sponge will become more fully incorporated. Use your bowl scraper from time to time to scrape the sticky dough from the sides of the bowl into the center. Keep rotating the bowl and squeezing the dough until everything is fully incorporated, 1 to 2 minutes. It will remain a shaggy and sticky mass.

The dough should be medium-soft, having definite give but also some resistance; you should be able to feel a core when you squeeze it.

Turn out the dough onto an unfloured counter, using the bowl scraper to get it all out of the bowl and scraping as much off your hands as you can. Resist the urge to add flour to the work surface or the dough at this stage.

Starting with the edge closest to you, grab the dough with both hands, palms down, and pull it gently toward you. Stretch it up and flip it over the top of the dough mass by 2 or 3 inches. Grab the closer edge and stretch it gently up and flip it over the top. Repeat this stretching and flipping of the dough four or five times, working your way to the far side of the mass. The stretches should be gentle enough not to tear the dough apart. As you continue this process, the dough will hold together better and be easier to stretch.

Scrape up the dough with a dough scraper, rotate it a quarter turn, and repeat the stretching and flipping through the mass again four or five times, 3 to 4 minutes. With each stretch and flip of the dough, you will feel it developing, becoming more cohesive and less sticky. However, because of the rye flour, it will not become as elastic and stretchy as dough made mostly with wheat.

Dust the work surface lightly with all-purpose flour. Work the dough into a ball by folding the edges into the center.

Fermentation

Return the ball to the bowl, smooth side up, cover with a tea towel or plastic wrap, and let sit in a warm, draft-free place for 30 minutes.

Preheat the oven to 475°F with the baking stone and steaming pan in place (see page 22).

Dust the work surface lightly with all-purpose flour and turn out the dough so the smooth side is down.

Gently press the dough into a flat circle. Fold the opposite edge of the dough to the center and press gently into the dough. Fold the edge closest to you to the center, overlapping the last fold slightly, and press gently into the dough. Rotate the dough and repeat the folds with the remaining two edges. Turn the dough over and fashion into a ball by cupping the dough with your hands and rotating it counterclockwise, returning it to the bowl, seam side down. Cover with a tea towel and let rest and rise until full, rounded, and well risen, but not quite doubled in size, 30 to 40 minutes.

Shaping

Dust the work surface lightly with all-purpose flour and turn out the dough, smooth side down. Divide the dough into two pieces with a bench knife or bowl scraper. Gently press the first piece of dough to flatten it into a round about 2 inches thick. Fold the sides in to form a ball. Turn over and mold into a ball, sealing the seam underneath as best you can. Without the gluten structure, you are molding the dough more than stretching it into shape.

Let the ball rest with the seam side down and repeat with the second ball. Let that one rest for a couple of minutes while you prepare the baskets for proofing. Evenly flour your baskets or bowls with a light coat of flour. Invert the balls into the baskets so that the seam side is up.

Proofing

Cover the loaves with a tea towel and let rise for 20 minutes. The loaves will be about one and a half times larger.

Baking

Dust the peel with rice flour (see page 17) and turn out one loaf onto the peel, seam side down.

Using a funnel (see page 14), steam the oven with about 60 grams (¼ cup) water.

Open the oven and place the tip of the peel on the baking stone where you want the loaf to end up. Leave room for the second loaf if the stone is large enough; center the loaf if it is not. Quickly pull the peel out from under the loaf, letting it gently drop onto the baking stone. Close the oven door immediately. If your stone can fit two loaves at once, place the second one on the baking stone.

Using the funnel, add 235 grams (1 cup) more water to the steaming pan. Close the oven door as soon as the water hits the pan. After 5 minutes, lower the oven to 400°F. Put the second loaf in the refrigerator if it does not fit.

After about 50 minutes, check your loaf. You want the crust to be a deep brown color and the loaf to sound hollow when it is tapped on the bottom. If it still gives a heavy thud, return it to the oven for 5 to 10 minutes. Wrap the loaves in tea towels and cool completely on a wire rack, preferably for 24 hours, before slicing.

RUGBRØD

Danish Rye Bread

MAKES 1 PULLMAN LOAF
OR 2 STANDARD LOAVES

STARTER 12 to 14 hours
(24 to 26 hours if starter needs a
wake-up feed)

SOAKER 2 to 24 hours

MIXING & KNEADING 10 minutes

FERMENTATION 1 hour

PROOFING 45 minutes to 1 hour

BAKING 1 hour 10 minutes to
1 hour 25 minutes

Compact, moist, and toothsome, this bread is the base for most Danish *smørrebrød*, the open-faced sandwiches ubiquitous around the country. Many different grains and seeds can be added, but I prefer a simple version with either whole rye berries or whole barley, also called hulless barley. You need to cook these whole grain kernels before adding them in the dough, which is called a soaker, or they will remain too hard to chew. Some recipes for this bread say to put the wet dough directly into the pan for a single rise, but I prefer to ferment the dough before shaping. For a traditional Pullman loaf, use a 16 by 4-inch Pullman loaf pan; you can also use two 8½ by 4½-inch loaf pans. Unlike other breads with this shape in the book, this bread is baked without a cover.

This recipe requires a mature rye sourdough starter, which must be made 4 to 5 days in advance, and making a soaker, which is best done a day in advance. In addition, it's best to rest the loaves overnight before slicing.

STARTER

RYE SOURDOUGH STARTER (PAGE 100)	33 grams	2 tablespoons plus 2 teaspoons
WHOLE RYE FLOUR	330 grams	3 cups
WATER AT 80°F OR SLIGHTLY WARMER THAN ROOM TEMPERATURE	330 grams	1⅓ cups plus 1½ tablespoons

If your rye sourdough starter is refrigerated, feed it the wake-up feed (page 102). After the 12-hour wake-up feed or if you are using an unrefrigerated mature starter, measure out 33 grams (2 tablespoons plus 2 teaspoons) of the starter into a small bowl; return the rest to your storage container and put it back in the refrigerator.

Add the flour and warm water to the starter and mix by hand until you have a smooth paste. Cover with a tea towel or plastic wrap and let ferment in a warm, draft-free place for 12 to 14 hours.

Soaker

You can make this at the same time you do the final feeding for the starter (above).

WHOLE RYE BERRIES	220 grams	1⅓ cups
WATER	440 grams, plus more as needed	2 cups, plus more as needed

Combine the grains and water in a heavy pot and bring to a boil, then lower to a simmer and cook until tender, about 30 minutes. Add more water as needed so that the grains do not scorch.

Strain the berries and reserve the liquid. Store, covered in the refrigerator.

DOUGH

WHOLE RYE FLOUR	555 grams	5 cups plus 1 tablespoon
ALL-PURPOSE FLOUR	222 grams	1¾ cups
SALT	27 grams	1 tablespoon plus 2 teaspoons
INSTANT YEAST	8 grams	2 teaspoons
RYE SOURDOUGH STARTER	All from above	
SOAKER	All from above	
WATER	555 grams	2⅓ cups

CONTINUED

Mixing and Kneading

Put the rye flour, all-purpose flour, salt, and yeast in a large bowl and blend together with your fingers to evenly distribute them. Add the starter and the soaker on top of the flour. Add the water, holding back a small amount (about 30 grams, or 2 tablespoons), until you see if the flour needs it all.

Make sure you have a plastic bowl scraper at hand. Plunge both hands in and squeeze the water, starter, and grains into the flour. Work from the side of the bowl closest to you across to the other side, squeezing with both hands. Rotate the bowl a quarter turn and squeeze through the dough again. You will feel the dough begin to come together as a more cohesive mass, and the water, starter, and grains will become more fully incorporated. Use your bowl scraper from time to time to scrape the dough from the sides of the bowl into the center. Keep rotating the bowl and squeezing the dough until everything is fully incorporated, 2 to 3 minutes. This is a very wet and sticky dough, so it is best to leave it in the bowl rather than turning it out onto the counter to stretch and fold it.

Fermentation

Return the ball to the bowl, smooth side up, cover with a tea towel or plastic wrap, and let sit in a warm, draft-free place for 1 hour.

Shaping

Spray the Pullman pan or two loaf pans generously with baking spray.

Dust the work surface generously with all-purpose flour and turn out the dough (it doesn't matter which side is down) and press the air out of it.

If using a Pullman pan, press the dough into a 14 by 8-inch rectangle. If using two loaf pans, divide the dough into two pieces with a bench knife or bowl scraper and pat out each piece into an 8 by 6-inch rectangle. For each rectangle, fold the long edge closest to you about two-thirds of the way to the opposite side, and press into the dough with the heels of your hands. Grab the opposite edge and fold it toward you over the first fold, about two-thirds of the way to the closest edge, and again seal it with the heel of your hand. Continue folding the opposite edge toward you two or three times to build up a cylinder. The dough will not stretch like a wheat-based dough, it is more a molding process. Roll the dough back and forth to make an even, straight cylinder the length of your pan. Keep the work surface dusted with all-purpose flour, as this is a sticky and loose dough. Carefully put the cylinder into the pan, seam side down. The dough will not hold the cylinder shape very well. Pat the dough to level out the top in the pan. Repeat with the second piece of dough if needed.

Proofing

Preheat the oven to 475°F with the steaming pan in place (see page 22). You do not need a baking stone.

Cover the pan(s) with a tea towel and let rise until the center of the loaf is just even with the top of the pan(s), 45 minutes to an hour.

Baking

Open the oven and slide the pan or pans onto the top oven rack. Close the oven door.

Using a funnel (see page 14), steam the oven with 235 grams (1 cup) water. After 5 minutes, lower the oven to 400°F and crack the oven door to let the steam out for a minute or two.

After 1 hour, check your loaves. If the sides are well set and have pulled away from the pans slightly, remove from the pans and give the bottoms a light thump. If they do not yet sound hollow or if the sides seem very soft, return the loaves to the oven without the pans for 5 to 10 minutes.

Cool the bread on a wire cooling rack until completely cool. Let sit 24 hours before slicing.

KNÄCKEBRÖD

Swedish Crispbread

**MAKES 2 LARGE
ROUND CRISPBREADS**

STARTER 12 to 14 hours (24 to 26
hours if starter needs a wake-up feed)

MIXING & KNEADING 25 minutes

SHAPING 25 minutes

PROOFING 30 minutes

BAKING 10 to 15 minutes
per crispbread

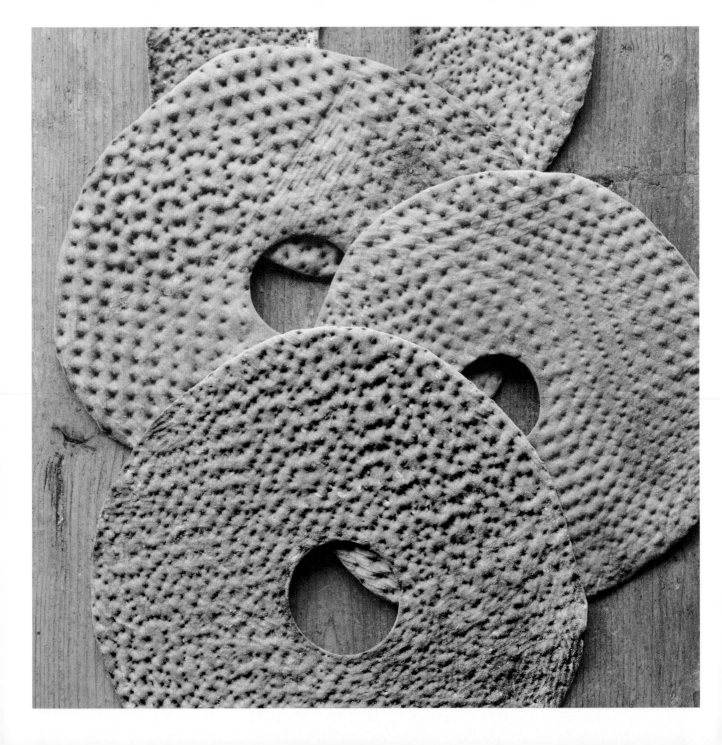

Even if you have never heard the word *knäckebröd*, you may be familiar with the Wasa brand crispbreads of many varieties, wrapped in rectangular packages and sold in the cracker section of your supermarket. That is *knäcke*, just baked in the small rectangular shape instead of the traditional large rounds. In the old days, *knäckebröd* was baked in large quantities a couple of times during the year and then strung on poles hung in the rafters to keep through the season; the hole in the center of the breads was for the pole to pass through. *Knäcke* bread also bakes best in the intense heat of a brick oven, with the fire still burning inside. That is what helps make them crispy. In a conventional home oven, preheating the oven and baking stone thoroughly at the hottest temperature possible and baking without steam produces good results. If the *knäckebröd* is still not crispy enough, you can dry it in a low oven after it has cooled.

This recipe requires a mature rye sourdough starter, which must be made 4 to 5 days in advance.

STARTER

RYE SOURDOUGH STARTER (PAGE 100)	10 grams	2 teaspoons
WHOLE RYE FLOUR	100 grams	¾ cup plus 2½ tablespoons
WATER AT 80°F OR SLIGHTLY WARMER THAN ROOM TEMPERATURE	100 grams	¼ cup plus 3 tablespoons

If your rye sourdough starter is refrigerated, feed it the wake-up feed (page 102).

After the 12-hour wake-up feed or if you are using an unrefrigerated mature starter, measure out 10 grams of the starter into a small bowl; return the rest to your storage container and put it back in the refrigerator.

Add the rye flour and warm water to the starter and mix by hand until you have a smooth paste. Cover with a tea towel or plastic wrap and let ferment in a warm, draft-free place for 12 to 14 hours.

DOUGH

WHOLE RYE FLOUR	75 grams	⅔ cup
ALL-PURPOSE FLOUR OR WHOLE WHEAT FLOUR	75 grams	½ cup plus 1 tablespoon and 1 teaspoon
SALT	5 grams	1 teaspoon
STARTER	All from above	
WATER	90 to 140 grams	6 to 9 tablespoons
RICE FLOUR	For dusting	

Mixing and Kneading

Put the rye flour, all-purpose flour, and salt in a large bowl and blend together with your fingers to evenly distribute them. Add the starter and water. You can mix with your fingers, but this wet, sticky dough can also be mixed with a wooden spoon. Mix to a cohesive dough, 2 to 3 minutes. You will not have gluten development.

Let rest for 15 minutes. You do not need to cover the bowl.

CONTINUED

Shaping

Preheat the oven to 500°F with the baking stone in place. You do not need a steaming pan. Dust a wooden board lightly with all-purpose flour or line a baking sheet with parchment paper; either needs to be large enough to fit two 12-inch circles.

Also dust the work surface lightly with all-purpose flour. Divide the dough into two equal pieces with a bench knife or bowl scraper and round each piece into a ball. Cover with a tea towel and let rest 15 minutes.

Flatten one ball with your hand and use a rolling pin to roll the ball into a 12-inch circle, always starting in the center and rolling outward in all directions. Bring the pin back to the center with each stroke. Transfer the circle carefully to the floured wooden board or parchment-lined baking sheet to make it easier to transfer the thin dough disk to a baking peel.

Cut a hole in the center of the circle with a 1½-inch or 2-inch round cookie or biscuit cutter. You can bake these small center pieces if you want; they make a fun little treat. Repeat with the second ball.

Dock the surface of the dough with a roller docker if you have one or a notched rolling pin, or use the blunt end of a wooden skewer or even a chopstick to poke holes in the top to let out steam.

Proofing

Cover the dough circles with tea towels and let rise for 30 minutes. You will not notice much rise in the dough, but it will be ready to bake.

Baking

Dust the peel with rice flour (see page 17). Carefully slide one circle onto the peel. Place the peel over the baking stone and quickly pull the peel out from under the circle of dough, letting it drop onto the baking stone. Close the door and bake until the round is well colored and set, 10 to 15 minutes. The crispbread may still be flexible; that is okay. Transfer the crispbread to a wire cooling rack to cool completely. Repeat with the second circle of dough.

If the cooled crispbreads are still more chewy than crisp, bake them at 250°F on a baking sheet until crispy, 15 to 20 minutes.

VÖRTBRÖD

Swedish "Wort" Bread

MAKES 2 OBLONG LOAVES

WORT (OPTIONAL) 1¼ hours plus cooling time

SCALD 1 to 24 hours

SPONGE 35 to 50 minutes

MIXING & KNEADING 20 minutes

FERMENTATION 1 to 1¼ hours

PROOFING 30 to 45 minutes

BAKING 30 to 45 minutes

The name for this bread came from the traditional use of brewer's wort, the malt extract that is diluted with water, boiled, flavored with hops, and then fermented into beer. The bread is sweet, rich with maltiness, and spiced with warm winter spices like ginger and cloves; often it includes raisins. Yet it is not generally eaten by itself as a coffee or dessert bread. Instead, it is used for the ritual *dopp i grytan* (literally "dip in the pot"), dunking the bread slices into the Christmas ham broth (see page 135).

At one time, wort could easily be purchased from a local brewery in Sweden, but now home bakers there find it easier to source powdered or liquid wort extract. Much easier, and almost as good, is to simply use a malty dark beer like a porter or stout in place of the wort in the following recipe.

With my past experience home brewing, I make a version of *vörtbröd* for one of our special Christmas breads at Easy Tiger in which I cook up my own batch of wort to use as the liquid in the bread dough. I use a Baltic porter extract kit from Austin Home Brew Supply, and this lends great flavor to the bread. The only problem is that it makes five gallons of wort, which is enough for an awful lot of bread. You could look for a similar dark, malty beer kit in a one-gallon size if you wanted, or you could brew the remaining wort into beer (see Note on page 120).

This is a good time to use Saf-Instant Gold yeast (see page 19), which is more tolerant of high sugar levels than regular instant yeast is. If you have this yeast on hand, use 8 grams (2 teaspoons) instead of the instant yeast in the sponge. Regular instant yeast works fine too.

WORT

1 beer-making kit such as for a porter or stout

Follow the instructions that come with the brewing kit. Add the malt extract to the water and bring to a boil. Cook at a steady boil for 1 hour, adding the hops (this is optional, but I like the subtle bitterness that balances the sweetness of this bread) when directed. If you are only using the wort for making the bread, you can allow the wort to cool at room temperature until it is 90°F or cooler. (If it is any warmer, it will kill the yeast.) It can be refrigerated up to a week if you want to make it ahead.

Scald

Although you can make this the same day, it is best to let it sit overnight.

WHOLE RYE FLOUR	140 grams	1¼ cups
WATER	280 grams	1 cup plus 3 tablespoons

Place the flour in a large heatproof bowl with at least a 1-gallon capacity. Bring the water to a rolling boil in a small saucepan, then carefully pour over the flour, immediately stirring with a wooden spoon. Stir until there are no lumps; the mixture will be quite thick.

Cover with a tea towel and leave in the bowl at room temperature overnight (up to 24 hours) for the best results.

If making the dough straightaway, let the scalded flour rest for 20 minutes in the bowl, then turn out onto a rimmed baking sheet, spreading it out to let it cool to room temperature before proceeding. Return the scalded flour to a large clean bowl just before mixing and kneading.

CONTINUED

SPONGE

WORT OR PORTER	356 grams	1½ cups
INSTANT YEAST	12 grams	1 tablespoon
UNSALTED BUTTER	35 grams	2½ tablespoons
SCALDED FLOUR	All from page 117	
ALL-PURPOSE FLOUR	210 grams	1⅔ cups
GROUND BITTER ORANGE PEEL	9 grams	3 teaspoons
GROUND GINGER	6 grams	2 teaspoons
GROUND CLOVES	3 grams	1 teaspoon

DOUGH

ALL-PURPOSE FLOUR	476 grams	3¾ cups
SALT	11 grams	2 teaspoons
DARK BEET-SUGAR SYRUP OR CANE SYRUP	78 grams	¼ cup
SPONGE	All from above	
RAISINS (OPTIONAL)	125 grams	1 cup
RICE FLOUR	For dusting	

If the wort or porter was refrigerated, warm it in a small saucepan until it reaches between 90°F and 95°F (be careful not to let it get too hot). Remove from the heat. Measure out 35 grams of the warm wort into a small bowl, leaving the rest in the pan.

Make a yeast slurry by sprinkling the yeast on top of the measured wort, whisking briefly to wet all the yeast, and let stand for 5 minutes. Whisk again until you have a creamy mixture and all of the yeast is hydrated.

Add the butter to the remaining wort and gently cook over medium heat just until the butter starts to melt. Remove from the heat and stir to melt the butter completely.

Add about half of the wort-butter mix to the scalded flour and mix and squeeze with your hands until just combined. Add the all-purpose flour, orange peel, ginger, cloves, and the yeast slurry. Gradually pour in the remaining wort-butter mix as you mix and squeeze with your hands until there are no lumps. You should have a smooth sponge. Cover with a tea towel and let stand in a warm, draft-free place until doubled in volume, 30 to 45 minutes.

Mixing and Kneading

Put the flour and salt in a small bowl and blend together with your fingers to evenly distribute them. Add this flour mixture and the syrup to the bowl on top of the sponge.

Make sure you have a plastic bowl scraper at hand. Plunge both hands in and start squeezing the flour and syrup into the sponge. Work from the side of the bowl closest to you across to the other side, squeezing with both hands. Rotate the bowl a quarter turn and squeeze your way through the dough again. You will feel the dough starting to come together as a more cohesive mass, and the syrup and sponge will become more fully incorporated. Use your bowl scraper from time to time to scrape the sticky dough from the sides of the bowl into the center. Keep rotating the bowl and squeezing the dough until everything is fully incorporated, 1 to 2 minutes. It will remain a shaggy and sticky mass.

Turn out the dough onto an unfloured counter, using the bowl scraper to get it all out of the bowl and scraping as much off your hands as you can. Resist the urge to add flour to the work surface or the dough at this stage.

Starting with the edge closest to you, grab the dough with both hands, palms down, and pull it gently toward you. Stretch it up and flip it over the top of the dough mass by 2 or 3 inches. Grab the closer edge again and stretch it gently up and flip it over the top.

Repeat this stretching and flipping of the dough four or five times, working your way to the far side of the mass. The stretches should be gentle enough not to tear the dough apart. As you continue this process, the dough will hold together better and be easier to stretch.

Scrape up the dough with a dough scraper, rotate it a quarter turn, and repeat the stretching and flipping through the mass four or five times, 3 to 4 minutes. With each stretch and flip of the dough, you will feel it developing, becoming more cohesive and less sticky.

If you are including the raisins, let the dough rest for 10 minutes, then work the raisins in to the dough by hand, folding and lightly kneading until the raisins are evenly distributed.

Dust the work surface lightly with all-purpose flour and flour your hands. Work the dough into a ball by folding the edges into the center.

Fermentation

Return the ball to the bowl, smooth side up, cover with a tea towel, and let sit in a warm, draft-free place for 30 minutes.

Turn out the dough onto a lightly floured surface, smooth side down. Gently press the dough into a flat circle and fold the opposite edge of the dough to the center and press gently into the dough. Fold the edge closest to you to the center, overlapping your last fold slightly, and press gently into the dough. Rotate the dough and repeat the folds with the remaining two edges. Turn the dough over and fashion into a ball by cupping the dough with your hands and rotating it counterclockwise. Return the ball to the bowl with the smooth side up and cover with a tea towel. Let rest and rise until it is full,

rounded, and well risen, but not quite doubled in size, 30 to 40 minutes.

Shaping

Preheat the oven to 480°F with the baking stone and steaming pan in place (see page 22).

Dust the work surface lightly with all-purpose flour and turn out the dough so that the smooth side is down. Divide the dough into two equal pieces with a bench knife or bowl scraper and round each piece into a ball by cupping the dough with your hands and rotating it counterclockwise. Place the balls of dough, seam side down, on the work surface, cover with a tea towel, and let rest for 5 to 10 minutes.

Gently press one piece of the dough with the heels of both hands into a rough rectangle. Grab the long edge closest to you and stretch and fold it about two-thirds of the way to the opposite side,

CONTINUED

and gently press into the dough with the heels of your hands. Grab the edge opposite you and stretch it over the first fold, about two-thirds of the way toward you, pressing it into the dough with the heels of your hands. Again, grab the opposite edge and fold toward you, this time all the way to meet the closest edge and seal the seam where the two edges meet with the heel of your hand from one end to the other. Gently roll the loaf back and forth to make a cylinder and further seal the seam. Keep the cylinder as even and straight as you can, not tapering the ends. The dough will be more clay-like. Place the loaf with the seam side up on a lightly floured baking cloth or tea towel. Repeat the shaping with the second piece of dough.

Proofing

With a fold of the towel pulled up to separate the two loaves, place the second loaf, seam side up, on the towel next to the first. Fold the ends of the cloth over the top of the loaves (you can add a second towel over the top of the loaves if the ends do not cover the tops to prevent the loaves from forming a skin) and let rise until doubled in size, 30 to 45 minutes.

Baking

Dust the peel with rice flour (see page 17). Turn out one of the loaves onto the peel with the seam side down.

Using your funnel (see page 14), steam the oven with 60 grams (¼ cup) of water. Let the steam settle for 30 seconds or so while you score the loaf.

Score your loaf with 4 cuts straight across with a razor blade.

Open the oven and place the tip of the peel on the baking stone where you want the loaf to end up. Leave room for the second loaf if the stone is large enough; center the loaf if it is not. Quickly pull the peel out from under the loaf, letting it gently

drop onto the baking stone. Close the oven door immediately. If your stone can fit two loaves at once, quickly place onto the baking stone. Place the second loaf in the refrigerator if it does not fit.

Using the funnel again, add 235 grams (1 cup) more water to the steaming pan. Close the oven door tightly as soon as the water hits the pan.

After 5 minutes, lower the oven to 375°F.

After about 25 minutes, check your loaves. You want the crust to be a deep brown color and the loaf to sound hollow when it is tapped on the bottom. If it still gives a heavy thud, return it to the oven for 5 to 10 minutes more.

Wrap the loaves in tea towels and cool completely on a wire cooling rack.

NOTE If you get the kit for making 5 gallons of wort and you are not planning to bake a hundred plus loaves as we do at the bakeshop in the weeks before Christmas, you may want to brew the rest of the wort into beer. In that case, follow the kit's directions, especially the cooling of the wort and the sanitation measures, carefully. Remove the amount of wort you need for the recipe and use the rest with the recommended brewer's yeast. You should not have to adjust the amount of yeast for the small amount of wort you took out. Cheers!

LEFSE

Norwegian Flatbreads, Olsen Family Style

MAKES 12 FLATBREADS

MIXING 20 minutes
RESTING 30 minutes
COOKING 2 to 3 minutes per lefse

A lefse is an unleavened flatbread that is cooked on a griddle instead of baked in an oven. Like many of the Nordic flatbreads, in the past, large quantities were made on baking day and then preserved, sometimes for months over the winter. To soften the lefse so it was pliable again, it was quickly moistened under running water—and then placed between tea towels.

Immigrant populations, even as they become well assimilated, often keep food traditions alive for holiday celebrations. For Norwegians in the Upper Midwest, making lefse is one Christmas tradition with an almost cult-like following. According to my mother-in-law, Julie, Norwegian-American families in Iowa make two types of lefse, one from potatoes and one made with plain wheat flour. Her relatives always made the flour version, and the following recipe is adapted from a recipe that Julie provided.

One winter, we headed up north so our daughter could have a white Christmas with their grandparents and cousins, and I requested a lefse-making tutorial, putting the requisite tools on my Christmas list. You can find many specialized lefse tools that are helpful, but by no means necessary, including round electric griddles with diameters wide enough for large flatbreads; corrugated or square-cut rolling pins that help roll the dough super thin; pastry boards with cloths that help you roll the dough to a specific diameter; and lefse turning sticks.

Any griddle or large heavy skillet will work, although you may have to make the lefse smaller. In lieu of a specialized rolling pin, I have been successful at rolling them out with a smooth pin on a well-floured wooden table. The most helpful tool, especially if you have a larger griddle and want to roll the dough into large, thin disks, is the lefse turning stick.

Flat on the bottom and beveled on top, it slips easily under the dough on the griddle to let you check cooking progress and then flip the lefse when it is time. You can certainly use a flat spatula instead.

ALL-PURPOSE FLOUR	512 grams	4 cups
SUGAR	60 grams	¼ cup
SALT	8 grams	1½ teaspoons
WATER	355 grams	1½ cups
UNSALTED BUTTER	114 grams	8 tablespoons

Mixing

Put the flour, sugar, and salt in a large bowl and blend together with your fingers to evenly distribute them. Combine the water and butter in a small saucepan and cook over high heat until the butter is melted. Remove from the heat.

Make a well in the center of the flour. Add the butter mixture and stir with a wooden spoon until there are no lumps.

Cover with plastic wrap and let rest for 20 minutes.

Shaping

Dust the work surface lightly with all-purpose flour and turn out the dough. Knead briefly to make a smooth dough. Divide the dough into twelve equal pieces with a bench knife or bowl scraper and round each piece into a ball. If your pan is 12 inches or less in diameter, divide the dough into fourteen pieces.

Resting

Place the balls on a floured surface and cover with plastic wrap. Let rest for 30 minutes.

CONTINUED

Cooking

You will need twelve tea towels for this step. Preheat a griddle or a heavy 12-inch skillet over medium-high heat or heat an electric griddle to 450°F. Spread four tea towels on a table or other work surface and have four additional towels ready for covering the lefse as they cool.

Place one ball on a well-floured work surface or lefse pastry board with its cloth and roll into a 14-inch circle, always starting in the center and rolling outward in all directions. (If you are making the smaller lefse, roll the ball into a 12-inch circle or the size that will fit your pan, as long as the dough is rolled out thinly.) Bring the pin back to the center with each stroke and use plenty of all-purpose flour so the dough does not stick to the pin or work surface. The circle should be thin enough that you can see through the dough.

To transfer to the hot griddle, brush the flour from the surface and roll the dough loosely around the lefse turning stick, if you have one, or your rolling pin and then unroll onto the griddle. Cook until bubbly and lightly specked with brown spots on the bottom, 1 to 2 minutes, then flip with the lefse stick, if you have it, and cook the other side until the lefse are opaque and lightly speckled with brown spots, 45 seconds to 1 minute more. Do not overcook, or they will be too dry and shatter when folded. Transfer to the tea towels and cover with additional towels. As the rounds cool, fold them into quarters like you would fold a napkin and keep stacked on one end under the towels as you continue to roll out, cook, and cool the remaining rounds.

Serve right away or cool completely and dry.

To reconstitute lefse, briefly run the rounds under cool water to moisten and place each on top of a waxed paper round and stack between tea towels. Let sit for at least 30 minutes to fully soften. Do not reheat before serving.

SCANDINAVIAN BREAD ON THE TABLE

IN SWEDEN, both breakfast and the evening meal were built around bread—always with a generous spread of toppings laid out on the table. There would be a selection of three or four loaf breads as well as *knäckebröd* or another thin crispbread. Each person made their own open-faced sandwiches, or *smörgås* as they're called in Sweden, as they went.

In a proper *smörgås,* bread is the star, the toppings are merely meant to complement and pair with the slice underneath. Swedish breads are hearty, often dense, and flavorful. Each variety has its own texture, and more often than not, they are somewhat sweet. A slice of bread is spread with butter, then topped with a single ingredient, such as a thin slice or two of ham, salami, or summer sausage; some shaved cheese; a smear of pâté; or a squeeze of caviar from a tube. Rarely is more than one topping put on the same slice of bread, unless there is a complementary garnish, such as pickled cucumber or beets. Honey often garnishes cheese, a combination I thought strange at first but then came to enjoy.

Following tradition, our hot meal was eaten midday. In fact, the meal is called *middag* (literally "midday"), even if it is eaten in the evening, as it is more frequently these days with changing work and eating habits. When I was in Sweden, bread was seldom served at these heavier meals. Even though they almost always included some gravy or sauce, you sopped it up with potatoes rather than a piece of bread, as in France or Italy.

For meals out, fancier versions of open-faced sandwiches are found in deli cases throughout Scandinavia, from ferry boat canteens to department stores. In Denmark, they have taken the *smørrebrød*—the Danish version of open-faced sandwiches—to almost artistic heights. Unlike the build-it-yourself Swedish *smörgås*, these prepared *smørrebrød* are piled high with several toppings and garnishes, sometimes so many that you cannot even tell if there is a slice of bread underneath. Some combinations have fanciful nicknames, such as *dyrlægens natmad*, "the veterinarian's dinner" (liver pâté, salted meat, gelatin, and rings of raw onion) or *sol over Gudhjem*, or "sun over Gudhjem" (smoked herring, onions, chives, and radishes topped with a raw egg yolk).

Several traditional restaurants in Denmark have entire menus made up mostly of *smørrebrød* and you can make a meal of them, one served after the other as separate courses. The typical order is herring, followed by warm fish, then meat and finally cheese. On a family trip, we ate lunch at Restaurant Kronborg, a charming and quaint restaurant in a cellar in the heart of Copenhagen. With blue and white china filling the shelves of a wooden hutch in the dining room and pictures of sailing ships hung above the banquettes, it had a full menu of *smørrebrød* and a collection of aquavit, many flavored in-house, to savor with each sandwich. After starting with herring, I enjoyed eel with scrambled eggs followed by pickled veal tongue with pickles and horseradish.

Many European cultures have special holiday breads that are richer and sweeter than daily breads, with added eggs, butter, milk, and sugar, as well as dried fruits or nuts; stollen in Germany, panettone in Italy, and *julekage* in Norway are all examples. In Sweden, Vörtbröd (page 116) is associated with Christmastime, as it's traditionally served with the cooking liquid from the Christmas ham, or Julskinka (page 135).

Another Scandinavian holiday meal includes *lutfisk* (lutefisk), which like pretzels (page 164), is made with a culinary application of lye (*lut*). Dried stockfish such as cod or ling is soaked and cured in a lye solution for several days, then rinsed in pure water, and changed daily for several more days. We lived in my dad's hometown of Cloquet, in northern Minnesota, until we moved to Florida when I was ten. All four of my father's grandparents came from Sweden, and we always celebrated Christmas Eve at my great aunts' house. Aunt Alma and her sister, Aunt Edie, made the feast that always included lutefisk. Somehow the Minnesotans adopted the Norwegian spelling no matter who was making it, but it was served with white sauce by the Swedes and drawn butter by the Norwegians.

As I kid, I remember not liking it, or maybe not even ever really trying it. My host mother in Sweden, Britt, cured her own *lutfisk* in the basement. The way she prepared it, the *lutfisk* was flavorful, yet delicate, and not too gelatinous or overpowering—I loved it. Later, when I lived in Minneapolis, I bought some frozen *lutfisk* and tried to replicate that wonderful holiday meal with potatoes and white sauce, but it turned out to be a gelatinous mess. My takeaway from that has been what a difference making something yourself can have and has fueled my own interest in trying so many projects from making sausage to brining hams and, of course, bread baking. So far, I have not tackled *lutfisk*, though.

Paula, my wife, grew up in Iowa and has Scandinavian roots, mostly Norwegian (since I have Swedish roots, we have what in the Upper Midwest is called a mixed marriage). Fish and Lefse (page 122) have long been a traditional part of her family's Christmas celebrations, and I have enjoyed it at a table together with four generations of Olsens, from her Grandma Millie to our own children. A piece of softened lefse is spread with butter, followed by mashed potatoes. We add a piece of codfish to the middle and then fold the lefse around the fillings, burrito style. The final touch is a dip into melted butter.

BUILD YOUR OWN SANDWICHES, SWEDISH STYLE

To replicate an authentic Swedish meal of *smörgås* for breakfast (or any time of day), you should have at least three varieties of bread and a crispbread on hand. If you have a local bakery that makes Scandinavian-style (or other similar) rye bread, you could supplement two of your own creations. Since most of these recipes make a couple of loaves, you can also wrap one loaf well and freeze it as you try the different recipes, until you have a few different loaves stored up.

For the toppings, pick your favorite cold cuts (such as a good boiled ham), some salami, summer sausage, liver pâté, a semisoft cheese (such as Jarlsberg or a Swedish farmer cheese), honey, Gravlax (page 132), and perhaps a marmalade or other fruit preserve. I like to have a tube of salmon roe "caviar" on hand too. Kalles is the most famous brand, which you can order online; Ikea has its own brand now as well. Some sliced fresh cucumbers or pickles are a nice garnish. And good butter is a must, either homemade (page 137) or a fine European variety like Kerrygold, Lurpak, or one of the better butters from France.

These days, especially on weekday mornings, my breakfast is often a couple of slices of rye bread, spread with butter, one topped with meat or maybe cured or smoked fish and the other with slices of cheese. From time to time, I put out a whole spread for my family at supper, slicing up several loaves of bread (I know, it is easier when you work at a bakery) and using toppings we already have on hand. Much of the food is not Scandinavian, per se, but even the kids enjoy these picnic-style meals.

GRAVLAX

MAKES 2.2 POUNDS | CURING 48 to 72 hours

One of the most widely known Swedish dishes, gravlax is raw salmon cured with salt and sugar, typically flavored with white pepper and dill. The name comes from *gravad lax*, meaning buried salmon, and is only one of an endless variety of cured fish dishes throughout the Nordic countries.

While I was an exchange student in Sweden, I heard that at one time salmon was so abundant in the area that workers made contracts limiting the numbers of days that they could be paid with fish instead of hard currency. I have since read that is a myth, but the story demonstrates how important the fish is in the region. A small town, Laholm, within biking distance of the village where I lived, had three salmon on its coat of arms and a hatchery on the river.

Serve this gravlax on thin slices of lightly buttered Scandinavian rye bread garnished with fresh dill and a thin slice of lemon if you wish.

20 white peppercorns

1 (1-kg/2.2-pound) skin-on salmon fillet

2 tablespoons (39 g) coarse sea salt

1 tablespoon plus 1 teaspoon (20 g) sugar

1 bunch dill, fronds only, plus more for garnish

Using a mortar and pestle, crush the peppercorns.

Inspect the salmon to be sure the skin is completely scaled and that the pin bones are removed. Pat dry with paper towels and place, skin side down, on a piece of aluminum foil more than three times as long as the fillet, with extra foil for sealing the packet. Scatter the crushed pepper over the salmon and lightly rub into the flesh.

To make the cure, stir together the salt and sugar in a small bowl. Sprinkle the cure over the salmon and lightly rub into the flesh. Place the dill fronds on top and press down. Fold the foil over the fillet lengthwise and roll the edges together to form a tight seal that fits snugly with the fillet (the foil will help press the cure into the flesh, so be sure the foil packet is tight). Roll the short ends up tight to seal the packet.

Place the packet in a shallow dish or on a plate and place a second plate on top of the foil packet. Then place something heavy on top to press the cure into the salmon and flatten it. (I use a pair of nesting oval stoneware dishes.)

Curing

Refrigerate for 24 to 36 hours. Unwrap the salmon and gently scrape off the dill and cure with the back of a butter knife. Rinse under cold water and pat dry with paper towels. Cover tightly in plastic wrap and return to the refrigerator for the same amount of time that the fish has already cured; this will even out the cure throughout the fillet and refine the flavor.

Unwrap the salmon. Cut very thin slices at an angle across the fillet. Cover leftovers, preferably unsliced, in plastic wrap and refrigerate for up to 2 weeks or freeze for up to 2 months. Thaw for about 1 hour before slicing (this makes it easier to slice) or up to overnight in the refrigerator.

JULSKINKA

Christmas Ham

SERVES 10 TO 12

Taking center stage on the Swedish Christmas table is a regal ham, coated with mustard and bread crumbs. Make the bread crumbs from the leftover heels of your Rugbrød (page 108). Typically, this ham is brine-cured but unsmoked and brought home raw from the butcher, but a lightly smoked ham will also do. It is simmered in water alongside onions studded with cloves, bay leaves, and white peppercorns before being coated and baked for the final presentation. The cooking liquid, which we would call potlikker in the South, is reserved and used for cooking the Christmas Kale (page 136) or for dipping with Vörtbröd (page 116). I like to use Swedish mustard, but you can substitute a mild German mustard or a honey Dijon.

1 large ham (3.6 to 4.5 kg/8 to 10 pounds), preferably brined and unsmoked

2 yellow onions, cut in half

6 cloves

3 bay leaves

2 teaspoons white peppercorns

2-inch (5-cm) piece fresh ginger

1 teaspoon allspice berries

3 tablespoons Swedish mustard

2 egg yolks

3 tablespoons fine fresh bread crumbs, preferably from rye bread

Put the ham in a large pot and add enough water to cover. Stud the onion halves with the cloves and put in the pot, along with the bay leaves, peppercorns, ginger, and allspice. Bring to a simmer over high heat, lower to a simmer, and cook until the center of the ham reaches 150ºF, 3 to 4 hours. (If you are using a fully cooked ham, simmer until the broth is fragrant and flavorful, 1 to 1½ hours.) Remove the ham from the pot and transfer to a platter to cool. Discard the onion and other aromatics and reserve the cooking liquid for another recipe.

Preheat the oven to 400ºF.

Using a sharp knife, cut the rind from the ham, leaving an even layer of fat. Place the ham in a roasting pan. Whisk together the mustard and egg yolks in a small bowl and use a brush to evenly spread over the ham. Evenly sprinkle the bread crumbs all over the ham, pressing them gently if needed to make them stick.

Bake the ham until evenly browned, 10 to 15 minutes. Let cool for about 20 minutes before slicing and serving.

Make sandwiches on *Vørtbrød* with mustard and any leftover ham.

CHRISTMAS KALE, HALLAND STYLE

SERVES 4 TO 6

In Halland, the west coast province of Sweden where I lived, this dish, called *grönkål*, was also a specialty of the Christmas meal along with Julskinka (page 135). Literally translated, it would mean green cabbage, but the curly-leafed plant they showed me did not look like what we call green cabbage—in Swedish that is *vitkål*, or white cabbage. That sent me to the dictionary, where I learned it was something called kale—which was still quite foreign to me at the time. In other parts of Sweden, kale is prepared with cream and some of the ham broth and called *långkål*, but in Halland, it was cooked in the ham broth alone and reminded me of Southern-style greens, part of the reason I still like it.

Remove the stems from the kale and discard. Wash the leaves and chop into large pieces.

Melt the butter in a large sauté pan over medium-low heat. Add the onion and cook until softened, about 8 minutes. Add the kale, a handful at a time, and sauté until wilted, 3 to 4 minutes.

Add the ham broth and simmer until the kale is very tender, about 1 hour, adding more ham broth as needed.

Remove from the heat and serve.

2 bunches curly kale

1 tablespoon unsalted butter

1 small yellow onion, chopped

1 cup ham broth (see page 135), plus more as needed

CULTURED BUTTER

MAKES ABOUT 1 CUP BUTTER AND 1 CUP BUTTERMILK

CULTURING 8 to 20 hours

CHURNING AND WASHING 20 minutes

The heart of a Scandinavian open-faced sandwich is butter. It is right there in the name, *smör* in Swedish or *smør* in Danish and Norwegian, and it is omnipresent between the bread and the toppings, whether you are building a simple sandwich or composing an elaborate spread of *smørrebrød*. European butters are often made from cultured cream, which gives them more depth of flavor than sweet cream butter. Although there are excellent imported European butters and European-style butters made in the United States, it can be fun to make your own. In this recipe, you ferment the cream with a small amount of *filmjölk* or kefir, which contains active cultures. Avoid using ultra-pasteurized cream for this recipe, because the high heat used in processing changes the flavor and makes the separation of the fat from the whey more difficult.

2 cups heavy cream

2 tablespoons *filmjölk* or kefir

Coarse sea salt (optional)

Culturing

Let cream come to room temperature. Put the cream in a sterilized jar, add the *filmjölk* or kefir, and stir together with a clean spoon. Let sit at room temperature overnight. The cream should thicken and smell pleasantly sour. If it has not thickened, let sit for 6 to 12 more hours.

Churning and Washing

Place the cultured cream, still at room temperature, in the bowl of a stand mixer and attach the whisk. If you have a splash guard for your mixer, you might want to put that on. Whip the cream on medium speed, keeping a careful eye on it. It will thicken like whipped cream, though it will not get as light and fluffy. Suddenly, the butterfat will break free from the liquid and form little globules that slosh around. This usually happens in 10 to 15 minutes. Lower the speed to medium-low and let the butter come together briefly, then turn off the mixer.

Remove as much of the butter solids as you can and transfer them to a medium bowl, then strain the liquid into a separate jar. This is buttermilk, and since you cultured the cream before churning the butter, it will be deliciously tangy, ready for drinking as is or to use in a recipe.

To wash the butter, pour cold tap water over the top to cover and knead the butter under the water, which will turn cloudy. Pour off the water, pressing the butter together into a ball with your hands. Repeat washing the butter one or two more times or until the water remains clear. Knead the butter a final time, pressing out as much of the water as possible. I like to press the butter into a ceramic butter keeper or terra-cotta dish. If you like, stir in coarse sea salt to taste.

Well rinsed, the butter will keep at room temperature for up to 4 days, or wrap well and refrigerate for up to 1 week.

German
Bread

A Regimented Approach

GERMANY HAS an incredible variety of bread. Most loaves include some amount of rye flour, but white rolls are common for breakfast, white tin bread is common for toasting, and many other whole grains are used as well. Ancient grains such as einkorn and spelt are also popular. All sorts of seeds such as flax, sunflower, pumpkin, poppy, and sesame are also mixed in or sprinkled on top of many breads.

When I arrived in Munich to study during my junior year of college, I was thrilled to find rye breads that were similar to those I had grown to love in Sweden three years before, yet also unique. As I arrived a few weeks before the school term began, I enjoyed buying bread, cheese, and charcuterie; practicing my college German; and eating the way I had become accustomed to during my year in Sweden. When school finally began and the fellow students arrived in the student housing, my new friends introduced me to fresh pretzels. My only reference was those we got while shopping in the American mall growing up, and these were as wonderfully different as the hearty rye breads were from the white bread of my childhood.

German bread is very systematic. Varieties are divided into several categories according to the proportion of grains they contain. There is *Weizenbrot*, or breads made with wheat (*Weizen*) flour, which most often refers to white breads, like pan breads for toasting, but can also include loaves made from up to 10 percent rye flour. Breads with a more balanced mix of wheat flour and rye flour are called *Weizenmischbrot*. Meanwhile, breads made with a minimum of 90 percent rye (*Roggen*) are called *Roggenbrot*.

As the percentage of rye flour increases, the proportion of rye sourdough starter also increases. Charts advise the baker on the correct amount of sourdough to use for each flour combination, as well as the dough yield and the temperature range best suited to the category of blend. Within that framework, the individual baker can vary the results with the choice of flours, meals, whole grains, seeds, and spices, and the method used to maintain and use the sourdough.

Although there are several methods of feeding rye sourdough cultures used by German bakers, I like to use the same starter that I use in the Scandinavian rye breads, so refer back to the previous chapter for instructions on building and maintaining the Rye Sourdough Starter (page 100).

In addition to larger loaves, there are myriad *Kleingebäck* or "small bakeworks" that German bakers produce. They include all sorts of rolls, made with varying ratios of wheat and rye, a gambit of seeds, and added grains. Under the umbrella of *Kleingebäck* are the special *Laugengebäck*, the category that includes pretzels and all their variations.

LANDBROT

German Country Bread with 30 Percent Rye

MAKES 2 OBLONG LOAVES

STARTER 12 to 14 hours (24 to 26 hours if starter needs a wake-up feed)

MIXING & KNEADING 1¼ hours

FERMENTATION 1½ to 2 hours

PROOFING 30 minutes to 1 hour

BAKING 30 to 35 minutes

As systematic as the German approach to bread is, I find it interesting that the most common bread names are not used consistently. What one baker might call *Landbrot* could have 50 percent rye flour, while a baker across town could have a *Landbrot* he makes with 80 percent rye flour. I decided to call my 30 percent rye Landbrot and my 70 percent rye Bauernbrot (page 148), even though those names are not definitive for those particular breads. Instead, it's a way of calling attention to the different ways you handle the dough and comparing the final flavor and texture of the two breads.

With a majority of wheat flour, this dough handles more like a wheat dough than the Bauernbrot, and will develop enough gluten to become smooth and elastic.

This recipe requires a mature rye sourdough starter, which must be made 4 to 5 days in advance.

STARTER

RYE SOURDOUGH STARTER (PAGE 100)	18 grams	1 tablespoon plus 1½ teaspoons
WHOLE RYE FLOUR	180 grams	1⅔ cups
WATER AT 80°F OR SLIGHTLY WARMER THAN ROOM TEMPERATURE	180 grams	¾ cup

If your rye sourdough starter is refrigerated, feed it the wake-up feed on page 102. After the 12-hour wake-up feed, measure out 18 grams (1 tablespoon plus 1½ teaspoons) of the starter into a medium bowl; return the rest to your storage container and refrigerate.

Add the rye flour and water to the starter and mix by hand until you have a smooth paste. Sprinkle the surface with a little rye flour, then cover with a tea towel or plastic wrap and let rest in a warm place for 12 to 14 hours.

The starter will rise and dome, breaking the flour on the surface into a patchwork, but should not collapse.

DOUGH

ALL-PURPOSE FLOUR	700 grams	5½ cups
WHOLE RYE FLOUR	120 grams	1 cup plus 1 tablespoon
SALT	18 grams	1 tablespoon plus ½ teaspoon
INSTANT YEAST	6 grams	1½ teaspoons
STARTER	All from above	
WATER	560 grams	2⅓ cups
RICE FLOUR	For dusting	

Mixing and Kneading

Put the all-purpose flour, rye flour, salt, and yeast in a large bowl and blend together with your fingers to evenly distribute them. Make a well in the center of the flour and add the starter and the water into the well, holding back a small amount of the water (about 28 grams, or 2 tablespoons) until you see if the flour needs it all.

Make sure you have a plastic bowl scraper at hand then start to blend the water and starter into the flour with your fingers. As the flour begins to absorb the water and the mixture starts to thicken, plunge both hands in and squeeze the dough between your thumbs and fingers. Work from the side of the bowl closest to you across to the other side, squeezing with both hands. Rotate the bowl a quarter turn and squeeze your way through the dough again. You will feel the dough starting to come together

CONTINUED

as a more cohesive mass, and the water and starter will become more fully incorporated. Use your bowl scraper from time to time to scrape the sticky dough from the sides of the bowl into the center. Keep rotating the bowl and squeezing the dough until everything is fully incorporated, 1 to 2 minutes. It will remain a shaggy and sticky mass.

The dough should be medium-soft, having definite give but still having some resistance; you should be able to feel a core when you squeeze it. Add the reserved water if the dough is not soft enough. Add the water a little at a time, squeezing it into the dough as you have been. You may even have to add more water to get the right consistency if it still feels too stiff. It is better to have a dough that is a little wet than one that is too dry.

Turn out the dough onto an unfloured work surface, using the bowl scraper to get it all out of the bowl and scraping as much off your hands as you can. Resist the urge to add flour to the work surface or the dough at this stage.

Starting with the edge closest to you, grab the dough with both hands, palms down, and pull it gently toward you. Stretch it up and flip it over the top of the dough mass by 2 or 3 inches and press it into the surface. Grab the new edge closest to you and stretch it gently up and flip it over the top. Repeat this stretching and flipping of the dough four or five times, working your way to the far side of the mass. The stretches should be gentle enough not to tear the dough apart. As you continue this process, the dough will hold together better and be easier to stretch.

Scrape up the dough with a dough scraper, rotate it a quarter turn, and repeat the stretching and flipping through the mass four or five times, 3 to 5 minutes. With each stretch and flip of the dough, you will feel it developing, becoming more cohesive and less sticky. Because there is rye in this dough, it will not become as elastic as dough with mostly wheat, but at 30 percent rye you will still get some

nice development, especially after the following folds. When most of the dough holds together and pulls off the work surface when you stretch it, slide the dough scraper under it and gather it into a ball. The dough will not be fully developed yet and will still be a little sticky.

Cup your hands around the bottom of the far side of the ball and pull it gently toward you, allowing the dough to grip the work surface, then move your hands to the left, rotating the dough counterclockwise. Return your hands behind the dough and pull and rotate again one or two times. This will tighten the surface and help shape the dough into a smooth ball. Put the ball back into the bowl with the smooth side up and let it rest for 15 minutes.

Dust the work surface lightly with all-purpose flour and turn out the dough with the smooth side down. Gently press out the dough to flatten it into a round about 2 inches thick. Grab the edge closest to you and stretch it up and over the top of the dough, about two-thirds of the way to the opposite side, and press into the surface. Grab the edge opposite you and stretch and fold it toward you over the first fold, about two-thirds of the way to the closest edge, and press into the surface. Rotate the dough a quarter turn and repeat two more folds, one away from you and one toward you.

Turn the dough over so the seam side is down. Form a ball by cupping your hands around the bottom of the far side of the dough and pulling it toward you, rotating the dough counterclockwise. Repeat one or two times to form a ball. You will notice that the dough is more developed and will stretch tighter than before. Be careful not to stretch too tight; if the surface starts to tear, stop tightening. Return the ball to the bowl, smooth side up, and let rest for 15 minutes.

CONTINUED

Repeat this stretching and folding three times at 15-minute intervals for a total of four folds over an hour. This will develop into a smooth, elastic dough with a good gluten network.

Fermentation

Return the ball to the bowl, smooth side up, cover with a tea towel or plastic wrap, and let sit in a warm, draft-free place until the dough has doubled in volume and feels airy when gently touched, about 1 hour.

Turn out the dough onto a lightly floured surface, smooth side down. Grabbing the edge opposite you, stretch the dough and fold it over the top, about halfway toward you. Gently press the dough down, then stretch the edge closest to you and fold it over the first fold. Press it in gently. Rotate the dough a quarter turn and repeat two more folds, one away from you and one toward you.

Turn the dough over so the seam side is down. Cup your hands behind the dough and gently pull it toward you to stretch the surface. At the same time, move your hands to the left, rotating the dough counterclockwise about a quarter turn, rounding it. Repeat one or two times to form a ball. Return the ball to the bowl and cover with a tea towel until it doubles in volume again, 30 minutes to 1 hour.

Shaping

Dust the work surface lightly with all-purpose flour again and turn out the dough so the smooth side is down. Divide the dough into two equal pieces with a bench knife or bowl scraper.

Starting with one of the pieces, grab the edge farthest from you and gently fold it toward you about two-thirds of the way and press it gently with the heel of your hand. Rotate the dough piece a quarter turn and grab the edge opposite you again, folding it over the previous flap and about two-thirds of the way toward you, pressing down gently with the heel of your hand. Repeat a couple more times, rotating and folding a flap over the previous flap. You will be building a round, ball shape.

Now turn the ball over, cup your hand under the far side of it, and pull it gently toward you, letting it grip slightly on the countertop. This will start to give the surface some tension. Rotate the ball between 90 and 180 degrees and pull toward you again. Now place the ball on a lightly floured work surface to rest and repeat with the other piece of dough.

Cover both pieces of dough with a tea towel and let them rest for 15 to 20 minutes.

When the pieces have rested, turn the first one over and repeat the stretching and rotating process you did in the previous step. Start with the far side of the round, stretch and fold a tab about two-thirds of the way toward you, rotate the round counterclockwise a little less than 90 degrees (you want to make five folds) and stretch a second tab over the first about two-thirds of the way toward you. Lightly seal with the heel of your hand and repeat for a total of five folds. You should have built up a nice ball shape. Now turn it over so the seams are underneath.

This time, put the heel of your right hand at the base of the ball and push gently away from you, letting the ball grip slightly on the counter. If it sticks too much, add a small dusting of flour, but too much flour won't allow it to grip and tighten properly. As you push the base of the round away from you, it should also be rotating counterclockwise. Bring the ball back close to you one or two times and continue the pushing and rotating until the surface is fairly tight. If it starts to tear, you are overdoing it and you should stop.

Let the first ball rest on its seam and repeat with the second ball. Let that one rest on its seam for a couple of minutes while you prepare the baskets for proofing. Evenly flour your baskets or liners with a light coat of flour. Invert the balls into the baskets so that the seams are now on top.

Proofing

Preheat the oven to 500°F with the baking stone and steaming pan in place (see page 22).

Cover the loaves with a tea towel and let them rise for 30 minutes to 1 hour. Check the loaves after 30 minutes, and again every 15 to 20 minutes if they are not ready. They should feel lighter and full of air.

Baking

Dust the peel with rice flour (see page 17) and turn out one of the loaves onto the peel with the seam side down.

Using a funnel (see page 14), steam the oven with about 60 grams (¼ cup) water. Let the steam settle for 30 seconds or so while you score the loaf.

Score your loaf with a razor blade.

Open the oven and place the tip of the peel on the baking stone where you want the loaf to end up. Leave room for the second loaf if the stone is large enough; center the loaf if it is not. Quickly pull the peel out from under the loaf, letting it gently drop onto the baking stone. Close the oven door immediately. If your stone can fit two loaves at once, quickly score the second loaf and place it onto the baking stone.

Using the funnel, add 235 grams (1 cup) more water to the steaming pan. Close the oven door tightly as soon as the water hits the steaming pan. Lower the oven to 450°F. Place the second loaf in the refrigerator if it does not fit.

Close the door and bake until evenly browned and slightly hollow sounding when rapped on the bottom, about 25 minutes. If it still gives a heavy thud, return it to the oven for 5 to 10 minutes. Cool the bread on a wire cooling rack until completely cool.

BAUERNBROT

German Farmer's Bread with 70 Percent Rye

**MAKES 2 LARGE
ROUND LOAVES**

STARTER 12 to 14 hours (24 to 26 hours
if the starter needs a wake-up feed)

MIXING & KNEADING 30 minutes

FERMENTATION 15 to 20 minutes

SHAPING 15 minutes

PROOFING 30 to 45 minutes

BAKING 55 to 65 minutes

When the ratio of rye becomes more than the amount of wheat flour, the Germans categorize the bread as *Roggenmischbrot* (mixed rye bread). The characteristics of the rye flour take over and little gluten is formed (even the gluten-producing proteins in the wheat flour have a difficult time forming much of a network with the presence of so much rye), and the dough will be stickier and much less elastic.

This recipe requires a mature rye sourdough starter, which must be made 4 to 5 days in advance.

STARTER

RYE SOURDOUGH STARTER (PAGE 100)	39 grams	3 tablespoons plus ½ teaspoon
WHOLE RYE FLOUR	390 grams	3½ cups
WATER AT 80°F	390 grams	1⅔ cups

If your rye sourdough starter is refrigerated, feed it the wake-up feed on page 102. After the 12-hour wake-up feed, measure out 39 grams (3 tablespoons plus ½ teaspoon) of the starter into a small bowl and return the rest to your storage container and refrigerate.

Add the rye flour and warm water to the starter and mix by hand until you have a smooth paste. Cover with a tea towel and let rest in a warm place for 12 to 14 hours.

The starter will rise and dome, breaking the flour on the surface into a patchwork, but should not collapse.

DOUGH

WHOLE RYE FLOUR	590 grams	5⅓ cups
ALL-PURPOSE FLOUR	420 grams	3¼ cups
SALT	25 grams	1 tablespoon plus 2 teaspoons
INSTANT YEAST	7 grams	2 teaspoons
STARTER	All from above	
WATER	720 grams	3 cups plus 2 teaspoons
RICE FLOUR	For dusting	

Mixing and Kneading

Put the rye flour, all-purpose flour, salt, and yeast in a large bowl and blend together with your fingers to evenly distribute them. Make a well in the center of the flour and add the starter and water into the well, holding back a small amount (about 36 grams, or 2½ tablespoons) until you see if the dough needs it all.

Make sure you have a plastic bowl scraper at hand, then start to blend the water and starter into the flour with your fingers. As the flour begins to absorb the water and the mixture starts to thicken, plunge both hands in and squeeze the dough between your thumbs and fingers.

As the dough comes together, add the reserved water if it seems too stiff or dry. Add the water a little at a time, squeezing it into the dough as you have been. You may even have to add more water to get the right consistency if it still feels too stiff. It is better to have a dough that is a little wet than one that is too dry.

Use a plastic dough scraper to lift the mixture from the sides and bottom of the bowl onto itself from time to time.

CONTINUED

This dough will remain more clay-like than wheat dough and you will not be able to stretch it in the same way. Work from side to side and around the bowl, squeezing and folding until the ingredients are thoroughly incorporated, 4 to 5 minutes. You can also turn out on the work surface and squeeze and fold the dough. Return the ball to the bowl, cover with a damp tea towel, and let rest for 20 minutes.

Dust the work surface lightly with all-purpose flour and turn out the dough. Fold the dough repeatedly into itself, working it to a smooth consistency, 1 to 2 minutes. This is not the same stretch and fold that is used with wheat dough, but more of a folding and pressing. Resist the urge to add flour to the work surface or the dough; use a bowl scraper or bench knife to scrape the dough off the work surface instead. Form the dough into as smooth a ball as you can and return to the bowl, seam side down.

Fermentation

Return the ball to the bowl, seam side down, cover with a tea towel or plastic wrap, and let sit in a warm, draft-free place for 15 to 20 minutes. The dough will expand and feel airy. The surface may start to look mottled, with small fissures, but it should not collapse at all.

Shaping

Preheat the oven to 500°F with the baking stone and steaming pan in place (page 22).

Dust the work surface generously with all-purpose flour and turn out the dough so the smooth side is down. Divide the dough into two equal pieces with a bench knife or bowl scraper.

Gently press out one of the dough pieces into a circle and fold the edges in all the way around to start to build a ball. Incorporating some flour into the folds is desirable for this bread, as this will let the seams open into a swirled pattern. Because of the high rye content, you will not be able to stretch the dough as you would a wheat dough. It is more a molding into shape, and the dough will be sticky.

Let the ball rest with the seam side down and repeat with the second ball. Let that one rest while you prepare the baskets for proofing. Evenly flour the baskets or bowls with a light coat of flour. Invert the balls into the baskets, seam side down.

Proofing

Cover the loaves with a tea towel and let them rise, until they look full and about 1½ times the volume, 30 to 45 minutes. If your baking stone is not large enough to bake both loaves at once, put one loaf into the refrigerator immediately.

Baking

Dust the peel with rice flour (see page 17) and turn out one of the proofed loaves onto your peel with the seam side up. The seams will open in the oven so you don't need to score the loaf.

Using a funnel (see page 14), steam the oven with about 60 grams (¼ cup) water; let the steam settle for a moment.

Open the oven and place the tip of the peel on the baking stone where you want the loaf to end up. Leave room for the second loaf if the stone is large enough; center the loaf if it is not. Quickly pull the peel out from under the loaf, letting it gently drop onto the baking stone. Close the oven door immediately. If your stone can fit two loaves at once, place the second loaf onto the baking stone.

Using the funnel, add 235 grams (1 cup) more water to the steaming pan. Close the oven door tightly as soon as the water hits the pan. After 5 minutes, lower the oven to 400°F and crack the door for a moment to allow the steam to escape.

After about 50 minutes, check your loaf. This loaf will be quite dark and should sound hollow when it is tapped on the bottom. If it still gives a heavy thud, return it to the oven for 5 to 10 minutes. Cool on a wire cooling rack, and let sit overnight before slicing.

LEINSAATBROT

Whole Wheat Bread with Flaxseeds

**MAKES 1
STANDARD LOAF**

STARTER 12 to 14 hours (24 to 26 hours if starter needs a wake-up feed)

SOAKER 8 to 12 hours

MIXING & KNEADING 45 minutes

FERMENTATION 45 minutes to 1 hour

SHAPING 15 minutes

PROOFING 45 minutes to 1 hour

BAKING 1 hour to 1½ hours

Here is my interpretation of a wonderful bread I was given by Dirk Eimer, a manager at Weichardt Brot in Berlin, after a tour and long chat at the bakery. It is made from all whole wheat, but it's more like a German-style rye bread and loaded with flaxseeds. It has the texture and crumb of a loaf with a high percentage of rye, but is made almost entirely with wheat ground on-site with one of their three beautiful stone mills. One employee is designated as the miller, and that person spends up to five hours a day milling wheat, rye, and spelt for that evening's production. All of their breads are whole grain and most are made with a sourdough starter. Though this version uses rye sourdough starter, the rest of the flour is whole wheat.

This recipe requires a mature rye sourdough starter, which must be made 4 to 5 days in advance.

STARTER

RYE SOURDOUGH STARTER (PAGE 100)	8 grams	2 teaspoons
WHOLE RYE FLOUR	75 grams	⅔ cup
WATER AT 80°F OR SLIGHTLY WARMER THAN ROOM TEMPERATURE	75 grams	⅓ cup

If your rye sourdough starter is refrigerated, feed it the wake-up feed on page 102. After the 12-hour wake-up feed, measure out 8 grams (2 teaspoons) of the starter into a small bowl and return the rest to your storage container and refrigerate.

Add the rye flour and warm water to the starter and mix by hand until you have a smooth paste. Sprinkle the surface with a little rye flour, then cover with a tea towel or plastic wrap and let rest in a warm place for 12 to 14 hours.

The starter will rise and dome, breaking the flour on the surface into a patchwork, but should not collapse.

SOAKER

FLAXSEEDS	50 grams	¼ cup
WATER	150 grams	⅔ cup

You can make this at the same time you do the final feeding for the starter (above). In a small bowl, soak the flaxseeds in the water at room temperature overnight.

DOUGH

WHOLE WHEAT FLOUR	425 grams	3¾ cups plus 2 tablespoons
SALT	10 grams	2 teaspoons
INSTANT YEAST	3 grams	1 teaspoon
STARTER	All from above	
SOAKER	All from above	
WATER	400 grams	1⅔ cups

Mixing and Kneading

Put the whole wheat flour, salt, and yeast in a large bowl and blend together with your fingers to evenly distribute them. Make a well in the center of the flour and add the starter, soaker, and water into the well, holding back a small amount of the water (about 20 grams, or 4 teaspoons) until you see if the flour needs it all.

Make sure you have a plastic bowl scraper at hand, then start to blend the water, soaker, and starter into the flour with your fingers. As the flour begins to absorb the water and the mixture starts to thicken, plunge both hands in and squeeze the

CONTINUED

dough between your thumbs and fingers. Work from the side of the bowl closest to you across to the other side, squeezing with both hands. Rotate the bowl a quarter turn and squeeze your way through the dough again. You will feel the dough starting to come together as a more cohesive mass, and the water and starter will become more fully incorporated. Use your bowl scraper from time to time to scrape the sticky dough from the sides of the bowl into the center. Keep rotating the bowl and squeezing the dough until everything is fully incorporated, 1 or 2 minutes. It will remain a shaggy and sticky mass.

The dough should be medium-soft to soft, having definite give but still having some resistance; you should be able to barely feel a core when you squeeze it. Add the reserved water if the dough is not soft enough. Add the water a little at a time, squeezing it into the dough as you have been. You may even have to add more water to get the right consistency if it still feels too stiff. It is better to have a dough that is a little wet than one that is too dry.

Turn out the dough onto an unfloured work surface, using the bowl scraper to get it all out of the bowl and scraping as much off your hands as you can. Resist the urge to add flour to the work surface or the dough at this stage.

Starting with the edge closest to you, grab the dough with both hands, palms down, and pull it gently toward you. Stretch it up and flip it over the top of the dough mass by 2 or 3 inches and press it into the surface. Grab the new edge closest to you and stretch it gently up and flip it over the top. Repeat this stretching and flipping of the dough four or five times, working your way to the far side of the mass. The stretches should be gentle enough not to tear the dough apart. As you continue this process, the dough will hold together better and be easier to stretch.

Scrape up the dough with a dough scraper, rotate it a quarter turn, and repeat the stretching and flipping through the mass four or five times, 3 to 5 minutes. Even though the flour is whole wheat, we are treating this more like a rye dough and not looking for a lot of gluten development. Stretch gently, and as the dough starts to pull apart, flip it over onto itself. With each stretch and flip of the dough, it will become smoother, more cohesive, and less sticky. Keep using your scraper to scrape the dough off the work surface and rotate it. When the dough feels uniform and cohesive, scrape it up completely from the work surface and lightly dust the work surface with all-purpose flour.

Put the dough on the floured work surface and fold the edges into the center. Turn it over, seam side down. Form a ball by cupping your hands around the bottom of the far side of the dough and pull it toward you, rotating the dough counterclockwise. Repeat one or two times to form a ball. You won't be able to pull the surface tight, but you will be able to make it smooth. Return the ball to the bowl, with the seam side down. Cover with a tea towel and let rest for 30 minutes.

Dust the work surface lightly again with all-purpose flour and turn out the dough so that the smooth side is down. Gently press out the dough to flatten it into a round about 2 inches thick. Grab the edge closest to you and stretch it up and over the top of the dough, about two-thirds of the way to the opposite side, and press into the surface. Grab the edge opposite you and stretch and fold it toward you over the first fold, about two-thirds of the way to the closest edge, and press into the surface. Rotate the dough a quarter turn and repeat two more folds, one away from you and one toward you.

Turn the dough over so the seam side is down. Form a ball by cupping your hands around the bottom of the far side of the dough and pulling it toward you, rotating the dough counterclockwise.

Be careful not to stretch it too tight; if the surface starts to tear, stop tightening. Repeat one or two times to form a ball.

Fermentation

Return the ball to the bowl, smooth side up, cover with a tea towel or plastic wrap, and let sit in a warm, draft-free place until the dough expands and feels airy, 45 minutes to 1 hour. The surface may start to look mottled, with small fissures, but it should not collapse at all.

Shaping

Spray one 8½ by 4½-inch loaf pan generously with baking spray.

Dust the work surface lightly with all-purpose flour and turn out the dough so the smooth side is down. Gently press the dough with the heels of both hands into a rough rectangle. Grab the long edge closest to you, stretch and fold it about two-thirds of the way to the opposite side, and gently press into the dough with the heels of your hands. Grab the opposite edge and stretch it over the first fold, about two-thirds of the way to the closest edge, and seal it with the heels of your hands. Again, grab the opposite edge and fold toward you, this time all the way to meet the closest edge and seal the seam where the two edges meet with the heel of your hand from one end to the other.

With the seam side down, cup both hands over the top of the loaf in the center and roll the loaf back and forth on the work surface. The dough will still be sticky and soft and a little hard to handle, so use as much flour as you need to prevent it from sticking to the work surface and roll with very little pressure. Keep your hands parallel to the work surface and use even pressure to achieve a straight cylinder the length of your pan. Carefully put the cylinder into the pan with the seam down.

Proofing

Preheat the oven to 475°F with the steaming pan in place (see page 22). You do not need a baking stone.

Cover the pan with a tea towel and let rise until the center of the loaf is just even with the top of the pan, 45 minutes to 1 hour.

Baking

Slide the pan onto the top oven rack. Using a funnel (see page 14), steam the oven with 235 grams (1 cup) of water. After 5 minutes, lower the oven to 400°F and crack the oven door to let the steam out for 30 seconds or so. Bake until the sides are well set and have pulled away from the pan slightly, 1 hour to 1 hour 10 minutes. The loaf should sound hollow when rapped on the bottom. If not, return the loaf directly to the oven rack without the pan for 5 to 10 minutes to finish baking.

Cool the bread on a wire cooling rack until completely cool. Let sit overnight before slicing.

SEMMELN

White Breakfast Rolls

MAKES 12 ROLLS

MIXING & KNEADING 1¼ hours

FERMENTATION 1½ to 2 hours

SHAPING 30 to 40 minutes

PROOFING 1 to 2 hours

BAKING 15 to 20 minutes

Semmeln is the southern German word for what people in the rest of the country call *Brötchen*, which translates to "small breads." Usually *semmeln* are white rolls with a thin crackly crust, and they are ubiquitous at breakfast with butter and jam or a slice of cheese or meat. If they are stamped on top, or more traditionally knotted, they are called *Kaisersemmeln*, what we call kaiser rolls.

It can be difficult to find the superlight crumb and thin, crackly crust in the *semmeln* prevalent in Germany today, mostly because the dough is mixed intensively by high-speed commercial mixers, oxidizing the dough in a way that cannot be done by hand. This roll, however, will be more flavorful and have a wonderful, crunchy crust.

If you want to add poppy or sesame seeds to the tops, spread the seeds on a plate or a separate rimmed baking sheet. When you are done shaping the rolls, moisten a tea towel and gently roll the top of each roll on the towel to wet it, then roll in the seeds.

This recipe calls for milk powder, which makes the rolls softer and helps caramelize the crust.

DOUGH

ALL-PURPOSE FLOUR	720 grams	5⅔ cups
MILK POWDER	22 grams	2 tablespoons
SALT	13 grams	1 tablespoon
INSTANT YEAST	7 grams	2 teaspoons
WATER	432 grams	1¾ cups plus 1½ tablespoons

Mixing and Kneading

Put the flour, milk powder, salt, and yeast in a large bowl and blend together with your fingers to evenly distribute them. Make a well in the center of the flour and add the water, holding back a small amount (about 20 grams, or 4 teaspoons) until you see if the flour needs it all.

Make sure you have a plastic bowl scraper at hand, then start to blend the water into the flour with your fingers. As the flour begins to absorb the water and the mixture starts to thicken, plunge both hands in and squeeze the dough between your thumbs and fingers. Work from the side of the bowl closest to you across to the other side, squeezing with both hands. Rotate the bowl a quarter turn and squeeze your way through the dough again. You will feel the dough starting to come together as a more cohesive mass, and the water will become more fully incorporated. Use your bowl scraper from time to time to scrape the sticky dough from the sides of the bowl into the center. Keep rotating the bowl and squeezing the dough until everything is fully incorporated, 1 to 2 minutes. It will remain a shaggy and sticky mass.

The dough should be medium-stiff, having some give but also a pretty solid core, like a rubber bouncy ball.

Turn out the dough onto an unfloured work surface, using the bowl scraper to get it all out of the bowl and scraping as much off your hands as you can. Resist the urge to add flour to the work surface or the dough at this stage.

Starting with the edge closest to you, grab the dough with both hands, palms down, and pull it gently toward you. Stretch it up and flip it over the top of the dough mass by 2 or 3 inches and press it into the surface. Grab the new edge closest to you and stretch it gently up and flip it over the top. Repeat this stretching and flipping of the dough

CONTINUED

four or five times, working your way to the far side of the mass. The stretches should be gentle enough not to tear the dough apart. As you continue this process, the dough will hold together better and be easier to stretch.

Scrape up the dough with a dough scraper, rotate it a quarter turn, and repeat the stretching and flipping through the mass four or five times, 3 to 5 minutes. With each stretch and flip of the dough, you will feel it developing, becoming more cohesive and less sticky. When most of the dough holds together and pulls off the work surface when you stretch it, slide the dough scraper under it and gather it into a ball. The dough will not be fully developed yet and will still be a little sticky.

Cup your hands around the bottom of the far side of the ball and pull it gently toward you, allowing the dough to grip the work surface, then move your hands to the left, rotating the dough counter-clockwise. Return your hands behind the dough and pull and rotate again one or two times. This will tighten the surface and help shape the dough into a smooth ball. Return the ball to the bowl with the smooth side up and let it rest for 15 minutes.

Dust the work surface lightly with all-purpose flour and turn out the dough so that the smooth side is down. Gently press out the dough to flatten it into a round about 2 inches thick. Grab the edge closest to you and stretch it up and over the top of the dough, about two-thirds of the way to the opposite side, and press into the surface. Grab the edge opposite you and stretch and fold it toward you over the first fold, about two-thirds of the way to the closest edge, and press into the surface. Rotate the dough a quarter turn and repeat two more folds, one away from you and one toward you.

Turn the dough over so the seam side is down. Form a ball by cupping your hands on the far side of the dough and pulling toward you, rotating the dough counterclockwise. Repeat one or two times to form a ball. You will notice that the dough is

more developed and will stretch tighter than before. Be careful not to stretch it too tight; if the surface starts to tear, stop tightening. Return the ball to the bowl, smooth side up, and let rest for 15 minutes.

Repeat this stretching and folding three times at 15-minute intervals for a total of four folds over an hour. This will develop into a smooth, elastic dough with a good gluten network.

Fermentation

After the final fold, return the ball to the bowl, cover with a tea towel or plastic wrap, and let sit in a warm, draft-free place until the dough has doubled in volume and feels airy when gently touched, 1 hour. Turn out the dough onto a lightly floured surface and gently press out the air. Grabbing the edge opposite you, stretch the dough and fold it over the top, about halfway toward you. Gently press the dough down, then stretch the edge closest to you and fold it over the first fold. Press it in gently. Rotate the dough a quarter turn and repeat the folds with the other two sides.

Turn the dough over so the seam side is down. Cup your hands behind the dough and gently pull it toward you to stretch the surface. At the same time, move your hands to the left, rotating the dough counterclockwise about a quarter turn, rounding it. Repeat one or two times to form a ball. Return the ball to the bowl, smooth side up, and cover with a tea towel until it doubles in volume again, 30 minutes to 1 hour.

Shaping

Dust the work surface lightly with all-purpose flour and turn out the dough.

Divide the dough into twelve equal pieces (about 100 grams each) with a bench knife or bowl scraper and round each piece into a ball. Cover with a tea towel and let rest for 15 to 20 minutes.

Line a rimmed baking sheet with parchment paper.

For the final shape, take a ball, turn it over so the smooth side is down, and flatten it out with the heel of your hand. Pull the top edge up and into the center and press into the dough with the heel of your hand. Rotate the dough and pull another flap over the top and press it in; repeat two or three times to make a rough ball shape. Turn the ball over and make a cage around it with the fingers of one hand. The ball of your hand should just lightly touch the top of the roll. With only a little pressure on the top of the roll, rotate your hand counterclockwise so that the roll turns inside your caged fingers, gripping slightly on the work surface and stretching tighter. When you have a nice tight roll, place it, seam side down, on the lined baking sheet.

Proofing

Preheat the oven to 500°F with the steaming pan in place (see page 22). You do not need a baking stone.

Cover the rolls with a tea towel and let rise until they have doubled in size and spring back slowly when poked with your finger, 1 to 2 hours.

Baking

Using a funnel (see page 14), steam the oven with 60 grams (¼ cup) of water. Let the steam settle for a moment.

Open the oven door and place the baking sheet with the rolls on the oven rack. Add 117 grams (½ cup) water to the steaming pan. Close the door tightly as soon as the water hits the steaming pan.

Bake the rolls until evenly browned, 15 to 20 minutes.

Cool the rolls on a wire cooling rack until completely cool.

PFENNIGMUCKERLN

Rye Pull-Apart Rolls

MAKES 12 ROLLS

RYE STARTER 16 hours (28 hours if starter needs a wake-up feed)

LEVAIN STARTER 3 hours (11 to 14 hours if starter needs a wake-up feed)

MIXING & KNEADING 40 minutes

FERMENTATION 30 minutes

SHAPING 30 minutes

PROOFING 50 minutes to 1 hour

BAKING 17 to 20 minutes

When I was researching recipes to go along with our Easy Tiger Oktoberfest sausage board one year, I came across a rye pull-apart roll called *Pfennigmuckerln* that I was not familiar with. In Munich, they are a traditional accompaniment to *Brotzeit*, a midmorning between-the-meals meal. Oblong rolls made with a wheat and rye mix are placed side by side to proof into a chain of four or five or six rolls together. I adapted the recipe to use both the rye sourdough and the *levain* starters for a complex flavor. Rye malt powder, which you can find online, and caraway seeds also add to the flavor.

This recipe requires both a mature rye sourdough starter and a mature *levain*; the latter must be started 1 week in advance.

RYE STARTER

RYE SOURDOUGH STARTER (PAGE 100)	12 grams	1 tablespoon
WHOLE RYE FLOUR	120 grams	1 cup plus 1 tablespoon
WATER AT 80°F OR SLIGHTLY WARMER THAN ROOM TEMPERATURE	120 grams	½ cup

If your rye sourdough starter is refrigerated, feed it the "Wake-Up Feed" (see page 102). After the 12-hour wake-up feed, measure out 12 grams (1 tablespoon) of the starter into a small bowl and return the rest to your storage container and refrigerate.

Add the rye flour and warm water to the starter and mix by hand until you have a smooth paste. Cover with a tea towel and let rest in a warm, draft-free place for 12 to 14 hours.

LEVAIN

LEVAIN (PAGE 64)	60 grams	2 tablespoons
ALL-PURPOSE FLOUR	60 grams	½ cup minus ½ tablespoon
WATER	36 grams	2½ tablespoons

You can do this while the rye starter is going. If your *levain* is refrigerated, feed it the "Maintaining Your Starter" feed (page 68). About 3 hours before you want to make your bread dough, place the *levain* in a clean bowl and mix in the flour and water by hand, stirring and blending with your fingers, until well incorporated. Cover with a tea towel and let ferment at room temperature for 3 hours.

DOUGH

ALL-PURPOSE FLOUR	220 grams	1¾ cups
WHOLE RYE FLOUR	120 grams, plus more for dusting	1 cup plus 1 tablespoon
SALT	10 grams	2 teaspoons
RYE MALT POWDER	8 grams	1 teaspoon
CARAWAY SEEDS, GROUND	5 grams	½ teaspoon
INSTANT YEAST	3 grams	1 teaspoon
LEVAIN	All from above	
RYE STARTER	All from above	
WATER	180 grams	¾ cup
RICE FLOUR	For dusting	

CONTINUED

Mixing and Kneading

Put the all-purpose flour, rye flour, salt, malt powder, caraway, and yeast in a large bowl and blend together with your fingers to evenly distribute them. Divide the *levain* into six pieces and scatter them on top of the flour. Make a well in the center of the flour and add the rye starter and the water, holding back a small amount (9 grams, or about 2 teaspoons) until you see if the flour needs it all.

Make sure you have a plastic bowl scraper at hand, then start to blend the water and starter into the flour with your fingers. As the flour begins to absorb the water and the mixture starts to thicken, plunge both hands in and squeeze the dough between your thumbs and fingers. Work from the side of the bowl closest to you across to the other side, squeezing with both hands. Rotate the bowl a quarter turn and squeeze your way through the dough again. You will feel the dough starting to come together as a more cohesive mass, and the water and starter will become more fully incorporated. Use your bowl scraper from time to time to scrape the sticky dough from the sides of the bowl into the center. Keep rotating the bowl and squeezing the dough until everything is fully incorporated, 1 to 2 minutes. It will remain a shaggy and sticky mass.

The dough should be medium-soft, having definite give but also some resistance; you should be able to feel a core when you squeeze it. If the dough is not soft enough, add the reserved water a little at a time, squeezing it into the dough as you have been. You may even have to add more water to get the right consistency if it still feels too stiff. It is better to have a dough that is a little wet than one that is too dry.

Turn out the dough onto an unfloured work surface, using the bowl scraper to get it all out of the bowl and scraping as much off your hands as you can. Resist the urge to add flour to the work surface or the dough at this stage.

Starting with the edge closest to you, grab the dough with both hands, palms down, and pull it gently toward you. Stretch it up and flip it over the top of the dough mass by 2 or 3 inches and press it into the surface. Grab the new edge closest to you and stretch it gently up and flip it over the top. Repeat this stretching and flipping of the dough four or five times, working your way to the far side of the mass. The stretches should be gentle enough not to tear the dough apart. As you continue this process, the dough will hold together better and be easier to stretch.

Scrape up the dough with a dough scraper, rotate it a quarter turn, and repeat the stretching and flipping through the mass four or five times, 3 to 5 minutes. With the rye flour, the dough will not stretch and become elastic in the same way as wheat-based dough. Stretch gently, and as the dough starts to pull apart, flip it over onto itself. With each stretch and flip of the dough, you will feel it developing, becoming more cohesive and less sticky. Keep using your scraper to scrape the dough off the work surface and rotate it. When the dough feels uniform and cohesive, scrape it up completely from the work surface and dust the work surface lightly with all-purpose flour.

Put the dough on the floured work surface and fold the edges into the center. Turn it over, seam side down. Form a ball by cupping your hands around the bottom of the far side of the dough and pull it toward you, allowing the dough to grip the work surface, then move your hands to the left, rotating the dough counterclockwise. Repeat one or two times to form a ball. Again, because of the rye flour, you won't be able to pull the surface tight, but you will be able to make it a smooth surface. Put the ball back into the bowl, seam side down. Cover with a tea towel and let rest for 30 minutes

Dust the work surface lightly again with all-purpose flour and turn out the dough so that the smooth side is down. Gently press out the dough to flatten it into a round about 2 inches thick. Grab the edge closest to you and stretch it up and over the top of the dough, about two-thirds of the way to the opposite side, and press into the surface. Grab the edge opposite you and stretch and fold it toward you over the first fold, about two-thirds of the way to the closest edge, and press into the surface. Rotate the dough a quarter turn and repeat two more folds, one away from you and one toward you.

Turn the dough over so the seam side is down. Form a ball by cupping your hands around the bottom of the far side of the dough and pulling it toward you, rotating the dough counterclockwise. Be careful not to stretch it too tight; if the surface starts to tear, stop tightening. Repeat one or two times to form a smooth ball.

Fermentation

Return the ball to the bowl, smooth side up, cover with a tea towel or plastic wrap and let sit until the dough is full, rounded, and well risen, but not quite doubled in size, about 30 minutes.

Shaping

Dust the work surface lightly with all-purpose flour and turn out the dough so the smooth side is down.

With a bench knife or bowl scraper, divide the dough into twelve pieces (about 75 grams each) and round each piece into a ball. Cover with a tea towel and let rest for 10 minutes.

Dust a cutting board or rimmed baking sheet with rice flour. Place some rye flour on a plate.

For the final shape, take a ball and cup one hand over the top. Roll the ball back and forth on the work surface with a gentle pressure to elongate it a little. You do not need to fold or reshape the ball, just roll it into an oblong shape. Roll the top of the roll lightly in rye flour and place on the floured board or baking sheet. Shape the second roll and place it next to the first with the long sides touching, but shifted to the right so the end

of the second roll is even with the middle of the first. The third roll should touch the second, but be shifted left so its ends are even with the first. Place the fourth offset to the right, even with the second. Make two more strands of four rolls in the same way. You could make two total strands of six rolls each instead, but for my baking stone, three strands of four rolls each fit better front to back.

Proofing

Preheat the oven to 500°F with the baking stone and steaming pan in place (see page 22). Cover the rolls with a tea towel and let sit until well risen and doubled in size, 50 minutes to 1 hour.

Baking

Dust the peel with rice flour (see page 17), then carefully transfer one strand of rolls all the way to the right side of the peel. The rolls should have grown and stuck together, but you will still need to take care so that they don't detach from each other.

Using a funnel (see page 14), steam the oven with 60 grams (¼ cup) of water. Let the steam settle for 30 seconds or so.

If you have three strands, put the other two on the peel and slide them in to the left. Open the oven and place the tip of the peel on the baking stone. Quickly pull the peel out from under the strand of rolls, letting them gently drop onto the baking stone. Close the oven door immediately.

Using the funnel, add 235 grams (1 cup) more water to the steaming pan. Close the door tightly as soon as the water hits the steaming pan. Lower the oven to 450°F.

After 10 minutes, open the door for a moment to let any remaining steam escape. Bake until well browned, 7 to 10 minutes.

Cool the rolls on a wire cooling rack.

EASY TIGER PRETZELS

**MAKES ABOUT
14 INDIVIDUAL OR
3 LARGE PRETZELS**

STARTER 13 to 37 hours

MIXING & KNEADING 1¼ hours

FERMENTATION 15 minutes

SHAPING 30 minutes

PROOFING 2¼ hours to 12 hours

DIPPING & BAKING 30 minutes

The word pretzel, or *Brezel* in German, comes from the Latin word for arms, which are crossed as in the medieval pose for prayer. While the familiar twisted shape can be given to many baked goods sweet and savory, soft and crunchy, our Easy Tiger pretzels are based on the Bavarian tradition of soft *Laugenbrezeln*. Made with a somewhat stiff yeasted dough, usually containing a little lard or butter, what sets these apart from other baked goods is the *Laugen*, or lye, in which the dough pieces are briefly dipped before they are baked in the oven.

That is right, the same lye, or sodium hydroxide (NaOH), that is used in soap making is used in a weak (3 to 5 percent) solution. The alkaline solution hydrolyzes the proteins on the surface of the dough enhancing the Maillard reaction (browning effect), giving the pretzel its deep mahogany color and its unique minerally flavor.

If it seems strange or intimidating to be introducing strong, caustic chemicals into your kitchen, there are other culinary uses for lye: Olives are sometimes cured with it, and to make *lutfisk*, the Scandinavians cure dried stockfish in lye (see page 129).

I am fond of paraphrasing Los Angeles chef Hans Röckenwagner, who, in an article featuring his pretzel recipe, pointed out that when lye is properly handled, it is no more dangerous than the sharp knives or open flames we use in everyday cooking. Just be sure to wear rubber gloves and eye protection.

Once the lye is dissolved in water, even if you get a little of the solution on your skin, it should do no more than cause a little irritation; you can put your skin under running water for a few minutes to rinse it off. Heed the label though, and make sure to add the lye slowly into the water rather than adding water to

the lye, as it can react quickly and splatter that way.

At Easy Tiger, we use a small amount of *pâte fermentée* (see page 41) in the dough, mainly to help extend the shelf life of the pretzels. Even so, we bake pretzels multiple times a day, as they are much better fresh. For this recipe, a very small amount of starter is used, so it can be omitted entirely if you wish.

STARTER

ALL-PURPOSE FLOUR	120 grams	1 cup
SALT	3 grams	½ teaspoon
INSTANT YEAST	½ gram	Pinch
WATER	82 grams	⅓ cup

Put the flour, salt, and yeast in a large bowl and blend together with your fingers to evenly distribute them. Make a well in the center of the flour and add the water.

Using your hand, draw the flour into the water, stirring and blending with your fingers. As it begins to come together, squeeze the dough with your hands to better incorporate the water into the flour. Starting at the near side of the bowl, grasp the dough with both hands and squeeze it between your thumbs and fingers. Rotate the bowl and continue to squeeze the dough, working in the water and working out any clumps of flour. Use a plastic bowl scraper to scrape down the sides and bottom of the bowl, folding the dough over on top of itself.

This dough should be medium-stiff, having some give but also a pretty solid core, like a rubber bouncy ball.

Because this dough will ferment a long time, you do not need to develop the gluten much; just squeeze

CONTINUED

and work the dough until it is fully combined with no lumps. Form the dough into a rough ball in the bowl and cover it with plastic wrap, or place in a container with a lid.

Let the dough sit at room temperature for 1 hour, then refrigerate for at least 12 hours or up to 36 hours.

DOUGH

ALL-PURPOSE FLOUR	680 grams	5⅓ cups
SALT	10 grams	2 teaspoons
INSTANT YEAST	12 grams	1 tablespoon
STARTER	All from page 165	
UNSALTED BUTTER	32 grams	2 tablespoons
MALT SYRUP	9 grams	1½ teaspoons
MILK	200 grams	¾ cup plus 1½ tablespoons
WATER	195 grams	¾ cup plus 1 tablespoon
LYE	30 grams	2 tablespoons plus 2 teaspoons
LUKEWARM WATER FOR LYE SOLUTION	1 liter	1 quart
PRETZEL SALT OR OTHER COARSE SALT	12 grams	2 teaspoons

Mixing and Kneading

Put the flour, salt, and yeast in a large bowl and blend together with your fingers to evenly distribute them. Divide the starter into six pieces and scatter them on top of the flour. Make a well in the center of the flour and add the butter and malt syrup, followed by the milk and water, holding back a small amount (50 grams, or about 3 tablespoons) of the water until you see if the flour needs it all.

Make sure you have a plastic bowl scraper at hand, then start to blend the liquids and starter into the flour with your fingers. As the flour begins to absorb the water and the mixture starts to thicken, plunge both hands in and squeeze the dough between your thumbs and fingers. Work from the side of the bowl closest to you across to the other side, squeezing with both hands. Rotate the bowl a quarter turn and squeeze your way through the dough again. You will feel the dough starting to come together as a more cohesive mass, and the water and starter will become more fully incorporated. Use your bowl scraper from time to time to scrape the sticky dough from the sides of the bowl into the center. Keep rotating the bowl and squeezing the dough until everything is fully incorporated, 1 to 2 minutes. You can add the reserved water if necessary, but this should be a fairly stiff dough.

This dough should be stiff; it should feel solid with little give.

Turn out the dough onto an unfloured work surface, using the bowl scraper to get it all out of the bowl and scraping as much off your hands as you can. Resist the urge to add flour to the work surface or the dough.

Starting with the edge closest to you, grab the dough with both hands, palms down, and pull it gently toward you. Stretch it up and flip it over the top of the dough mass by 2 or 3 inches and press it into the surface. Grab the new edge closest to you and stretch it gently up and flip it over the top. Repeat this stretching and flipping of the dough four or five times, working your way to the far side of the mass. The stretches should be gentle enough not to tear the dough apart. As you continue this process, the dough will hold together better and be easier to stretch.

Scrape up the dough with a dough scraper, rotate it a quarter turn, and repeat the stretching and flipping through the mass four or five times,

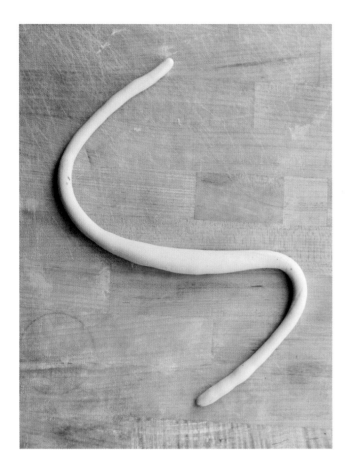

down. Gently press out the dough to flatten it into a round about 2 inches thick. Grab the edge closest to you and stretch it up and over the top of the dough, about two-thirds of the way to the opposite side, and press into the surface. Grab the edge opposite you and stretch and fold it toward you over the first fold, about two-thirds of the way to the closest edge, and press into the surface. Rotate the dough a quarter turn and repeat two more folds, one away from you and one toward you.

Turn the dough over so the seam side is down. Form a ball by cupping your hands around the bottom of the far side of the dough and pulling it toward you, rotating counterclockwise. Repeat one or two times to form a ball. You will notice that the dough is more developed and will stretch tighter than before. Be careful not to stretch it too tight; if the surface starts to tear, stop tightening. Return the ball to the bowl, smooth side up, and let rest for 15 minutes.

Repeat this stretching and folding three times at 15-minute intervals for a total of four folds over an hour. This will develop into a smooth, elastic dough with a good gluten network.

Fermentation

After the final fold, return the ball to the bowl, cover with a tea towel or plastic wrap, and let sit in a warm, draft-free place for 15 minutes. Pretzel dough gets its flavor mainly from the lye dip and the ingredients, rather than a long fermentation.

Shaping

Dust the work surface lightly with all-purpose flour and turn out the dough so the smooth side is down.

With a bench knife or bowl scraper, divide the dough into four pieces (about 300 grams each) for large Oktoberfest pretzels or fourteen pieces (about 85 grams each) for small pretzels. Roll each piece into a ball, cover with a tea towel, and let rest for 15 minutes.

3 to 5 minutes. With each stretch and flip of the dough, you will feel it developing, becoming more cohesive and less sticky. When most of the dough holds together and pulls off the work surface when you stretch it, slide the dough scraper under it and gather it into a ball. The dough will not be fully developed yet and will still be a little sticky.

Cup your hands around the bottom of the far side of the ball and pull it gently toward you, allowing the dough to grip the work surface, then move your hands to the left, rotating the dough counterclockwise. Return your hands behind the dough and pull and rotate again one or two times. This will tighten the surface and help shape the dough into a smooth ball. Return the ball to the bowl with the smooth side up and let it rest for 15 minutes.

Dust the work surface lightly with all-purpose flour and turn out the dough so that the smooth side is

CONTINUED

Press one ball out with the heels of your hand into a rough rectangle. Grab the long side closest to you and stretch and fold it about two-thirds of the way to the opposite side, and gently press into the dough with the heel of your hand. Grab the edge opposite you and stretch it over the first fold, about two-thirds of the way toward you, pressing it into the dough with the heel of your hand. Grab the opposite edge and fold toward you, this time all the way to meet the closest edge and seal the seam where the two edges meet with the heel of your hand from one end to the other.

Place your hands on the middle of the strand, leaving a 1½- to 2-inch gap between them. Roll the dough piece back and forth with light pressure. While rolling, move your hands gradually outward, lengthening the dough strand. Repeat from the center one or two times until the strand is about 36 inches long for the large pretzels or 18 inches long for the small ones. Remember to leave the gap between your hands each time you return to the center. This leaves a bulge in the bottom of the pretzel. Roll the ends thinner than the middle. One of the pleasures of eating a pretzel is the contrast between the thin "arms" and the thicker "belly." Repeat the shaping with the remaining pieces of dough.

Lightly dust two cutting boards or rimmed baking sheets with rice flour. (Do not line the sheets with parchment paper, because the dough will stick to it.)

Once the strands are rolled out, grab each end and lift off the work surface, holding at nearly arm's length away from each other. In a quick motion, move your hands together, which will cause the strand to twist. Lay the twisted strand down on the table, folding the ends over and onto the sides of the thicker portion. Press the ends into the dough underneath with your thumbs. Press hard, making a deep indent. Place the twisted pretzels on the floured boards or baking sheets.

Proofing

Cover the pretzels with tea towels and let rise until they rise to 1½ times their original size, 15 to 20 minutes. Uncover and put the pans or boards in the refrigerator for at least 2 hours or up to overnight. The pretzels should be firm and a light skin should have formed. The skin keeps the lye from penetrating too much into the dough.

Baking

Preheat the oven to 450°F. You do not need a baking stone or steaming pan.

Wearing rubber gloves, fill up a large bowl with the lukewarm water and add the lye. *Always* add the lye to the water, rather than pouring the water onto the lye, as that can cause a reaction that can splash lye on you. Stir the solution with a whisk until all the lye is dissolved.

Still wearing gloves, place the pretzels into the lye solution, as many as you can fit and still have them submerged. Swish the pretzels in the water gently (no splashing) briefly, 5 to 10 seconds. Lift them out carefully one at a time, allowing the lye solution to drain off, then place on a rimmed baking sheet. Repeat with any pretzels left.

Sprinkle the tops with pretzel salt. Bake until deep brown, about 15 minutes. Cool the pretzels on a wire cooling rack until completely cool.

You can pour the lye solution right down your sink's drain—lye is an ingredient in most drain cleaners, so it will not hurt the drain; it might even help it.

GERMAN BREAD
ON THE TABLE

Chef Drew's Easy Tiger
Beer Cheese 175

Wurstsalat | *Biergarten*
Sausage Salad 176

WITH HUNDREDS of varieties baked daily throughout the country, bread is eaten all day long in Germany. In Bavaria, most days start with a light breakfast of *Brötchen* (rolls) or Semmeln (page 156), split in half and spread with butter and jam or draped with a slice of cheese or some meat. When I was a student in Munich, pretzels became one of my favorite breakfast foods, with flecks of cool, sweet butter that tamed the salt and mineral bite.

Traditionally, a *zweites Frühstück* or *Brotzeit* (second breakfast or bread time) is eaten mid-morning. In Munich, a classic *Brotzeit* includes *Weißwurst*, delicate poached veal sausages served with a sharp, sweet mustard and a pretzel or roll. Another favorite is a simple sandwich of *Leberkäse*, a type of pork meatloaf. While the first breakfast is served with coffee or tea, *Brotzeit* can provide the excuse for the day's first beer.

Abendbrot (evening bread) is often a lighter meal of bread and cured meat and cheese eaten later in the day, especially if a hot meal was eaten midday. In traditional taverns and casual restaurants in Bavaria, a basket with rolls and pretzels is commonly in the middle of the table when you sit down. You help yourself and then tell the server at the end of your meal how many you ate.

More and more, throughout German cities—in train and subway stations, in department stores, and along the streets—you can find all kinds of snack and sandwich cases. *Laugengebäck*, the category of baked goods that includes pretzels and other rolls dipped in lye, are split horizontally and sandwiched around meats and cheeses, perhaps with a leaf of lettuce and slice of tomato stuck in for good measure. Others have toppings baked right in, featuring chunks of salami and cheese.

On mild, sunny summer days, the people of Munich flock to the many biergartens throughout the city.

Besides bratwurst and other sausages, biergarten fare includes salads, cheeses, and other snacky foods. A classic is the cheese spread *Obatzda* (aka *Obatzter*), made from two parts of a soft-ripened cheese like Camembert and one part butter and flavored with paprika, caraway, beer, and sometimes horseradish. It is served with a pretzel or a roll and is a cousin of American beer cheese.

During Oktoberfest, I encountered a much larger version of the hand-size pretzels I loved so much in the morning. While the oompah band played onstage, we crowded around a long communal table in the beer tent of our favorite brewery, waiting for the Fräuleins to make their rounds with several liter-size steins in each hand and giant pretzels slipped over a forearm. We enjoyed the pretzels' chewy, salty goodness with our massive beer.

At Easy Tiger, pretzels have become a signature item since they are such a natural fit with the beer garden menu. Serving a pretzel with mustard is decidedly an American thing; perhaps it came from pretzels served alongside sausages with mustard, but you won't find it in Germany. Easy Tiger, though, is decidedly a beer garden, not a biergarten, and we make a fantastic grainy mustard with Brooklyn Lager that it is almost as popular a dip for the pretzels as our own version of Beer Cheese (page 175).

For Oktoberfest, we team up with our good friends at Austin Beerworks, who brew a special beer for the occasion, a Märzen style (the typical Oktoberfest beer in Munich) named Montecore. Small pretzels are retired for the day and we bake rack after rack of the large ones. Alongside the Montecore, we serve several other local Oktoberfest beers and usually an import or two from Germany.

CHEF DREW'S EASY TIGER BEER CHEESE

SERVES 4 TO 6

At Easy Tiger, our own version of beer cheese took a different path to our menu than through a Munich biergarten. Chef Andrew Curren, the partner who drives Easy Tiger's culinary programs and the rest of the ELM Restaurant Group, first discovered beer cheese in Louisville. He had just landed back in the States after a stint cooking and eating in Vietnam, and he went with some college buddies to the Kentucky Derby, where the mix of Cheddar, cream cheese, beer, and spices is a staple. Just how this delectable spread became ubiquitous in Central Kentucky is lost to history, but the resemblance to the Munich cheese spread *Obatzda* as well as to Welsh rabbit provides clues. From my own childhood, there was Win Schuler's bar cheese from the well-known restaurant that has been in Marshall, Michigan, for more than a hundred years. We stopped there at least once on family trips to visit my mother's folks, but even if we did not go through Marshall, we would come back from Michigan with enough crocks of that cheese to make it until the next summer.

Serve this cheese with the Easy Tiger Pretzels (page 164) and a Märzen-style beer, such as Brooklyn Lager.

1 cup lager beer (such as Brooklyn Lager)

1 pound sharp Cheddar cheese, grated

8 ounces cream cheese, at room temperature

½ yellow onion, minced

2 cloves garlic, minced

1½ teaspoons hot sauce (such as Tabasco)

1½ teaspoons salt

1 teaspoon cayenne pepper

1 teaspoon dry mustard

1 teaspoon Worcestershire sauce

½ teaspoon freshly ground black pepper

Pour the beer into a glass and let it sit until it loses its effervescence, about 15 minutes. Combine the Cheddar, cream cheese, onion, garlic, hot sauce, salt, cayenne, mustard, Worcestershire, and black pepper in a food processor and pulse until slightly blended. With the processor running, slowly pour in the beer. Transfer the mixture to a bowl, cover and refrigerate for at least 4 hours and up to 1 week. Serve cold or let soften at room temperature briefly before serving.

WURSTSALAT

Biergarten Sausage Salad

SERVES 2 TO 4

Another popular biergarten dish is *Wurstsalat*. I hesitated to even offer the translation into English, because "sausage" and "salad" are two words that just do not fit together in our language or cuisine. Sure, we have our Cobbs and our chef's salads with some cold cuts julienned on top, but in *Wurstsalat*, the sausage replaces the vegetables rather than merely garnish them. Yes, that is right, thinly sliced and finely cut strips of a cooked sausage are dressed with a vinaigrette and accompanied by onions and gherkins, sometimes also radish and some herbs, and served chilled with a buttered roll on the side.

Though this might not sound like a salad, it is a tasty biergarten treat, perfect for sitting outdoors on a sunny summer day with a frothy lager. Although there are regional variations in what type of sausage is used, *Fleischwurst*, a long, mild-tasting smoked sausage, is the most common. Coarse ring bologna makes a good substitution, but any fully cooked sausage works well, and even large slices of bologna lunch meat can be used.

Slice narrow sausages thinly into rounds or half rounds, and thicker sausages into strips. Dress the sausage and onions the night before serving to mellow the onions and meld the flavors even more. Add the gherkins the next day and shave the radishes and snip the chives over the top. Serve with a buttered roll, such as the Semmeln (page 156) and a hearty beer.

¼ cup vegetable oil

2 tablespoons white wine vinegar

1 teaspoon salt

¼ teaspoon paprika

Freshly ground black pepper

10 ounces fully cooked sausage, such as German Fleischwurst or ring bologna, thinly sliced, or cut into strips if slices are large

½ large white onion, thinly sliced

2 German gherkins or other pickles, thinly sliced

2 or 3 radishes, thinly sliced

Snipped fresh chives for garnish

In a large bowl, whisk together the oil, vinegar, salt, and paprika. Season with pepper to taste. Add the sausage and onion, and toss to evenly coat. (This is best done the night before, covered, and refrigerated, but it can be done the same day.)

Add the gherkins and refrigerate for at least 2 hours, then remove from the fridge and let sit at room temperature 30 minutes before serving. Just before serving, garnish with sliced radishes and chives.

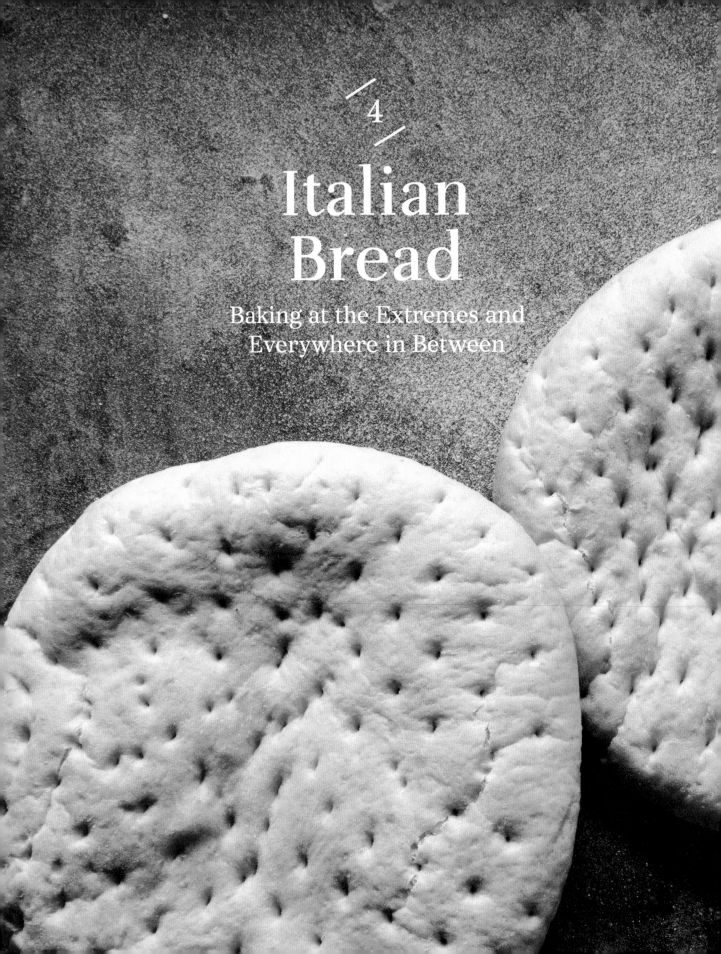

/4/

Italian Bread

Baking at the Extremes and
Everywhere in Between

Pane Toscano | *Saltless Tuscan Bread* 182

Ciabatta 188

Panini Press Bread 194

WHEN I WAS a college student at the University of Munich, I took advantage of our monthlong winter break to see more of Europe and to visit Sweden again. Armed with a student train pass that allowed me to travel for free outside of Germany, I headed south on an overnight train to Verona. I had my sights set on Paris, Belgium, and the Netherlands, and an integral part of my travel strategy was to sleep on night trains so I could avoid hotel expenses. As the train pulled into the city of Romeo and Juliet just as the sun was coming up over the stone buildings, I was smitten. For several hours, I wandered the ancient streets, drank cappuccino, and ate some gelato before continuing on to Milan and then on an overnight train to Paris.

I do not remember if I ate any bread during that short stop in Italy, but years later, when I began to think of baking as a creative and fulfilling career rather than just a stepping-stone to something else, I borrowed a copy of Carol Field's seminal book *The Italian Baker*. In it, I recognized something different from the breads I had been making up to that point, what with the use of starters and longer fermentation. I tried some of the recipes at home and started to fantasize about someday starting a bakery and making those kinds of breads. As fate would have it, I moved to Seattle that same year and came across Grand Central Bakery, where they were already making rustic breads, many of which were inspired by the book.

Fifteen years after that trip to Verona, I finally made it back to Italy. Paula and I vacationed in Venice, traveled to Rome and Tuscany, and visited a friend in Sardinia. One of my favorite parts of the trip was meeting a family who grew grapes for Mionetto Prosecco outside of Valdobbiadene in the Veneto. The farmhouse dated from the 1500s and had a wood-fired oven built into its side, which opened onto the courtyard. The family also cooked on a giant cast-iron wood-burning stove, which was clearly a choice and not out of necessity, as many of their other appliances were completely modern. The matriarch brought out some of that week's bread for us to sample and seemed perplexed by my fascination with her oven and bread baking. What to her was a weekly chore held little of the romanticism I felt sitting at their dining table, sipping the raw, young wine from their grapes.

Italian breads are very regional. They run the gamut, from very dense, stiff dough to extremely wet dough. Tuscan bread is still made without salt. Other regional breads incorporate semolina and even cornmeal. Of course there are also the many forms of focaccia and pizza. Sometimes the name of a bread in one area might be the same as in another region, but the bread itself is completely different.

In this chapter, we will explore some of the technical challenges that make Italian breads fun to bake. By omitting the salt from the Tuscan bread, for example, we see how salt affects the dough beyond lending it flavor. Ciabatta is typically made with a lot of water, but I like to add the water in stages in order to first develop the gluten properly. I then introduce more water into that gluten structure, which turns to steam in the heat of the oven, helping create the extremely open crumb structure typical for that loaf.

Many Italian breads use *bigas*, a type of leavener made with commercial rather than wild yeast. The main goal of a *biga* is to create extra flavor in the dough without, necessarily, a long fermentation time. And while you won't see any rye or many grains in this chapter, the breads do incorporate whole spelt, durum, and semolina flours along with wheat flour.

PANE TOSCANO
Saltless Tuscan Bread

**MAKES 1 LARGE
OBLONG LOAF**

BIGA 12 to 16 hours

MIXING & KNEADING 1½ hours

FERMENTATION 1 to 1½ hours

SHAPING 40 minutes

PROOFING 30 to 45 minutes

BAKING 25 to 35 minutes

Stories abound as to why the typical Tuscan bread is made without salt. Most involve the legendary frugality of the ancient Tuscans, who went without expensive salt or may have been unwilling to pay its tax. Some say it was their archrival, the city of Pisa, that controlled the supply and levied the tax that the Florentines rebelled against. The truth is that historically, much of the bread around the world was made without salt, which was either unavailable or too dear. What is more interesting in the case of Tuscan bread is why the tradition of baking bread without it continues.

Salt does several things to bread dough. Of course, it imparts flavor; bread without it can have a flat, bland taste. Salt helps strengthen gluten structure in the dough, and it also inhibits fermentation, providing a controlling effect. If you are serious about bread baking, I encourage you to make this bread if for no other reason than to experience these effects firsthand. You will learn to recognize the clues that alert you to dough where the salt has accidently been left out. This dough will be slacker and stickier than normal and will rise more quickly, making it a little harder to handle.

BIGA

ALL-PURPOSE FLOUR	300 grams	2⅓ cups
INSTANT YEAST	½ gram	Pinch
WATER	150 grams	⅔ cup

Put the flour and yeast in a large bowl and blend together with your fingers to evenly distribute them. Make a well in the center of the flour and add the water.

Using your hands, draw the flour into the water, stirring and blending with your fingers. As it begins to come together, squeeze the dough with your hands to better incorporate the water into the flour. You can use a more traditional kneading action with the heel of your hand, as well, to push down and bring the *biga* together. This is a stiff dough and it will take a bit to get the flour all hydrated. Add up to 15 grams (1 tablespoon) more water if you are really having trouble.

Form the dough into a tight ball. Return to the bowl and cover with plastic wrap, or place it in a container with a lid.

Let the *biga* sit at room temperature for 12 to 16 hours.

DOUGH

ALL-PURPOSE FLOUR	300 grams	2⅓ cups
INSTANT YEAST	2 grams	½ teaspoon
BIGA	All from above	
WATER	270 grams	1 cup plus 2 tablespoons
RICE FLOUR	For dusting	

Mixing and Kneading

Put the flour and yeast in a large bowl and blend together with your fingers to evenly distribute them. Divide the *biga* into four pieces and scatter them on top of the flour. Make a well in the center of the flour and add the water, holding back a small amount (13 grams or 2 to 3 teaspoons) until you see if the flour needs it all.

Make sure you have a plastic bowl scraper at hand, then start to blend the water and *biga* into the flour with your hands. As the flour begins to absorb the water and the mixture starts to thicken, plunge both hands in and squeeze the dough between your

CONTINUED

thumbs and fingers. Work from the side of the bowl closest to you across to the other side, squeezing with both hands. Rotate the bowl a quarter turn and squeeze your way through the dough again. You will feel the dough starting to come together as a more cohesive mass, and the water and *biga* will become more fully incorporated. Use your bowl scraper from time to time to scrape the sticky dough from the sides of the bowl into the center. Keep rotating the bowl and squeezing the dough until everything is fully incorporated, 1 to 2 minutes. It will remain a shaggy and sticky mass.

Do not confuse the stickiness of this dough with the hydration. The dough should be medium-soft, having definite give but also some resistance; you should be able to feel a core when you squeeze it. Add the reserved water if the dough is not soft enough. Add the water a little at a time, squeezing it into the dough as you have been. You may even have to add more water to get the right consistency if it still feels too stiff. It is better to have a dough that is a little wet than one that is too dry.

Turn out the dough onto an unfloured work surface, using the bowl scraper to get it all out of the bowl and scraping as much off your hands as you can. Resist the urge to add flour to the work surface or the dough at this stage.

Starting with the edge closest to you, grab the dough with both hands, palms down, and pull it gently toward you. Stretch it up and flip it over the top of the dough mass by 2 or 3 inches and press it into the surface. Grab the new edge closest to you and stretch it gently up and flip it over the top. Repeat this stretching and flipping of the dough four or five times, working your way to the far side of the mass. The stretches should be gentle enough not to tear the dough apart. As you continue this process, the dough will hold together better and be easier to stretch.

Scrape up the dough with a dough scraper, rotate it a quarter turn, and repeat the stretching and

flipping through the mass again four or five times, 3 to 5 minutes. With each stretch and flip of the dough, you will feel it developing, becoming more cohesive and less sticky. When most of the dough holds together and pulls off the work surface when you stretch it, slide the dough scraper under it and gather it into a ball. The dough will not be fully developed yet and will still be a little sticky.

Cup your hands around the bottom of the far side of the ball and pull it gently toward you, allowing the dough to grip the surface, then move your hands to the left, rotating the dough counterclockwise. Return your hands behind the dough and pull and rotate again one or two times. This will tighten the surface and help shape the dough into a smooth ball. Return the ball to the bowl with the smooth side up and let it rest for 15 minutes.

Dust the work surface lightly with all-purpose flour and turn out the dough so that the smooth side is down. Gently press out the dough to flatten it into a round about 2 inches thick. Grab the edge closest to you and stretch it up and over the top of the dough, about two-thirds of the way to the opposite side, and press into the surface. Grab the edge opposite you and stretch and fold it toward you over the first fold, about two-thirds of the way to the closest edge, and press into the surface. Rotate the dough a quarter turn and repeat two more folds, one away from you and one toward you.

Turn the dough over so the seam side is down. Form a ball by cupping your hands around the bottom of the far side of the dough and pulling it toward you, rotating the dough counterclockwise. Repeat one or two times to form a ball. You will notice that the dough is more developed and will stretch tighter than before. Be careful not to stretch too tight; if the surface starts to tear, stop tightening. Return the ball to the bowl, smooth side up, and let rest for 15 minutes.

CONTINUED

Repeat this stretching and folding three times at 15-minute intervals for a total of four folds over an hour. This will develop into a smooth, elastic dough with a good gluten network.

Fermentation

After the final fold, return the ball to the bowl, smooth side up, cover with a tea towel or plastic wrap, and let sit in a warm, draft-free place until the dough has doubled in volume and feels airy when gently touched, 30 to 45 minutes. Because of the absence of salt, it will ferment faster, so keep your eye on it.

Turn out the dough onto a lightly floured surface, smooth surface down. Grabbing the edge opposite you, stretch the dough and fold it over the top, about halfway toward you. Gently press the dough down, then stretch the edge closest to you and fold it over the first fold. Press it in gently. Rotate the dough a quarter turn and repeat two more folds, one away from you and one toward you. It is okay to press some of the air out of the dough as you fold it.

Turn the dough over so that the seam side is down. Cup your hands behind the dough and gently pull it toward you to stretch the surface. At the same time, move your hands to the left, rotating the dough counterclockwise about a quarter turn, rounding it. Repeat one or two times to form a ball. Return the ball to the bowl, smooth side up. Cover with a tea towel and let rest until it doubles in volume again, 30 to 45 minutes.

Shaping

Preheat the oven to 500°F with the baking stone and steaming pan in place (see page 22).

Dust the work surface lightly with all-purpose flour and turn out the dough so the smooth side is down.

Gently press the dough to flatten it into a round about 1 inch thick. Grab the edge opposite you and stretch it up and over the top of the dough, about two-thirds of the way toward you. Gently press into the surface with the heel of your hand. Rotate the dough a quarter turn and grab the edge opposite you again, stretching and folding over the first fold, about two-thirds of the way toward you, and gently press it in. Repeat two or three times until you have a loose ball shape, then turn over so the seam side is down.

Cup your hands behind the ball with your pinkie fingers and the sides of your hands on the table, then gently pull your hands toward you. At the same time as you are gently pulling, move your hands to the left, causing the ball to rotate counterclockwise about a quarter turn. The dough should grip the table and the surface will tighten. Move your hands behind the ball again, pulling gently and rotating the ball. Set aside and cover with a tea towel. Let the dough rest for 15 to 20 minutes so the gluten relaxes a bit.

Turn the dough ball over so the smooth side is down. Gently press the round piece flat with the heel of your hand, preserving most of the fermentation gases in the dough. Grab the closest edge with both hands and stretch and fold it about two-thirds of the way to the opposite edge and gently press into the surface with the heel of one hand. Grab the opposite edge and stretch it over the first fold, about two-thirds of the way toward you, pressing it into the surface. Return to the opposite edge and pull it toward you all the way so that it meets the closest edge. Using the heel of your hand, start at one of the long ends and gently press along where the two edges meet to form a seam, working from one end to the other. It is important to use the heel of your hand rather than your fingertips to seal the seam, so that you evenly seal it, rather than making lots of indentations along the seam, which will produce tight spots in the crumb.

With the seam side down, cup both hands over the center of the loaf and roll the loaf back and forth on the work surface to make a cylinder shape.

If it sticks, add a tiny dusting of flour. If it slides instead of rolls, there is too much flour, so you need to brush some away. Angle your hands downward slightly to help shape the tapered ends of the loaf. Roll a few more times until you have a smooth, even loaf with a well-sealed seam.

Lay a towel on top of a cutting board or baking sheet and dust with all-purpose flour. Place the loaf, seam side up, on the floured towel and pull the sides of the towel up and over the loaf. Position a loaf pan or other object on each side of the loaf to help it keep its shape while proofing.

Proofing

Let the loaf rise until doubled in size, 30 to 45 minutes. Watch carefully, because without the salt, this bread will rise faster.

Baking

Dust the peel with rice flour (see page 17) and turn out the proofed loaf onto your peel with the seam side down.

Using a funnel (see page 14), steam the oven with about 60 grams (¼ cup) water. Let the steam settle for 30 seconds or so while you score the loaf.

Score your loaf with a razor blade, making one long slash down the center from end to end, with the blade at an angle to the surface so that it cuts a shallow lip under the surface rather than a straight up and down cut.

Open the oven and place the tip of the peel on the center of the baking stone. Quickly pull the peel out from under the loaf, letting it gently drop onto the baking stone. Using the funnel, add 235 grams (1 cup) more water to the steaming pan. Close the oven door tightly as soon as the water hits the pan. Lower the oven to 450°F.

After about 25 minutes, check your loaf. You want the crust to be well set and the loaf to sound hollow when it is tapped on the bottom. If it still gives a heavy thud, return it to the oven for 5 to 10 minutes. Salt also affects the browning of the crust, so it will remain paler even when fully baked.

Cool the bread on a wire cooling rack until completely cool.

CIABATTA

**MAKES 2 OR
3 OBLONG LOAVES**

POOLISH 12 hours

MIXING & KNEADING 1¼ hours

FERMENTATION 2 hours

PROOFING 30 to 45 minutes

BAKING 30 to 35 minutes

While the origins of Tuscan bread stretch back into obscure Florentine history, ciabatta has a more modern story. Although some form of this bread has been made for a long time in different regions of Italy, the super-hydrated bread that we know today as ciabatta was developed in the 1980s as a response to the widespread importation of French baguettes for sandwich making in Italy. A group of bakers and millers got together to combat the imports and develop this native loaf.

With lots of extra water and very little shaping, a well-made ciabatta should have very large, irregular holes—it's really mostly crust and air. Sliced in half horizontally, it is the perfect sandwich bread. Nowadays it is commonly baked around the world, even by French bakers.

Ciabatta dough is a bit tricky to work with because of all the extra water, especially when mixing by hand. In the bakery, we use a double hydration technique known in French as a *bassinage*. First you develop the gluten using a normal range of hydration, then you add extra water in an extended mix. I tried several ways of mixing this dough by hand and found this to be the easiest and to give the best results. You begin by mixing together a medium to medium-soft dough, and then as you give it the folds to further develop the dough, you add in a little more water at each fold.

For this bread we use another type of yeasted starter called a *poolish* instead of a stiffer, more dough-like starter like *biga* or *pâte fermentée*. A *poolish* is more like a batter, made with equal parts (by weight) of flour and water.

A note on shaping: Depending on the size of your oven and baking stone, you can shape the dough into two longer loaves that may have to fit width-wise in your oven, or three shorter loaves that fit front to back. If you choose the first option, you may need to pull the oven rack out and slide the loaves sideways onto the baking stone; just make sure to do this very carefully.

POOLISH

ALL-PURPOSE FLOUR	145 grams	1 cup plus 2 tablespoons
INSTANT YEAST	½ gram	Pinch
WATER	145 grams	⅔ cup

Put the flour and yeast in a large bowl and blend together with your fingers. Make a well in the center of the flour and add the water.

Mix with your hands until all incorporated. The mixture will be more like a batter than a dough. Work the dough until most of the lumps are gone; some small lumps are okay. Cover with a tea towel and let sit at room temperature until bubbly, well risen, and just starting to dimple on top, about 12 hours. It should not be collapsing in on itself.

DOUGH

ALL-PURPOSE FLOUR	435 grams	3⅓ cups
SALT	12 grams	2 teaspoons
INSTANT YEAST	2 grams	½ teaspoon
POOLISH	All from above	
FIRST WATER	260 grams	1 cup plus 1½ tablespoons
SECOND WATER	100 grams	7 tablespoons
RICE FLOUR	For dusting	

CONTINUED

Mixing and Kneading

Put the flour, salt, and yeast into a large bowl and blend together with your fingers. Add the *poolish* on top of the flour mix. Add the first amount of water, holding back a small amount (13 grams or 2 to 3 teaspoons).

Make sure you have a plastic bowl scraper at hand. Using your hand, draw the flour into the water, stirring and blending with your fingers. As the flour begins to absorb the water and the mixture starts to thicken, plunge both hands in and start squeezing the dough. Work from the side of the bowl closest to you across to the other side, squeezing with both hands. Rotate the bowl a quarter turn and squeeze your way through the dough again. You will feel the dough starting to come together as a more cohesive mass, and the water and starter will become more fully incorporated. Use your bowl scraper from time to time to scrape the sticky dough from the sides of the bowl into the center. Keep rotating the bowl and squeezing the dough until everything is fully incorporated, 1 to 2 minutes. It will remain a shaggy and sticky mass.

The dough should be medium-soft, having definite give but also some resistance; you should be able to feel a core when you squeeze it. Add the reserved water if the dough is not soft enough.

Turn out the dough onto an unfloured work surface, using the bowl scraper to get it all out of the bowl and scraping as much off your hands as you can. Resist the urge to add flour to the work surface or the dough at this stage.

Starting with the edge closest to you, grab the dough with both hands, palms down, and pull it gently toward you. Stretch it up and flip it over the top of the dough mass by 2 or 3 inches and press it into the surface. Grab the new edge closest to you and stretch it gently up and flip it over the top. Repeat this stretching and folding of the dough four or five times, working your way to the far side of the mass. The stretches should be gentle enough not to tear the dough apart. As you continue this process, the dough will hold together better and be easier to stretch.

Scrape up the dough with a dough scraper, rotate it a quarter turn, and repeat the stretching and flipping through the mass four or five times, 3 to 5 minutes. With each stretch and flip of the dough, you will feel it developing, becoming more cohesive and less sticky. When most of the dough holds together and pulls off the work surface as you stretch it, slide the dough scraper under it and gather it into a ball. The dough will not be fully developed yet and will still be a little sticky.

Cup your hands around the bottom of the far side of the ball and pull it gently toward you, allowing the dough to grip the surface, then move your hands to the left, rotating the dough counterclockwise. Return your hands behind the dough and pull and rotate again one or two times. This will tighten the surface and help shape the dough into a smooth ball. Return the ball to the bowl with the smooth side up and let rest for 15 minutes.

Add 30 grams (about 2 tablespoons) of the second water to the bowl and squeeze it into the dough. With your palms facing up, push your hands underneath the dough on either side of the bowl and squeeze your fingers and thumbs together, forcing the dough through them. Move your hands under the dough 1 or 2 inches farther away from you and squeeze again, repeating until you have moved from the near side of the bowl to the far side. Rotate the bowl a quarter turn and squeeze your way through the dough again. Repeat until the water is fully incorporated.

Dust the work surface lightly with all-purpose flour and turn out the dough so that the smooth side is down. Gently press out the dough to flatten it into a round about 2 inches thick. Grab the edge closest to you and stretch it up and over the top of the dough, about two-thirds of the way to the opposite side,

CONTINUED

and press into the surface. Grab the edge opposite you and stretch and fold it toward you over the first fold, about two-thirds of the way to the closest edge, and press into the surface. Rotate the dough a quarter turn and repeat two more folds, one away from you and one toward you.

Turn the dough over so the seam side is down. Form a ball by cupping your hands around the bottom of the far side of the dough and pulling it toward you, rotating the dough counterclockwise. Repeat one or two times to form a ball. Return the ball to the bowl, smooth side up, and let rest for 15 minutes.

Add 50 grams (about 3 tablespoons) more water in the same way, turn out and fold, then return to the bowl and rest for 15 minutes. Add the remaining 30 grams (about 2 tablespoons) of water in the same way again, turn and fold, and return to the bowl for 15 minutes.

Finally, turn out the dough on a lightly floured surface and stretch and fold it again. Pull into a ball the best you can, as it will be a very soft dough at this point.

Fermentation

After the final fold, return the ball to the bowl, smooth side up, cover with a tea towel or plastic wrap, and let sit in a warm, draft-free place for 1 hour. After an hour, the dough will look much slacker than it did, almost batter-like.

Carefully, with the help of your plastic bowl scraper, turn out the dough onto a generously floured work surface, top side down. Grabbing the edge opposite you, stretch the dough and fold it over the top, about halfway toward you. Gently press the dough down, then stretch the edge closest to you and fold it over the first fold. Press it in gently. Rotate the dough a quarter turn and repeat two more folds, one away from you and one toward you. You will be surprised by the dough's resiliency, despite its appearance.

Turn the dough over so the seam side is down. Cup your hands behind the dough and gently pull it toward you to stretch the surface. At the same time, move your hands to the left, rotating the dough counterclockwise about a quarter turn, rounding it. Repeat one or two times to form a ball. Return the ball to the bowl smooth side up, cover with a tea towel, and let rest for 30 minutes.

Give another fold like you did after the dough fermented for 1 hour. The dough should be wet, but more cohesive and feel strong and somewhat elastic after this last fold.

Preheat the oven to 500°F with the baking stone and steaming pan in place (see page 22).

Return the ball to the bowl, smooth side up. Cover with a tea towel and let rest until it is billowy and feels looser again, 30 to 45 minutes.

Shaping

Dust the work surface generously with all-purpose flour, using more flour than usual. Gently turn out the dough so the smooth side is down. Press very lightly and gently on the top of the dough to even out the thickness, without pressing any of the gases out. Pull into a rough rectangle.

With a bench knife or bowl scraper, cut the dough into either two pieces lengthwise or three pieces across the width of the rectangle.

Dust a cutting board or baking sheet with all-purpose flour.

After dividing the dough, place one hand on each side of the length of the first dough piece, palms touching the dough, and very gently push the long sides in toward the center, working from top to bottom. Your goal is to make some floury wrinkles in the underside of the dough that is touching the work surface. With your fingertips, very gently dimple the top surface to widen it out again, trying to deflate the dough as little as possible. Repeat the pushing in of the sides one more time to get better wrinkles. Transfer the dough to the board or baking sheet, wrinkle side still down. Repeat with the second and third pieces of dough.

Proofing

Cover with a tea towel and let sit until well risen and full of air, but not starting to collapse, 30 to 45 minutes.

Baking

Dust the peel and the tops of the ciabattas with rice flour (see page 17). Turn out the proofed ciabattas onto the peel so that the wrinkled sides are up.

If you have two large loaves and need to bake them across the width of your oven, using heavy-duty oven mitts very carefully pull the rack and stone out no more than halfway (it is very heavy) and place the tip of the peel on the baking stone. Quickly pull the peel out from under the loaves, letting them gently drop onto the baking stone. Arrange them if necessary, then carefully and quickly slide the rack back in and close the door.

Using a funnel (see page 14), steam the oven with 60 grams (¼ cup) water if you desire. Ciabatta, with all the extra water in the dough, does not need a steamy oven, though it can help with the oven spring (see page 29).

If you have three pieces, follow the directions above but load the loaves front to back.

After 10 minutes, lower the oven to 450°F.

After about 20 minutes, check your loaves. You want the crust to be a golden brown color and the loaves to sound hollow when they are tapped on the bottom. If they still give a heavy thud, return them to the oven for 5 minutes.

Cool the bread on wire cooling racks until completely cool.

PANINI PRESS BREAD

MAKES 2 FLAT ROUND LOAVES

BIGA 12 to 16 hours

MIXING & KNEADING 1¼ hours

FERMENTATION 30 minutes to 1 hour

SHAPING 30 minutes

PROOFING 30 minutes

BAKING 25 to 35 minutes

Many types of bread, from sliced sandwich breads to rolls, can be put in a panini grill to make a toasted sandwich. Ciabatta, though popular for panini in the United States, is not my first choice for grilled sandwiches. With its crisp crust and floury surface, it is better for cold sandwiches. In Italy, I remember seeing stacks of ready-to-grill sandwiches on pale, flat round loaves of bread. This is my approximation of that bread. With a little bit of olive oil in the dough, it stays soft and flavorful, and underbaking them a little means they crisp up nicely in the grill press as the cheese melts inside and the other ingredients warm up.

To use these for a sandwich, split the rounds in half horizontally, lightly drizzle with olive oil, and line with a single layer of prosciutto or pancetta followed by thin slices of a complementary cheese like fontina or provolone. Cover with the top half of the bread and grill in a panini press until the bread is well marked and crisp and the cheese is melted.

BIGA

ALL-PURPOSE FLOUR	90 grams	¾ cup
INSTANT YEAST	½ gram	Pinch
WATER	45 grams	3 tablespoons

Put the flour and yeast in a large bowl and blend together with your fingers to evenly distribute them. Make a well in the center of the flour and add the water.

Using your hand, draw the flour into the water, stirring and blending with your fingers. As it begins to come together, squeeze the dough with both hands to better incorporate the water into the flour. You can use a more traditional kneading action with the heel of your hand, as well, to push down and bring the *biga* together. This is a stiff dough,

so it will take some time and a little more effort to incorporate all the flour. Add up to 15 grams (1 tablespoon) more water if you are really having trouble.

Because this dough will ferment a long time, you do not need to develop the gluten much; just squeeze and work the dough until it is fully combined with no lumps.

Form the dough into a ball the best you can. Return the ball to the bowl and cover with plastic wrap, or place it in a container with a lid.

Let the *biga* sit at room temperature for 12 to 16 hours.

DOUGH

ALL-PURPOSE FLOUR	210 grams	1⅔ cups
SALT	6 grams	1 teaspoon
INSTANT YEAST	2 grams	½ teaspoon
BIGA	All from above	
WATER	135 grams	½ cup plus 1 tablespoon
OLIVE OIL	12 grams	1 tablespoon
RICE FLOUR	For dusting	

Mixing and Kneading

Put the flour, salt, and yeast in a large bowl and blend together with your fingers to evenly distribute them. Divide the *biga* into three pieces and scatter them on top of the flour. Make a well in the center of the flour and add the water and olive oil, holding back a small amount of the water (7 grams or 1½ teaspoons) until you see if the flour needs it all.

Make sure you have a plastic bowl scraper at hand, then start to blend the water and *biga* into the flour

CONTINUED

with your hands. As the flour begins to absorb the water and the mixture starts to thicken, plunge both hands in and squeeze the dough between your thumbs and fingers. Work from the side of the bowl closest to you across to the other side, squeezing with both hands. Rotate the bowl a quarter turn and squeeze your way through the dough again. You will feel the dough starting to come together as a more cohesive mass, and the water and starter will become more fully incorporated. Use your bowl scraper from time to time to scrape the sticky dough from the sides of the bowl into the center. Keep rotating the bowl and squeezing the dough until everything is fully incorporated, 1 to 2 minutes. It will remain a shaggy and sticky mass.

The dough should be medium-stiff, having some give like a rubber bouncy ball. Add the reserved water if the dough is not soft enough. Add the water a little at a time, squeezing it into the dough as you have been. You may even have to add more water to get the right consistency if it still feels too stiff. It is better to have a dough that is a little wet than one that is too dry.

Turn out the dough onto an unfloured work surface, using the bowl scraper to get it all out of the bowl, and scraping as much off your hands as you can. Resist the urge to add flour to the work surface or the dough at this stage.

Starting with the edge closest to you, grab the dough with both hands, palms down, and pull it gently toward you. Stretch it up and flip it over the top of the dough mass by 2 or 3 inches and press it into the surface. Grab the new edge closest to you and stretch it gently up and flip it over the top. Repeat this stretching and folding of the dough four or five times, working your way to the far side of the mass. The stretches should be gentle enough not to tear the dough apart. As you continue this process, the dough will hold together better and be easier to stretch.

Scrape up the dough with a dough scraper, rotate it a quarter turn, and repeat the stretching and flipping through the dough mass four or five times, 3 to 5 minutes. With each stretch and flip through the dough, you will feel it developing, becoming more cohesive and less sticky. When most of the dough holds together and pulls off the work surface as you stretch it, slide the dough scraper under it and gather it into a ball. The dough will not be fully developed yet and will still be a little sticky.

Cup your hands around the bottom of the far side of the ball and pull it gently toward you, allowing the dough to grip the work surface, then move your hands to the left, rotating the dough counterclockwise. Return your hands behind the dough and pull and rotate again one or two times. This will tighten the surface and help shape the dough into a smooth ball. Return the ball to the bowl with the smooth side up and let it rest for 1 minutes.

Dust your work surface lightly with all-purpose flour and turn out the dough so that the smooth side is down. Gently press out the dough to flatten it into a round about 2 inches thick. Grab the edge closest to you and stretch it up and over the top of the dough, about two-thirds of the way to the opposite side, and press into the surface. Grab the edge opposite you and stretch and fold it toward you over the first fold, about two-thirds of the way to the closest edge, and press into the surface. Rotate the dough a quarter turn and repeat two more folds, one away from you and one toward you.

Turn the dough over so the seam side is down. Form a ball by cupping your hands around the bottom of the far side of the dough and pulling toward you, rotating the dough counterclockwise. Repeat one or two times to form a ball. You will notice that the dough is more developed and will stretch tighter than before. Be careful not to stretch too tight; if the surface starts to tear, stop

CONTINUED

tightening. Return the ball to the bowl, smooth side up, and let rest for 15 minutes.

Repeat this stretching and folding three times at 15-minute intervals for a total of four folds over an hour. This will develop into a smooth, elastic dough with a good gluten network.

Fermentation

After the final fold, return the ball to the bowl, smooth side up, cover with a tea towel or plastic wrap, and let sit in a warm, draft-free place until the dough has doubled in volume and feels airy when gently touched, about 30 minutes.

Shaping

Preheat the oven to 475°F with the baking stone and steaming pan in place (see page 22).

Dust the work surface lightly with all-purpose flour and turn out the dough so the smooth side is down. Divide the dough into two equal pieces with a bench knife or bowl scraper.

Gently press one piece of the dough to flatten it into a round about 2 inches thick. Grab the edge opposite you and stretch it up and over the top of the dough, about two-thirds of the way toward you. Gently press into the surface with the heel of your hand. Rotate the dough a quarter turn and grab the edge opposite you, stretching and folding it over the first fold, about two-thirds of the way toward you, pressing it gently. Repeat two or three times until you have a loose ball shape, then turn the ball over so the seam side is down.

Cup your hands behind the ball with your pinkie fingers and the sides of your hands on the table, then gently pull your hands toward you. At the same time as you are gently pulling, move your hands to the left, causing the ball to rotate counterclockwise about a quarter turn. The dough should grip the table and the surface will tighten. Move your hands behind the ball again, pulling

gently and rotating the ball. Set aside and cover with a tea towel, repeating with the second piece of dough. Let the dough rest for 15 to 20 minutes so the gluten relaxes a bit.

When the pieces have rested, dust a cutting board lightly with all-purpose flour or line a baking sheet with parchment paper and dust it lightly with flour.

Dust the work surface again with all-purpose flour. Flatten one ball on the work surface with your hand and use a rolling pin to roll into a 12-inch circle, always starting in the center and rolling outward in all directions. Bring the pin back to the center with each stroke and use plenty of all-purpose flour so the dough does not stick to the pin or work surface. Transfer the circle carefully to the floured board or parchment. Repeat with the second piece of dough.

Proofing

Cover the circles with tea towels and let rise in a warm, draft-free place, about 30 minutes.

Baking

Dust the peel with rice flour (see page 17) and transfer one of the loaves onto the peel with the seam side down.

Dock the surface of the dough with a roller docker if you have one or a notched rolling pin, or use the blunt end of a wooden skewer or even a chopstick to poke holes in the top to let out steam.

Using a funnel (see page 14), steam the oven with about 60 grams (¼ cup) of water.

Open the oven and place the tip of the peel on the center of the baking stone. Quickly pull the peel out from under the loaf, letting it gently drop onto the baking stone, leaving room for the second loaf if the stone is large enough; center the loaf if it is not. Close the oven door immediately. If your stone can fit two loaves at once, quickly dock the second loaf and slide it onto the stone.

Using the funnel, add 60 grams (¼ cup) more water to the steaming pan (less water than larger loaves). Close the door tightly as soon as the water hits the steaming pan. Lower the oven to 425°F.

After about 10 minutes, check the bread. The top should still be pale, while the bottom will just be starting to color and the crust will be set.

Cool the bread on a wire cooling rack until completely cool.

ITALIAN BREAD
ON THE TABLE

BREAD IS an integral part of the Italian meal, from the antipasto on through. Although you do not eat bread with your pasta, it will be there for you to *fare la scarpetta* (which literally translates "to form a little shoe," but means using a bit of bread to sop up the remaining sauce).

Bread is also a ubiquitous snack food in Italy. Sandwiches, called panini whether served cold or grilled and served warm, are everywhere from street carts to the local *enoteca*. In Rome, we watched bakers stretch *pizza bianca* from their peels the whole depth of their oven, and then went inside the shop to buy a couple of pieces to eat as we walked the *Campo de' Fiori* market. Focaccia and its many cousins make great street snacks as well and are topped with almost anything imaginable, from salty to sweet.

Italians are adept at using stale bread in many types of dishes, from giving body to soups to *panzanella*, the Tuscan bread salad made by soaking old bread in water, then squeezing it out and shredding it into a bowl, adding fresh tomatoes, and dressing it with oil and vinegar.

When my wife, Paula, and I traveled to Tuscany and were based in the small seaside town of Castiglione della Pescaia, of course, we bought some of the local bread. Though it was bland without the salt, it had more flavor than I expected, but it still wasn't something you would spread with butter and eat by itself for breakfast. Still, saltless Tuscan bread is omnipresent at the table alongside the boldly flavored foods of the region and is often the foil to the salty cured meats. Tuscan prosciutto is saltier than those made in other regions, as is much of the salumi produced there. It's another example of how the bread of Tuscany and many other parts of Italy goes along so well with the cuisine, fitting in with the food and the way it is eaten there.

A couple of years ago, as I was developing the ideas for this book, I held a talk for one of Slow Food Austin's Slow Sessions, a series of talks about different food topics. For treats for the audience and to illustrate my points, I made a small variety of breads, including Tuscan bread, and this *cinghiale alla cacciatora*, wild boar, hunter's style. After the talk, which I felt had gone well and people seemed to be enjoying the food and bread, I was upstairs in the café area of Easy Tiger when a woman approached me. She wanted to introduce me to her friend whom she had brought to the event. He shook my hand and said his name was Massi. Then his friend said he was a baker from Tuscany and for a moment my heart sank. Massi quickly put me back at ease, though, when he said that the boar and the bread were just like at home. Some weeks later, I joined Massi and his fiancée at their friends' house, where he baked bread and focaccia for me and we enjoyed great wine and Tuscan treats of salumi and cheeses.

Tuscany is also renowned for *cinghiale*, the black-bristled, fearsome wild boar of the Tuscan hills. Prized for their mildly gamey but tender meat, their meat is used to make sausages and ragouts and are an important part of Tuscan cuisine, but they also can wreak havoc on the farms in the region. This was familiar to me since starting on the ranch in Central Texas, where there is a large problem with wild pigs. Most of these are feral hogs rather than indigenous wild boar, though there are even some true European wild boar out there, descended from hunting ranch escapees. I witnessed the destructive power of the pigs, not only in the ruts, trenches, and broken fences they left behind, but up close. One day I was in the woods near the neighboring ranch and saw a pig scurry through the brush headed toward a fairly new, tightly built game fence delineating the property line. He barely slowed down as he seemingly magically slipped right under that fence and kept on his way. Hunting them was challenging, but I landed a few during my tenure and butchered them to make sausage.

Not far from Rio Frio, where we had lived on the guest ranch, is Broken Arrow Ranch, a company specializing in game meats, all harvested in the area. They have a rather unique mobile processing truck that travels to different ranches with everything they need, including a Federal USDA Inspector, to be able to process meat for sale all over the country. I remember seeing the big Styrofoam coolers dropped off by the UPS driver to the Bouley offices in New York before I had ever heard of Ingram, Texas, never imagining I would end up living in the ranch country where they sourced most of their game meat. I would recommend that you seek out a fuller-flavored heritage breed.

CINGHIALE ALLA CACCIATORA

SERVES 4 TO 6

1½ pounds wild boar stew meat, or loin, cut into cubes

Salt and freshly ground black pepper

¼ cup olive oil

1 cup Chianti or other dry red wine

2 cloves garlic, minced

1 medium onion, coarsely chopped

2 stalks celery, coarsely chopped

1 carrot, peeled and coarsely chopped

2 sprigs fresh rosemary, minced

3 fresh bay leaves

⅔ cup water

1 cup tomato puree

¼ cup briny black olives, such as kalamata

Crushed red pepper flakes

Season the meat with salt and pepper and let rest for 15 minutes. Pat dry with paper towels.

Heat the oil in a large braising pan or Dutch oven with a lid. Add the meat and brown on all sides. Add the wine and cook until it evaporates, scraping up all the browned bits from the bottom of the pan. Add the garlic, onion, celery, carrot, rosemary, and bay leaves and cook for 30 minutes uncovered, stirring from time to time. Add half the water, lower the heat, and cover, keeping at a slow simmer for another 30 minutes. Add additional water if needed.

Add the tomato puree, olives, and red pepper flakes to taste, stirring in well. Adjust seasonings and cook, covered, for another 30 minutes.

CROSTINI TOSCANI

Tuscan Chicken Liver Toasts

SERVES 4 TO 6

Stale Tuscan bread makes great toasts for an antipasto course. Crostini are sliced thinly and toasted in the oven until crisp but not browned. For bruschetta, the bread is cut thicker and can be grilled or toasted at a higher heat so the surface gets a bit charred but the middle stays soft. The rough surface makes a perfect grater for a clove of fresh garlic to be rubbed across the warm toast before you add a topping.

While the more delicate crostini are traditionally served with lighter toppings like a silky chicken liver pâté, the more rustic bruschette are classically combined with a chunky, fresh tomato and basil topping.

1 pound chicken livers	½ cup dry white wine
3 tablespoons olive oil	Pinch of red pepper flakes (optional)
1 red onion, diced	
3 or 4 anchovy fillets or 2 tablespoons anchovy paste	Salt and freshly ground black pepper
	1 loaf Pane Toscano (page 182), preferably at least a day old
1 tablespoon capers	

Rinse and drain the chicken livers and pat dry with paper towels.

In a large skillet, heat the oil over medium-low heat. Add the onion and cook until softened, about 8 minutes. Add the anchovies and capers and cook until the anchovies have dissolved and the flavors have combined well with the onions, 3 to 4 minutes. Increase heat to medium, add the chicken livers, stirring occasionally, and cook until all the sides are brown, 3 to 4 minutes.

Add the wine, bring to a gentle simmer, then decrease the heat to low; cover and simmer until the livers are fully cooked through, 15 to 20 minutes. Add the red pepper flakes, if using, and season with salt and black pepper to taste.

Put the mixture in a food processor and puree until smooth (you can leave the pâté a little bit chunky, if you prefer).

Preheat the oven to 200°F.

While the pâté cools, cut the bread into thin slices, then cut the slices into pieces that are about 3 inches across. Arrange the slices on a rimmed baking sheet pan and toast in the oven until crisp but not browned. Let the crostini cool.

Just before serving, spread the pâté on the crostini. Serve at room temperature.

PANINI

Italian Sandwiches

Panino, the diminutive form of *pane*, is the Italian term for a roll, but it also refers to a sandwich, and not just the kind grilled on a press but also many served at room temperature. Here are two suggestions for simple cold Italian sandwiches on ciabatta.

CAPRESE PANINI

Tomato and Mozzarella Sandwich

SERVES 2 TO 4

The best sandwiches I ate in Italy were never overloaded with ingredients; all of them displayed restraint and balance, the fillings harmonizing with the bread creating a whole better than the parts. This one is a classic combination of fresh mozzarella, tomatoes, and basil.

Olive oil for drizzling

1 Ciabatta (page 188), halved

1 (8-ounce) ball fresh mozzarella, sliced

1 ripe large tomato, sliced

Fresh basil leaves

Generously drizzle the olive oil on the cut sides of the bread. Layer the bottom half with cheese, tomatoes, and basil. Cover with the top half of the bread, press down lightly, and slice. Serve at room temperature.

MELANZANA PANINI

Grilled Eggplant Sandwich

SERVES 2 TO 4

This recipe calls for stuffing the bread with grilled eggplant and spring onions—the tender, long-stemmed young onions you can find in the farmers' market in the spring.

Salt

1 medium eggplant, cut widthwise into ½-inch slices

2 spring onions, trimmed

2 tablespoons olive oil

1 Ciabatta (page 188), halved

1 ripe medium tomato, sliced

Freshly ground black pepper

Preheat a charcoal or gas grill to medium heat.

Salt both sides of the eggplant slices, place on a cutting board, and let sit for 15 to 20 minutes to draw out some of the water. Blot dry with paper towels. Grill the eggplant, turning occasionally, until softened and lightly charred, 12 to 15 minutes. Grill the spring onions, turning often, until tender and well charred, about 15 minutes. When cool, slice the spring onions.

Generously drizzle the olive oil on the cut sides of the ciabatta. Layer the bottom half with eggplant, tomato, and spring onion. Season to taste with salt and pepper, keeping in mind that the eggplant may be salty. Cover with the top half of the ciabatta, press down lightly to hold the sandwich together, and slice. Serve at room temperature.

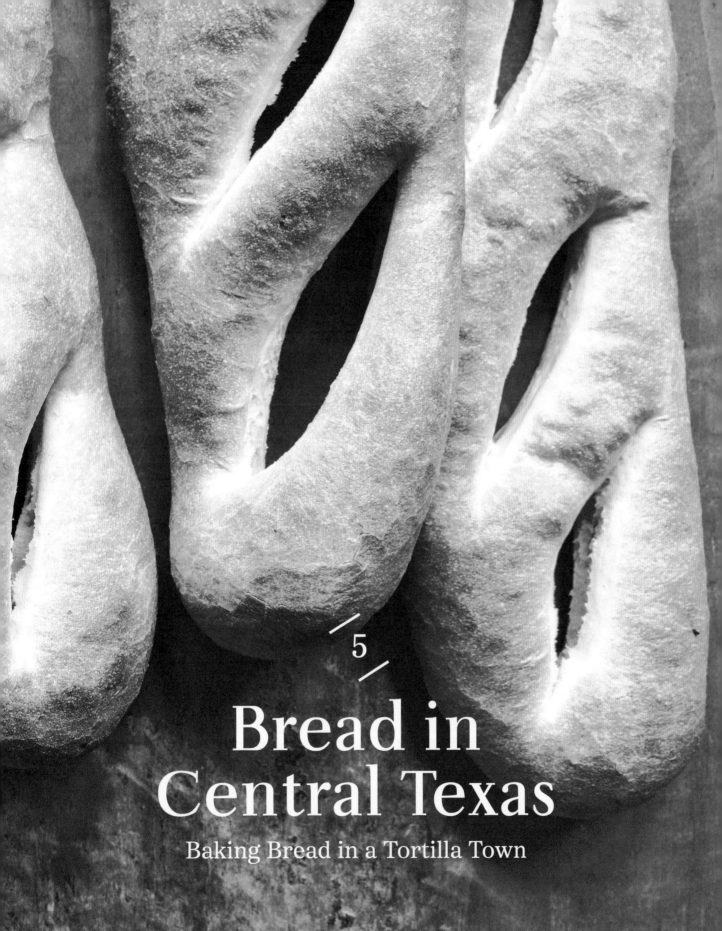

/ 5 /

Bread in Central Texas

Baking Bread in a Tortilla Town

White Pan Bread 212

Smoked Flour Fougasse 216

Birotes Salados | *Mexican Sourdough Rolls* 222

Flour Tortillas 228

MY WIFE, PAULA, and I have seen a lot of changes in the decade that we have made our home in Texas, which has one of the fastest growing populations in the country. Certainly, the food scene here is rapidly expanding too. Easy Tiger has been a part of that growth, providing bread to an ever more mature and sophisticated roster of restaurants.

When we first moved to Texas to run the guest operations at Kit and Carl Detering's fitness ranch in the Hill Country, one of my favorite activities became the campfire breakfasts I made for the guests. Like bread baking days, that involved getting up early and starting a fire. Once that was going, I would hang the enameled coffee pot on the triangle over the flames and start a pot for myself. I would make buttermilk biscuits in a cast-iron Dutch oven on the coals, cook some homemade turkey sausage, and then scramble a pan of eggs, before setting a second pot of coffee to boil for the guests.

I did not have to make all our bread; we also got to enjoy locally made tortillas. In Texas, tortillas are served at many places, not just at Mexican or Tex-Mex restaurants; in fact the gas station restaurant in Uvalde, the closest town to the ranch, made them on-site. From seats at the tables, we could watch tortillas being expertly rolled out and griddled to wrap breakfast tacos.

As we explored more Texas dining options, we encountered *tortas* (Mexican sandwiches), an alternative to tacos at many local restaurants. Unfortunately, most of the time the *bolillos*, the baguette-like rolls they are made with, consist of industrial bread that is overoxidized, cottony, and bland. That is why I was so delighted to learn about Birotes Salados (page 222), a roll that is made in Guadalajara using a sourdough culture and baked in brick ovens. I include a version of

the recipe I have since adapted that you can use in your own tortas at home.

Baking in Texas has provided other unexpected opportunities for creating new breads. Though originally inspired by French bread, my Smoked Flour Fougasse (page 216) pairs perfectly with Texas' smoked sausages, and Austin's pit masters inspired me to perfect a White Pan Bread (page 212) to sop up their barbecue.

WHITE PAN BREAD

MAKES 1 STANDARD LOAF

MIXING & KNEADING 1½ hours

FERMENTATION 2½ hours

PROOFING 1 hour

BAKING 35 to 45 minutes

In Central Texas, a barbecue plate usually comes with slices of white bread tossed on top of the meat (sometimes you have a choice of a sleeve of saltine crackers). With several young pit masters in the Austin area taking their skill to new levels, I always want a well-crafted version of the bread to go with the extraordinary meat.

This is my version of the first bread I ever made, the Basic White Bread from *Beard on Bread*. By applying the same principles and techniques, I created what is basically an artisan white bread with outstanding flavor.

Of course, in addition to being the best accompaniment to a slab of fatty brisket, this makes an excellent sandwich loaf and is also great for morning toast.

DOUGH

ALL-PURPOSE FLOUR	520 grams	4 cups plus 1 tablespoon
GRANULATED SUGAR	20 grams	1 tablespoon plus 1 teaspoon
SALT	11 grams	2 teaspoons
INSTANT YEAST	3 grams	¾ teaspoon
WATER	320 grams	1⅓ cups

Mixing and Kneading

Put the flour, sugar, salt, and yeast in a large bowl and blend together with your fingers to evenly distribute them. Make a well in the center of the flour and add the water, holding back a small amount (about 15 grams or 1 tablespoon) until you see if the flour needs it all.

Make sure you have a plastic bowl scraper at hand, then start to blend the water into the flour with your fingers. As the flour begins to absorb the water and the mixture starts to thicken, plunge both hands in and squeeze the dough between your thumbs and fingers. Work from the side of the bowl closest to you across to the other side, squeezing with both hands. Rotate the bowl a quarter turn and squeeze your way through the dough again. You will feel the dough starting to come together as a more cohesive mass, and the water and flour will become more fully incorporated. Use your bowl scraper from time to time to scrape the sticky dough from the sides of the bowl into the center. Keep rotating the bowl and squeezing the dough until everything is fully incorporated, 1 to 2 minutes. It will remain a shaggy and sticky mass.

The dough should be medium-soft, having definite give but also some resistance; you should be able to feel a core when you squeeze it. Add the reserved water if the dough is not soft enough. You may even have to add additional water to get the right consistency if it still feels too stiff. It is better to have a dough that is a little wet than one that is too dry.

Turn out the dough onto an unfloured work surface, using the bowl scraper to get it all out of the bowl and scraping as much off your hands as you can. Resist the urge to add flour to the work surface or the dough at this stage.

Starting with the edge closest to you, grab the dough with both hands, palms down, and pull it gently toward you. Stretch it up and flip it over the top of the dough mass by 2 or 3 inches and press it into the surface. Grab the new edge closest to you and stretch it gently up and flip it over the top. Repeat this stretching and flipping of the dough four or five times, working your way to the far side of the mass. The stretches should be gentle enough not to tear the dough apart. As you continue this process, the dough will hold together better and be easier to stretch.

Scrape up the dough with a dough scraper, rotate it a quarter turn, and repeat the stretching and flipping through the dough mass four or five times,

CONTINUED

3 to 5 minutes. With each stretch and flip of the dough, you will feel it developing, becoming more cohesive and less sticky. When most of the dough holds together and pulls off the work surface as you stretch it, slide the dough scraper under it and gather it into a ball. The dough will not be fully developed yet and will still be a little sticky.

Cup your hands around the bottom of the far side of the ball and pull it gently toward you, allowing the dough to grip the work surface, then move your hands to the left, rotating the dough counterclockwise. Return your hands behind the dough and pull and rotate again one or two times. This will help shape the dough into a smooth ball. Return the ball to the bowl with the smooth side up and let it rest for 15 minutes.

Dust your work surface lightly with all-purpose flour and turn out the dough so that the smooth side is down. Gently press out the dough to flatten it into a round about 2 inches thick. Grab the edge closest to you and stretch it up and over the top of the dough, about two-thirds of the way to the opposite side, and press into the surface. Grab the edge opposite you and stretch and fold it toward you over the first fold, about two-thirds of the way to the closest edge, and press into the surface. Rotate the dough a quarter turn and repeat two more folds, one away from you and one toward you.

Turn the dough over so the seam side is down. Form a ball by cupping your hands around the bottom of the far side of the dough and pulling it toward you, rotating the dough counterclockwise. Repeat one or two times to form a ball. You will notice that the dough is more developed and will stretch tighter than before. Be careful not to stretch it too tight; if the surface starts to tear, stop tightening. Return the ball to the bowl, smooth side up, and let rest for 15 minutes.

Repeat this stretching and folding three more times at 15-minute intervals for a total of four folds over

an hour. This will develop into a smooth, elastic dough with a good gluten network.

Fermentation

After the final fold, return the ball to the bowl, smooth side up, cover with a tea towel or plastic wrap, and let sit in a warm, draft-free place until the dough has doubled in volume and feels airy when gently touched, about 1 hour.

Turn out the dough onto a lightly floured work surface, smooth side down. Gently press out the dough to flatten until it's 2 inches thick. Grabbing the edge opposite you, stretch the dough and fold it over the top, about halfway toward you. Gently press the dough down, then stretch the edge closest to you and fold it over the first fold. Press it in gently. Rotate the dough a quarter turn and repeat two more folds, one away from you and one toward you.

Turn the dough over so that the seam side is down. Form into as smooth and round a ball as you can. Return the ball to the bowl with the smooth side up, cover with a tea towel, and let rest until it doubles in size again, about 1 hour. Repeat the fold one more time, then let rest for 30 minutes more.

Shaping

Spray one 8½ by 4½-inch loaf pan generously with baking spray.

Dust the work surface lightly with all-purpose flour and turn out the dough so the smooth side is down.

For this bread, you should press out the gases evenly and thoroughly to achieve a more even crumb structure, without any large holes. Press the dough out with the palms of your hands. Shape the loaf into a round by folding the edges into the center three or four times around the circle. Flip the dough over with your hands cupped around the dough, pulling a slight tension into the surface. Place the ball, seam

Proofing

Preheat the oven to 475°F with the steaming pan in place (see page 22). You do not need a baking stone.

Cover the pan with a tea towel and let rise until the center of the loaf has crested about 1 inch above the top of the pan, about 1 hour.

Baking

Using a funnel (see page 14), steam the oven with 60 grams (¼ cup) water. Let the steam settle for 30 seconds or so.

Open the oven and slide the pan onto the oven rack. Close the oven door. Using the funnel, add 117 grams (½ cup) more water to the steaming pan. Close the oven door tightly as soon as the water hits the pan. After 5 minutes, lower the oven to 425°F.

After about 30 minutes, check your loaf. The top should be golden brown while the sides just above the rim of the pan will remain lighter. The sides should be well set and have pulled away from the pan slightly. The loaf should sound hollow when rapped on the bottom. If not, return the loaf directly to the oven rack without the pan for 5 to 10 minutes to finish baking.

Cool the bread on a wire cooling rack until completely cool.

side down, on the work surface, cover with a tea towel, and let rest for 15 to 20 minutes.

Turn the dough over and, with the palms of your hands, press the dough out flat, pulling into a rough rectangle about 7 inches wide and 12 inches long.

Fold the closest edge away from you about two-thirds of the way up and press into the dough. Fold the opposite edge over the first flap about two-thirds of the way toward you and press into the dough. Start again with the opposite edge and bring it over and all the way to meet the closest edge. With the heel of your hand, press along the edge from one side to the other to make and seal the seam. Roll the log shape back and forth on the work surface to make an even cylinder the length of the pan. Place in the pan with the seam down.

SMOKED FLOUR FOUGASSE

MAKES 3 FOUGASSES

SMOKING THE FLOUR 1 hour
plus time to cool

STARTER 12 to 36 hours

MIXING & KNEADING 1¼ hours

FERMENTATION 1½ hours

PROOFING 30 to 40 minutes

BAKING 20 to 25 minutes

On a trip to Paris to watch the baking team from the United States compete in the *Coupe du Monde de la Boulangerie* (aka the World Cup of Baking), I went on a tour of Parisian bakeries that the Bread Bakers Guild of America had put together. One of the bakeries had a wood-fired oven, and while I was there, I tasted a fougasse, the large Provençal bread that resembles a ladder or sometimes a leaf. The bread had a faint yet distinct smokiness that has remained stuck in my taste memory ever since.

At the French Culinary Institute, I was reminded of that loaf when some of the chef instructors had become interested (obsessed, actually) in smoking food; they were rigging together all kinds of contraptions to smoke things on their stoves. Besides fish and meat, they were smoking salt and other ingredients, so I thought I should have a go at adding smoked flavor to some bread. At first, I tried adding some wood chips in a tray directly in the bread ovens to see if that would impart flavor into the breads, but it was too faint to detect. Talking with one of the chefs, who had smoked some salt, we thought smoking some of the flour might work. It added a good aroma to the flour and the flavor was in the loaf after baking. After some trial and error, I settled on using about 20 percent smoked flour.

Around that time, we had the opportunity to make the bread for the James Beard Foundation Journalism Awards ceremony. The smoked flour fougasse seemed like the perfect pairing for Bobby Flay's porterhouse steaks, and so we made individual-size breads with two small cuts in the middle.

Of course, at Easy Tiger we have a smoker for sausages and our pastrami and other meats from time to time, so I revived my smoked fougasse there as a special. It has a nice smoky flavor that is not overbearing and the bread makes a great accompaniment to steak or other grilled meats.

I like to use either oak or hickory chips for this, but fruitwood would also be nice.

Smoking the Flour

Spread the flour in an even layer on a rimmed baking sheet. Place in a smoker at 250°F to 350°F (the cooler temperature is better) or preheat a grill to 250°F and fill a wood chip smoking box with oak or hickory chips and smoke the flour in the grill.

Smoke for about 1 hour, stirring the flour halfway through so that more of it is exposed to the smoke.

The flour should brown slightly and have a good smoky aroma.

Cool completely. If sealed well in a plastic bag, the smoked flour will keep at room temperature for several months.

STARTER

ALL-PURPOSE FLOUR	132 grams	1 cup
SALT	3 grams	½ teaspoon
INSTANT YEAST	½ gram	⅛ teaspoon
WATER	90 grams	⅓ cup

Put the flour, salt, and yeast in a large bowl and blend together with your fingers to evenly distribute them. Make a well in the center of the flour and add the water.

Using your hand, draw the flour into the water, stirring and blending with your fingers. As it begins to come together, squeeze the dough with your hands to better incorporate the water into the flour. Starting at the near side of the bowl, grasp the dough with both hands and squeeze it between your thumbs

CONTINUED

and fingers. Rotate the bowl and continue to squeeze the dough, working in the water and working out any clumps of flour. Use a plastic bowl scraper to scrape down the sides and bottom of the bowl, folding the dough over on top of itself.

This dough should be medium-stiff at this point, having some give but also a pretty solid core, like a rubber bouncy ball.

Because this dough will ferment a long time, you do not need to develop the gluten much, just squeeze and work the dough until it is fully combined with no lumps. Form the dough into a rough ball in the bowl and cover it with plastic wrap, or place in a container with a lid.

Let the dough sit at room temperature for 1 hour, then refrigerate for at least 12 hours or up to 36 hours.

DOUGH

ALL-PURPOSE FLOUR	375 grams	3 cups
ALL-PURPOSE FLOUR, SMOKED	125 grams	1 cup
SALT	11 grams	2 teaspoons
INSTANT YEAST	2 grams	½ teaspoon
STARTER	All from above	
OLIVE OIL	30 grams	2½ tablespoons
WATER	340 grams	1½ cups
RICE FLOUR	For dusting	

Mixing and Kneading

Put the regular and smoked all-purpose flours, the salt, and yeast in a large bowl and blend together with your fingers to evenly distribute them. Divide the starter into six pieces and scatter them on top of the flour. Make a well in the center of the flour

and pour in the olive oil and then the water, holding back a small amount of the water (about 15 grams or 1 tablespoon) to see if the flour needs it all.

Make sure you have a plastic bowl scraper at hand, then start to blend the water and starter into the flour with your fingers. As the flour begins to absorb the water and the mixture starts to thicken, plunge both hands in and squeeze the dough between your thumbs and fingers. Work from the side of the bowl closest to you across to the other side, squeezing with both hands. Rotate the bowl a quarter turn and squeeze your way through the dough again. You will feel the dough starting to come together as a more cohesive mass, and the water and starter will become more fully incorporated. Use your bowl scraper from time to time to scrape the sticky dough from the sides of the bowl into the center. Keep rotating the bowl and squeezing the dough until everything is fully incorporated, 1 to 2 minutes. It will remain a shaggy and sticky mass.

The dough should be medium-soft, having definite give but still having some resistance; you should be able to feel a core when you squeeze it. Add the reserved water if the dough is not soft enough. Add the water a little at a time, squeezing it into the dough as you have been. You may even have to add additional water to get the right consistency if it still feels too stiff. It is better to have a dough that is a little wet than one that is too dry.

Turn out the dough onto an unfloured work surface, using the bowl scraper to get it all out of the bowl and scraping as much off your hands as you can. Resist the urge to add flour to the work surface or the dough at this stage.

Starting with the edge closest to you, grab the dough with both hands, palms down, and pull it gently toward you. Stretch it up and flip it over the top of the dough mass by 2 or 3 inches and press it into the surface. Grab the new edge closest to you and stretch it gently up and flip it over the top.

CONTINUED

Repeat this stretching and flipping of the dough four or five times, working your way to the far side of the mass. The stretches should be gentle enough not to tear the dough apart. As you continue this process, the dough will hold together better and be easier to stretch.

Scrape up the dough with a dough scraper, rotate it a quarter turn, and repeat the stretching and flipping through the dough mass four or five times, 3 to 5 minutes. With each stretch and flip of the dough, you will feel it developing, becoming more cohesive and less sticky. When most of the dough holds together and pulls off the work surface as you stretch it, slide the dough scraper under it and gather it into a ball. The dough will not be fully developed yet and will still be a little sticky.

Cup your hands around the bottom of the far side of the ball and pull it gently toward you, allowing the dough to grip the work surface, then move your hands to the left, rotating the dough counterclockwise. Return your hands behind the dough and pull and rotate again one or two times. This will tighten the surface and help shape the dough into a smooth ball. Return the ball to the bowl with the smooth side up and let it rest for 15 minutes.

Dust your work surface lightly with all-purpose flour and turn out the dough so that the smooth side is down. Gently press out the dough to flatten it into a round about 2 inches thick. Grab the edge closest to you and stretch it up and over the top of the dough, about two-thirds of the way to the opposite side, and press into the surface. Grab the edge opposite you and stretch and fold it toward you over the first fold, about two-thirds of the way to the closest edge, and press into the surface. Rotate the dough a quarter turn and repeat two more folds, one away from you and one toward you.

Turn the dough over so the seam side is down. Form a ball by cupping your hands around the bottom of the far side of the dough and pulling it

toward you, rotating the dough counterclockwise. Repeat one or two times to form a ball. You will notice that the dough is more developed and will stretch tighter than before. Be careful not to stretch it too tight; if the surface starts to tear, stop tightening. Return the ball to the bowl, smooth side up, and let rest for 15 minutes.

Repeat this stretching and folding three times at 15-minute intervals for a total of four folds over an hour. This will develop into a smooth, elastic dough with a good gluten network.

Fermentation

After the final fold, return the ball to the bowl smooth side up, cover with a tea towel or plastic wrap, and let sit in a warm, draft-free place until the dough has doubled in volume and feels airy when gently touched, about 1 hour.

Turn out the dough onto a lightly floured work surface, smooth side down. Gently press out the dough to flatten until it's 2 inches thick. Grabbing the edge opposite you, stretch the dough and fold it over the top, about halfway toward you. Gently press the dough down, then stretch the edge closest to you and fold it over the first fold. Press it in gently. Rotate the dough a quarter turn and repeat two more folds, one away from you and one toward you.

Turn the dough over so that the seam side is down. Form into as smooth and round a ball as you can. Return the ball to the bowl with the smooth side up, cover with a tea towel, and let rest for 30 minutes.

Shaping

Preheat the oven to 500°F with the baking stone and steaming pan in place (see page 22).

Dust the work surface lightly with all-purpose flour and turn out the dough. Divide the dough into three equal pieces with a bench knife or bowl scraper. Pat the first piece out into a rectangle, then fold the top long edge toward you about two-thirds of the way. Gently press the fold with the heel of your hand, then fold once more from the top down to the bottom edge and gently seal the seam with the heel of your hand.

Dust a wooden board lightly with all-purpose flour or line a baking sheet with parchment paper and dust it lightly with flour. Place the loaf, seam side down, on a floured wooden board or parchment. Repeat with the remaining two pieces of dough.

Proofing

Cover the pieces with a tea towel and let rise in a warm, draft-free place until doubled in size, 30 to 40 minutes.

Baking

Dust the peel with rice flour (see page 17) and carefully transfer the first loaf to your peel.

Using a funnel (see page 14), steam the oven with 60 grams (¼ cup) of water. Let the steam settle for 30 seconds while you score your loaf.

Using the straight side of a bowl scraper or a bench knife, press through the dough to make a cut all the way through from about ½ inch from the top of the loaf at an angle until the bottom of the cut is ½ inch from the side. Make a second cut parallel to the first, starting about halfway from the top of the first cut, and make a third cut parallel to the first two that should reach to about ½ inch of the bottom of the loaf. All three cuts should go all the way through the dough. Gently lift the sides of the loaf to stretch open the holes you have cut.

Open the oven and place the tip of the peel on the baking stone where you want the loaf to end up. Leave room for the other two loaves if the stone is large enough; center the loaf if it is not. Quickly pull the peel out from under the loaf, letting it gently drop onto the baking stone. Close the oven door immediately. If your stone can fit two or even three loaves at once, quickly score the second loaf and slide it onto the baking stone. Repeat with the third loaf, if there is space.

Using the funnel, add 235 grams (1 cup) more water to the steaming pan. Close the oven door tightly as soon as the water hits the steaming pan.

After about 20 minutes, check your loaves. The crusts should be a golden color and the holes should have color, but may be slightly paler than the top, but they should not still be white. If not, return them to the oven for 5 minutes.

Cool the bread on a wire cooling rack until completely cool.

BIROTES SALADOS

Mexican Sourdough Rolls

MAKES 8 SMALL OR 4 LARGE ROLLS

STARTER 12 hours (23 to 25 hours if starter needs a wake-up feed)

MIXING & KNEADING 1¼ hours

FERMENTATION 2 hours

PROOFING 1 to 1½ hours

BAKING 20 to 30 minutes (may require two bakes depending on the size of your oven)

One Thanksgiving at the house of our dear friends, we had the pleasure of sitting next to Mariana McEnroe and her husband, Ian. In addition to having a food blog, *Yes, More Please*, with Ian, Mariana is a proud Tapatio, what the people from Guadalajara call themselves. When the subject came around to bread and food, the gleam in her eye seemed to turn up two notches as she told me about *birote salado* and the *tortas ahogadas* made with them.

As I soon learned, *birotes* are long, baguette-like rolls made from a sourdough, unique to Guadalajara and the state of Jalisco. Supposedly, a French (or possibly Belgian) officer in Emperor Maximilian's army by the name of Pirotte, who also happened to be a baker, brought this bread to Guadalajara. Today, there are two types of *birote*, one called *Fleiman*, which is sweeter and less crusty, and the *salado*, salty with a thick crust and dense, rather spongy interior that stands up well in the "drowned sandwich," or *torta ahogada*. Although you can find cheaper, quicker versions of these rolls made with yeast, the traditional version is made with a sourdough starter that has some beer in the mix. One version I came across in my research also includes eggs and lime juice in the starter, which create a unique flavor profile.

The following recipe started with a version Mariana had developed with a sourdough-based starter and some yeast added to the final dough mix. I played around with it by baking her samples, as well as tasting the rolls her friend had sent by UPS from Guadalajara. By adjusting the fermentation schedule for the sponge, I was able to take out the added yeast altogether.

This recipe requires a mature sourdough starter, which must be made at least 1 week in advance. The wake-up feed and final-feed resting times are different for this bread than for other recipes using this starter.

Sourdough Starter | *Levain*

If you are making this bread from the Levain Naturel that you have been maintaining and storing in your refrigerator, take it out and feed it as follows, 11 to 13 hours before you want to make your bread dough. After this step, you will need to feed it again and let it ferment another 12 hours before making the dough. If your starter is already active—either because you just brought a new starter to maturity or you just used it for baking another bread and have been actively feeding it—skip to the final feed step.

WAKE-UP FEED

LEVAIN (PAGE 64)	200 grams	7 ounces
ALL-PURPOSE FLOUR	200 grams	1½ cups
WATER AT 90°F	120 grams	½ cup

Place the starter in a clean bowl and mix in the flour and water by hand, stirring and blending with your fingers, until well incorporated. Cover with a tea towel and let ferment at room temperature for 8 to 10 hours, depending on your schedule.

FINAL FEED

LEVAIN	20 grams	1 tablespoon
ALL-PURPOSE FLOUR	270 grams	2 cups plus 1 tablespoon
MEXICAN LAGER BEER, SUCH AS MODELO ESPECIAL	175 grams	¾ cup

Twelve hours before you want to make your bread dough, measure out 20 grams (1 tablespoon) of the starter in a clean bowl and mix in the all-purpose

CONTINUED

flour and beer by hand, stirring and blending with your fingers, until well incorporated. Cover with a tea towel and let ferment at room temperature for 12 hours. Return the remaining starter to your storage container and refrigerate.

DOUGH

ALL-PURPOSE FLOUR	430 grams	3⅓ cups
GRANULATED SUGAR	20 grams	1 tablespoon plus 1 teaspoon
SALT	18 grams	1 tablespoon plus ½ teaspoon
STARTER	All from above	
WATER	212 grams	¾ cup plus 1 tablespoon
RICE FLOUR	For dusting	

Mixing and Kneading

Put the flour, sugar, and salt in a large bowl and blend together with your fingers to evenly distribute them. Divide the starter into four pieces and scatter on top of the flour. Make a well in the center of the flour and add the water, holding back a small amount (10 grams, or 2 teaspoons) until you see if the flour needs it all.

Make sure you have a plastic bowl scraper at hand, then start to blend the water and starter into the flour with your fingers. As the flour begins to absorb the water and the mixture starts to thicken, plunge both hands in and squeeze the dough between your thumbs and fingers. Work from the side of the bowl closest to you across to the other side, squeezing with both hands. Rotate the bowl a quarter turn and squeeze your way through the dough again. You will feel the dough starting to come together as a more cohesive mass, and the water and starter will become more fully incorporated. Use your bowl scraper from time to time to scrape the sticky dough

from the sides of the bowl into the center. Keep rotating the bowl and squeezing the dough until everything is fully incorporated, 1 to 2 minutes. It will remain a shaggy and sticky mass.

The dough should be medium-soft, having definite give but also some resistance; you should be able to feel a core when you squeeze it. Add the reserved water if the dough is not soft enough. You may even have to add more water to get the right consistency if it still feels too stiff. It is better to have a dough that is a little wet than one that is too dry.

Turn out the dough onto an unfloured work surface, using the bowl scraper to get it all out of the bowl and scraping as much off your hands as you can. Resist the urge to add flour to the work surface or the dough at this stage.

Starting with the edge closest to you, grab the dough with both hands, palms down, and pull it gently toward you. Stretch it up and flip it over the top of the dough mass by 2 or 3 inches and press it into the surface. Grab the new edge closest to you and stretch it gently up and flip it over the top. Repeat this stretching and flipping of the dough four or five times, working your way to the far side of the mass. The stretches should be gentle enough not to tear the dough apart. As you continue this process, the dough will hold together better and be easier to stretch.

Scrape up the dough with a dough scraper, rotate it a quarter turn, and repeat the stretching and flipping through the dough mass four or five times, 3 to 5 minutes. With each stretch and flip of the dough, you will feel it developing, becoming more cohesive and less sticky. When most of the dough holds together and pulls off the work surface as you stretch it, slide the dough scraper under it and gather it into a ball. The dough will not be fully developed yet and will still be a little sticky.

Cup your hands around the bottom of the far side of the ball and pull it gently toward you, allowing the dough to grip the work surface, then move your hands to the left, rotating the dough counterclockwise. Return your hands behind the dough and pull and rotate again one or two times. This will tighten the surface and help shape the dough into a smooth ball. Return the ball to the bowl with the smooth side up and let it rest for 15 minutes.

Dust your work surface lightly with all-purpose flour and turn out the dough so that the smooth side is down. Gently press out the dough to flatten it into a round about 2 inches thick. Grab the edge closest to you and stretch it up and over the top of the dough, about two-thirds of the way to the opposite side, and press into the surface. Grab the edge opposite you and stretch and fold it toward you over the first fold, about two-thirds of the way to the closest edge, and press into the surface. Rotate the dough a quarter turn and repeat two more folds, one away from you and one toward yourself.

Turn the dough over so the seam side is down. Form a ball by cupping your hands around the bottom of the far side of the dough and pulling it toward you, rotating the dough counterclockwise. Repeat one or two times to form a ball. You will notice that the dough is more developed and will stretch tighter than before. Be careful not to stretch it too tight; if the surface starts to tear, stop tightening. Return the ball to the bowl, smooth side up, and let rest for 15 minutes.

Repeat this stretching and folding three times at 15-minute intervals for a total of four folds over an hour. This will develop into a smooth, elastic dough with a good gluten network.

Fermentation

After the final fold, cover with a damp tea towel, and let sit in a warm, draft-free place until the dough has doubled in volume and feels airy when gently touched, about 1 hour. Turn out the dough

on a lightly floured surface, smooth side down. Press it gently to flatten a bit until it is about 2 inches thick. Grabbing the edge opposite you, stretch the dough and fold it over the top, about halfway toward you. Gently press the dough down, then stretch the edge closest to you and fold it over the first fold. Press it in gently. Rotate the dough a quarter turn and repeat two more folds, one away from you and one toward you.

Turn the dough over so that the seam side is down. Form into as smooth and round a ball as you can. Return the ball to the bowl with the smooth side up and cover again with a tea towel or plastic wrap until it doubles in volume again, about 1 hour.

Shaping

Dust the work surface lightly with all-purpose flour and turn out the dough.

For smaller rolls, divide the dough into eight pieces (about 150 grams each) with a bench knife or bowl scraper and round each piece into a ball. Alternately, if you want larger rolls, divide the dough into four pieces (about 300 grams each).

Press one ball out with the heels of your hand into a rough rectangle. Grab the long side closest to you and fold it about two-thirds of the way up to the opposite side, and gently press into the dough with the heel of your hand. Grab the edge opposite you and stretch it over the first fold, about two-thirds of the way toward you, pressing it into the dough with the heel of your hand. Again, grab the opposite edge and fold it toward you, this time all the way to meet the closest edge and seal the seam where the two edges meet with the heel of your hand from one end to the other.

Place your hands on top of the dough piece, overlapping them in the middle. Roll the cylinder back and forth, moving your hands outward to lengthen the rolls to about 8 inches. Return your

CONTINUED

hands to the center and roll a second time, this time with your hands at a slight angle, lower at the outside ends to give a slight taper to the ends as you roll them.

Proofing

Preheat the oven to 475°F with the baking stone and steaming pan in place (see page 22).

Lay a towel on top of a cutting board or baking sheet and dust with all-purpose flour. Place the rolls, seam side up, on a floured towel. With a fold of the towel in between, place the second roll, seam side up, next to the first. Continue with the remaining rolls, pulling up a tuck of the towel in between each roll and placing them side by side lengthwise. This helps hold the shape of the rolls, while the fabric between them keeps them from sticking together. Use a second towel if they don't all fit on one.

Cover with another towel and let proof until they feel airy when gently poked (they will not double in size), 1 to 1½ hours.

Baking

You will probably need to bake these in two batches, depending on the size of your oven. Because they rise fairly slowly, you should be able to leave the second batch out at room temperature without overproofing.

Dust the peel with rice flour (see page 17). Turn out the rolls onto the peel, placing them seam side down with some space between them.

Using a funnel (see page 14), steam the oven with 60 grams (¼ cup) of water. Let the steam settle for 30 seconds or so while you score the rolls.

Score each loaf with a razor blade from end to end the length of the roll and down the center. The blade should lay almost flat on top of the roll, cutting at a sharp angle under the top surface of the roll.

Open the oven and use the peel to carefully slide the rolls onto the baking stone. Close the oven door immediately.

Using the funnel, add 235 grams (1 cup) more water to the steaming pan. Close the oven door tightly as soon as all the water hits the steaming pan. Lower the oven to 400°F.

After about 20 minutes, check your rolls. You want the crusts to be a deep brown color and the rolls to sound hollow when they are tapped on the bottom. If they still give a heavy thud, return them to the oven for 5 to 10 minutes.

Cool the rolls on a wire cooling rack until completely cool.

FLOUR TORTILLAS

MAKES 8 TORTILLAS

MIXING & KNEADING 45 minutes
SHAPING 40 minutes
COOKING 10 minutes per tortilla

I sometimes think baking handcrafted breads is an uphill battle in a town where the most common question after you have placed your food order is "flour or corn tortilla?" Still, I do love a good tortilla—most of the time I am a flour guy—and there is always a bag of them in our fridge. If you have a source for rendered lard, by all means use that for the best flavor.

ALL-PURPOSE FLOUR	215 grams	1¾ cups
SALT	7 grams	1½ teaspoons
BAKING POWDER	5 grams	¾ teaspoon
LARD, UNSALTED BUTTER, OR SHORTENING	40 grams	¼ cup
WATER	120 grams	½ cup

Mixing and Kneading

Put the flour, salt, and baking powder in a medium bowl and blend together with your fingers to evenly distribute them. Add the lard and cut it into the flour with your fingers until well incorporated (you do not want pebbles of fat left in).

Add the water and mix by hand until incorporated. Because of the fat worked into the flour, the water will not absorb into the gluten in the same way as in a bread dough. Turn out the dough onto an unfloured work surface. Stretch and fold the dough from one side to the other, three to four folds; rotate and stretch and fold across the dough again. Repeat rotating, stretching, and folding the dough for 1 to 2 minutes. Again, the gluten will not develop as much as in a bread dough, and the dough will seem rougher and may tear more easily. Form dough into a shaggy ball and return to the bowl, seam side down. Cover with a tea towel and let rest for 15 minutes.

Turn out the dough on a lightly floured counter, seam side up. Press out into a circle about 1 inch thick, then stretch the edge closest to you toward the center. Stretch the opposite edge toward you into the center to just overlap the first fold and press into the dough. Rotate a quarter turn and repeat the stretching and folding with the other two edges.

Turn the dough over, seam side down. Form a ball by cupping your hands around the bottom of the far side of the dough and pulling it toward you, rotating the dough counterclockwise. Repeat one or two times to form a ball. Let rest for 10 minutes.

Shaping

Preheat a griddle to 400°F or a heavy skillet over medium-high heat.

Divide the dough into eight equal pieces and form each piece into a small ball. Cover the pieces with a damp tea towel and let rest for 15 minutes.

Dust the work surface lightly with all-purpose flour. Flatten one ball on the work surface with your hand and flour the top. Use a rolling pin to roll into an 8-inch circle, always starting in the center and rolling outward in all directions. Bring the pin back to the center with each stroke and use plenty of flour so the dough does not stick to the pin or work surface.

If you are quick at rolling out the tortillas, you can roll one out while another is cooking, making sure to watch it carefully and flip before burning. Alternatively, you can roll them all out, stacking them with a piece of parchment or wax paper between them, and cook them one at a time.

Cooking

Brush off excess flour and transfer a tortilla carefully to the griddle or skillet. Cook until small brown blisters dot the underside, then flip to cook the other side, about 5 minutes per side.

Transfer to a tea towel–lined basket, pulling the towel to cover them while the next one cooks.

BREAD ON THE TABLE IN CENTRAL TEXAS AND SOUTH OF THE BORDER

THE **FOODS OF** Central Texas are infused by the diversity of immigrants who shaped the only state that was once a republic in its own right. Long before salsa supplanted ketchup as our most popular condiment and Mexican ingredients and dishes became mainstream across the country, many of these dishes were woven into what Texans ate daily. Tortillas have long been a household fixture and are served in restaurants beyond those with a Mexican or strictly Tex-Mex menu. The breakfast taco is a also staple. Although it has become a quick convenience food and can be purchased preassembled and wrapped in foil all over the state, the best are made to order and wrapped in freshly griddled tortillas. Scrambled eggs form the base for most, and additions of potatoes and bacon, sausage, or chorizo are very popular.

While on the ranch, I learned the versatility of the taco by observing the ranch hands we hired for larger jobs from time to time. For their lunch breaks, they would light a small fire, let it burn down, then toss their tortillas right on the hot coals to heat up. Most often, they would have something leftover from their dinner the night before to fill their impromptu tacos, everything from a few strips of grilled meat to *fideo*, a Mexican vermicelli dish. Just about anything cold can be folded up in a warm tortilla.

In Nuevo Laredo, just across the Mexican border, we ate goat meat feet away from the kid goats roasting in front of open fires. Large platters of the meat were served to us family style, with heaps of freshly made tortillas on the table. Goat has been an important part of the economy in the Texas Hill Country, where the jagged, rocky landscape is more suited for them than cattle. The meat, with a bold and mildly gamey flavor, has become a favorite of mine.

Of course, barbecue needs to be part of any discussion of food in Texas. In Central Texas, beef is king on the pit, though sausages are also important. A lot has been written and debated about the origins of Texas barbecue and the role that German and Czech meat markets played. The prevailing mythology says that meat that did not sell from the fresh case was smoked and sold, often for immediate consumption in the store. That is why many joints around here still serve their meat on butcher paper, even if you are just taking it to a table a few feet away. Clear to me, though, is that there must be other influences—African-American and Mexican for sure—at play in the methods we now think of as barbecue, as they diverge from typical German smoking tradition. Accompaniments usually include pickles, onions, and white bread, or sometimes saltine crackers, which would have been at hand in a market.

I debate with my good friend Aaron Franklin, owner of Franklin Barbecue, about the bread part of the equation. He is tied to the industrial white bread he slings on the tray, liking the spongy sweetness in contrast with the meat. I argue that he should be serving a white bread that is as well crafted as his brisket. I do not suggest that he serve a crusty hearth-baked sourdough, just well-made white pan bread, with good, natural ingredients. For a couple of events, I have prevailed and made the bread for him, but the point has remained moot for his daily restaurant bread, as I have not had the capacity to make that. Once Easy Tiger expands, we will have to see whether I can convince him to let me bake bread for him.

While I am no pit master, I have learned to smoke and grill fairly well. On the ranch, between the grill and the brick oven, I came to love cooking with fire. In that perennial debate over gas versus charcoal, I emphatically answer neither, always preferring to cook over real wood.

TORTA AHOGADA
Sandwich from Guadalajara

MAKES 4 SANDWICHES

Once my new friend Mariana (originally from Guadalajara) and I had the Birote Salado (page 222) recipe down, we got together for sandwich-making lessons. They say the *torta ahogada* was invented by accident when a sandwich vendor dropped a carnitas-filled roll into a vat of tomato salsa. It is now ubiquitous in the market stalls, street carts, and restaurants of Mexico's second largest city.

There are two sauces, one a flavorful but not spicy tomato sauce for "drowning" the sandwich, and a second made from arbol chiles, potent and fiery, used to customize the heat level. Some order an *ahogado todo*, fully dunked in just the arbol chile sauce, others get a *medio*, dunked in the tomato sauce and then drizzled with the arbol chile sauce, and some stick with just the tomato sauce. I read that a true Tapatio (a native of Guadalajara) supposedly can eat this sandwich by hand with only one napkin, but Mariana assures me that is ridiculous.

One important element in a *torta ahogada* is the refried beans used to coat the inside of the cut rolls. In Guadalajara, Mayocoba beans are traditionally used, and I have found them canned in Mexican grocers. You can use any variety except black beans.

4 small Birotes Salados (page 222)

½ cup refried Mayocoba or pinto beans

3 cups Carnitas (page 236)

4 cups warm Tomato Sauce (page 236)

Chile Arbol Salsa (page 237)

Quick Pickled Onions (page 237)

Split the rolls in half vertically, leaving a hinge on one edge. Spread the inside of each half with a thin layer of refried beans, as if you were buttering them. Stuff each roll with about ¾ cup carnitas and close together.

Place the tomato sauce in a deep bowl. Using tongs, dunk the whole sandwich into the tomato sauce. Place the *torta* on a plate and pour a little more tomato sauce over the top. Add the chile arbol salsa to taste and garnish with quick pickled onions.

CARNITAS

---

4 ounces lard

4 pounds boneless pork shoulder, cut into 2-inch cubes

4 cloves garlic, peeled

2 bay leaves

3 cloves

In a large pan or Dutch oven with a lid, melt the lard over medium-high heat. Add the pork and cook until browned on all sides, about 2 minutes per side. You may have to brown the pork in two batches so as to not overcrowd the pan. Lower the heat to medium, and return the pork from the first browning to the pan if you have cooked two batches. Add enough water so that it comes about halfway up the meat, and add the garlic, bay leaves, and cloves. Bring to a simmer and cover until the pork just starts to get tender, 1 to 1¼ hours.

Uncover the pot and turn the heat to medium-high. As the water boils and starts to evaporate, stir the meat so that it does not stick and burn, but colors evenly on all sides. Cook until all water has evaporated and meat is well browned all over, about 1 hour. Allow to cool, then discard the garlic, bay leaves, and cloves.

You can cover and refrigerate the carnitas for up to 1 week.

TOMATO SAUCE

---

3 pounds Roma tomatoes, cored

½ white onion, cut in half

3 cloves garlic, peeled and trimmed

2 teaspoons salt

¼ teaspoon cumin seeds

¼ teaspoon peppercorns

Pinch ground cloves

2 tablespoons olive oil

1 teaspoon dried marjoram

½ teaspoon dried Mexican oregano

Combine the tomatoes and onion in a large, heavy pot and add enough water to cover. Bring to a gentle boil over medium heat and cook until the tomatoes are tender and the skins just start to split. Drain, reserving the cooking water. Do not clean the pot.

Combine the tomatoes, onion, garlic, salt, cumin, peppercorns, and cloves in a blender and process until well pureed, adding some of the cooking water if needed.

Heat the oil over medium-high heat in the same pot you used to cook the tomatoes. Add the pureed sauce, marjoram, and oregano and cook, stirring occasionally, 4 minutes. Decrease the heat to low and thin the sauce with some of the remaining cooking water. Keep the sauce warm until ready to use. The sauce can be cooled, covered, and refrigerated for up to 3 days.

CHILE ARBOL SALSA

MAKES ENOUGH FOR 4 SANDWICHES

¾ ounce arbol chiles (about 40 dried chiles), stemmed and seeded

2½ cups water

2 cloves garlic, peeled

3 tablespoons white vinegar

1 teaspoon salt

¼ teaspoon ground cumin

¼ teaspoon peppercorns

Pinch of ground cloves

Combine the chiles, 2 cups of the water, and garlic in a small saucepan and bring to a boil over high heat. Boil until the chiles are soft, meaty, and have swollen to about twice their size when dried, about 30 minutes. Put the chiles, water, and garlic in a blender. Add the vinegar, salt, cumin, peppercorns, and cloves and puree until smooth. Strain through a fine-mesh sieve and thin with the remaining ½ cup water. Keep the sauce warm until ready to use. The sauce can be cooled, covered, and refrigerated for up to 2 weeks.

QUICK PICKLED ONIONS

MAKES ABOUT 1 CUP

1 large white onion, thinly sliced

Juice of 1½ limes

2 pinches dried oregano

1 tablespoon water

Place the onions in a colander and rinse well under running water. Put them in a small bowl. Add the lime juice, oregano, and water and toss until evenly coated. Set aside.

MIGAS

Migas is a Tex-Mex breakfast dish in itself, but it is often put in a flour tortilla and served as a taco. I like to use slightly stale tortillas that are cut or torn into strips. Broken tortilla chips make a fine substitute.

2 tablespoons vegetable oil

2 corn tortillas, preferably slightly stale, cut or torn into strips

½ medium yellow onion, chopped

½ cup chopped tomato

1 serrano chile, chopped

4 eggs

½ cup shredded Cheddar cheese

4 Flour Tortillas (page 228)

Your favorite salsa for serving

Heat the oil in a skillet over medium-high heat until hot but not smoking. Add the tortilla strips and fry until crispy, about 5 minutes, stirring occasionally. Lower the heat to medium-low and add the onion, tomato, and serrano and cook until onion is softened, about 5 minutes. Add the eggs and scramble until nearly set, about 5 minutes. Sprinkle the cheese over the top and remove from the heat. Serve in the flour tortillas topped with your favorite salsa.

BREAKFAST TACOS

Breakfast tacos are a special subgenre and belong squarely in the Tex-Mex tradition. They are ubiquitous in Austin, whether made to order at a destination taco stand or prewrapped in the local coffee shop. We often make them at home for breakfast or even sometimes for a quick dinner. Here are some of my favorite combinations, to serve with the Flour Tortillas (page 228).

Scrambled eggs with bacon and cheese. Scramble one or two eggs per serving and place in the tortilla. Sprinkle some shredded Cheddar or Oaxacan cheese on the hot eggs and top with a slice of cooked bacon and your salsa of choice.

Mexican chorizo and scrambled eggs. Remove the chorizo from the casing and cook in a skillet until browned. Add eggs and scramble with the sausage, then stuff into a tortilla and garnish with chopped fresh cilantro.

Bean and cheese. Pinto beans are the perennial favorite in Texas, but our family is partial to black beans. Heat some refried black beans, smear into a heated tortilla, sprinkle with shredded Cheddar, and top with salsa.

ACKNOWLEDGMENTS

Thank you to David Hale Smith, my agent, for getting this project from fanciful idea to concrete proposal and finding it a great home with Ten Speed Press.

Thanks to Emily Timberlake for your enthusiasm, encouragement, and guidance getting the book started, and to Kelly Snowden and Emma Rudolph for your hard work, stewardship, and (nearly) endless patience with a neophyte author and busy baker. Thanks for sticking with me and pushing to get this book out there. For the stunning design, thank you to Lisa Bieser. Thank you also to the rest of the team at Ten Speed, including Jane Chinn, David Hawk, Windy Dorresteyn, and Kara Plikaitis.

Johnny Autry, your photos add brilliance and clarity and show the boundless beauty that can come from flour, water, salt, and yeast. We sure had fun on the back porch. Thank you to Charlotte Autry for styling the beautiful food and table shots.

Thanks Aaron and Stacey Franklin for letting us shoot at the trailer and sharing BBQ with us.

Thank you so much to Mariana and Ian McEnroe for sharing recipes and a wonderful afternoon of learning, eating, and sharing in your lovely home.

Thank you to the many bakers who have guided and taught me so much through the years, including Jacqueline Dufty, who got me started; Lisa Berg and Dennis Gelpe in Minneapolis; Amy Scherber; Craig Kominiak; Mark Fiorentino; Gwen Bassetti; and especially Leslie Mackie. Special thanks to Michel Suas for being a mentor and genuine friend.

Thank you to Bob Gillett, Andrew Curren, Scott Hentschel, and Vince Ashwill for conceiving and building Easy Tiger. We made something magical together. Thank you to all the leads, managers, and eager bakers that have punched so much dough together to bring the highest quality bread to Austin.

Tack så mycket to Britt, Hans-Erik, Michael, and Marie Jonsén for sharing your home, your lives, and your warmth and for sparking a lifelong love for *bröd*.

Mike and Julie Disbrowe and the rest of the Minnesota clan, it is so wonderful to be a part of your family. Thanks for all the love and support and the helping hands always. *Uff da*, and for the lefse griddle.

To Jana Norman and Paul Turley way off in Adelaide, wish we could break bread more often.

Thank you so much to Fran Norman for all your love and support with everything I have wanted to pursue. Your belief in me always means so much. So wish that Dad could have read these pages. You both gave me so much growing up, not the least of which was a hearty, but discerning, appetite.

Most of all, thank you to Paula Disbrowe and our beautiful children, Flannery and Wyatt. Having a baker in the family means early mornings, late nights, lots of weekends and holidays cut short or missed, and dough clinging to forearms, but also wonderful smells, tasty treats in the morning, fresh bread on the table, and the best lunch box sandwiches. We have had many great adventures together. You are all my light and inspiration.

ABOUT THE AUTHOR

David Norman is the Head Doughpuncher and a founding partner of Easy Tiger Bake Shop and Beer Garden. Previously, he was the head baker at Grand Central Bakery in Seattle and TriBakery, Ecce Panis, and Bouley Bakery in New York City. He taught the International Bread program at the French Culinary Institute and was an instructor at the San Francisco Baking Institute.

He lives with his wife and two children in Austin, Texas.

INDEX

Published in the United States by Ten Speed Press, an imprint of
Random House, a division of Penguin Random House LLC, New York.
www.tenspeed.com

Ten Speed Press and the Ten Speed Press colophon are registered
trademarks of Penguin Random House LLC.

Library of Congress Cataloging-in-Publication Data
Names: Norman, David, 1963- author. | Easy Tiger Bake Shop &
Beer Garden.
Title: Bread on the table : a top Texas baker shares his favorite recipes /
  by David Norman.
Description: First edition. | Berkeley : Ten Speed Press, [2019] |
  Includes index.
Identifiers: LCCN 2019008705 | ISBN 9781607749257 (hardcover)
Subjects: LCSH: Bread—Texas. | LCGFT: Cookbooks.
Classification: LCC TX769 .N637 2019 | DDC 641.81/509764—dc23
  LC record available at https://lccn.loc.gov/2019008705

Hardcover ISBN: 978-1-60774-925-7
eBook ISBN: 978-1-60774-926-4

Printed in China

Design by Lisa Schneller Bieser
Food and prop styling by Charlotte Autry

10 9 8 7 6 5 4 3 2 1

First Edition

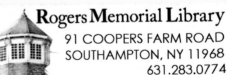